SOVIET CINEMATOGRAPHY
1918–1991

COMMUNICATION AND SOCIAL ORDER

An Aldine de Gruyter Series of Texts and Monographs

Series Editor

David R. Maines, Wayne State University

Advisory Editors

Bruce Gronbeck • Peter K. Manning • William K. Rawlins

David L. Altheide and Robert Snow, **Media Worlds in the Postjournalism Era**

Joseph Bensman and Robert Lilienfeld, **Craft and Consciousness: Occupational Technique and the Development of World Images** (*Second Edition*)

Valerie Malhotra Bentz, **Becoming Mature: Childhood Ghosts and Spirits in Adult Life**

Jörg R. Bergmann, **Discreet Indiscretions**

Herbert Blumer, **Industrialization as an Agent of Social Change: A Critical Analysis** (*Edited with an Introduction by David R. Maines and Thomas J. Morrione*)

Dennis Brissett and Charles Edgley (*editors*), **Life as Theater: A Dramaturgical Sourcebook** (*Second Edition*)

Richard Harvey Brown (*editor*), **Writing the Social Text: Poetics and Politics in Social Science Discourse**

Norman K. Denzin, **Hollywood Shot by Shot: Alcoholism in American Cinema**

Irwin Deutscher, Fred P. Pestello, and H. Frances G. Pestello, **Sentiments and Acts**

Bryan S. Green, **Gerontology and the Construction of Old Age: A Study in Discourse Analysis**

Pasquale Gagliardi (ed), **Symbols and Artifacts: Views of the Corporate Landscape** (paperback)

J. T. Hansen, A. Susan Owen, and Michael Patrick Madden, **Parallels: The Soldiers' Knowledge and the Oral History of Contemporary Warfare**

Emmanuel Lazega, **The Micropolitics of Knowledge: Communication and Indirect Control in Workgroups**

Niklas Luhmann, **Risk: A Sociological Theory**

David R. Maines (*editor*), **Social Organization and Social Process: Essays in Honor of Anselm Strauss**

Peter K. Manning, **Organizational Communication**

Stjepan G. Meštrović, **Durkheim and Postmodernist Culture**

R. S. Perinbanayagam, **Discursive Acts**

William K. Rawlins, **Friendship Matters: Communication, Dialectics, and the Life Course**

Dmitry Shlapentokh and Vladimir Shlapentokh, **Soviet Cinematography, 1918–1991: Ideological Conflict and Social Reality**

Anselm Strauss, **Continual Permutations of Action**

Jacqueline P. Wiseman, **The Other Half: Wives of Alcoholics and Their Social-Psychological Situation**

SOVIET CINEMATOGRAPHY
1918–1991

Ideological Conflict and Social Reality

Dmitry Shlapentokh and Vladimir Shlapentokh

ALDINE DE GRUYTER
New York

About the Authors

Dmitry Shlapentokh, Professor of History, Indiana University, South Bend, received his Ph.D. from the University of Chicago, and his Master's degrees in History from Moscow University and Michigan State University. The author of several articles on various issues in modern Russian history, Dr. Shlapentokh is also a writer of short stories and poetry in Russian.

Vladimir Shlapentokh, Professor of Sociology, Michigan State University. He is the author of numerous books, professional articles, and newspaper columns on Soviet issues.
Before emigrating to the United States in 1979, Dr. Shlapentokh was a Senior Fellow at the Sociological Institute in Moscow, and conducted the first nationwide public opinion surveys in the U.S.S.R.

ALDINE DE GRUYTER
A division of Walter de Gruyter, Inc.
200 Saw Mill River Road
Hawthorne, New York 10532

This publication is printed on acid-free paper ⊗

Library of Congress Cataloging-in-Publication Data

Shlapentokh, Dmitry.
    Soviet cinematogrpahy, 1918–1991 : ideological conflict and social
reality / Dmitry Shlapentokh, Vladimir Shlapentokh.
      p.   cm. — (Communication and social order)
    Filmography: p.
    Includes bibliographical references (p.   ) and index.
    ISBN 0-202-30461-2 (cloth). — ISBN 0-202-30462-0 (paper)
    1. Motion pictures—Soviet Union—History. 2. Motion pictures—
Political aspects—Soviet Union. 3. Communism and motion pictures.
4. Motion picture industry—Soviet Union. 5. Motion pictures—
Social aspects—Soviet Union. I. Shlapentokh, Vladimir.
II. Title. III. Series.
PN1993.5.R9S436   1993
791.43'0947—dc20   93-12309
                                                      CIP

Manufactured in the United States of America
10 9 8 7 6 5 4 3 2 1

*To Liuba, mother and wife, who shared, with us
the pleasure of viewing most of the movies
mentioned in this book*

Contents

PART III
Movies During Stalin's Time: Total Submission
to the Official Ideology

PART V

Soviet Cinematographers Reject Official Ideology:
Cinema during the Last Years of the Soviet Empire

Preface

The following work will explore the role of ideology and politics in Soviet movies, concentrating on the influence of certain ideologies on the movie industry. It examines the political activity of filmmakers in the seventy-plus years between 1917, when the Bolsheviks came to power, and 1991, when the Soviet empire collapsed.

WHAT WE WILL NOT EXAMINE

This work will not, however, address the artistic value of movies and the conflicts of various artistic schools in movies. Neither will we address the attitudes of Russians toward certain movies, and we will only briefly dwell on the influence of movies on the Soviet mentality. However, we hope that our analysis will lend insight into the mentality of Soviet filmmakers and the Soviet intellectual community as a whole.

Of course, we would prefer to address all of these issues in this book; certainly this would enable the reader to have a more complete understanding of the topic. It would be interesting, for instance, to examine the correlation between the artistic quality of a film and the degree of pressure that official ideology exerted on film directors. One hypothesis that could be tested in this way is that the peak of filmmakers' artistic innovations occurred in the 1920s, when they were seemingly "sincere believers," while the most realistic movies, made when repression was mild (in the 1960s and 1970s), were more traditional artistically. However, such an ambitious project is beyond our abilities, although we find some consolation in the fact that such an endeavor has yet to be undertaken.

Another limitation of this work is the cursory treatment of other areas of intellectual activity. Of course, the history of Soviet cinema is closely intertwined with the history of literature, theater, and social science. Unfortunately, the political activities of all intellectuals can only be touched upon here (for a detailed analysis of the political activity of intellectuals in the Soviet Union, see Shlapentokh 1990).

THE MAJOR GOAL OF THE BOOK

The major goal of this work is to examine the influence of official ideology, i.e. the ideology supported by the centralized state, on the presentation of social reality by Soviet cinema. This is also a subject that has not been thoroughly studied until now. Soviet historians of cinema, up until a few years ago, were unable to speak seriously on this issue. Their publications before 1987 should be regarded as products of official propaganda (see, for instance, Romanov 1971; Murian 1976; Zorkaya 1989; Groshev et al. 1969; Vorontsov and Rachuk 1980). However, after the beginning of *Glasnost* the situation changed drastically and Russian critics, especially in the journal *Iskusstvo Kino* (*Art of Cinema*), published a series of brilliant and insightful articles on ideological processes in the Soviet movie industry since its birth. Among the most prominent authors were Iurii Bogomolov, Daniil Dondurei, E. Levin (1990), L. Kozlov, S. I. Freilikh, and M. Iampol'skii.

Acknowledgments

We wish to convey our gratitude to Vladimir's graduate students Walter Russyk and Eric Dammann for their editing and useful comments, as well as to Neil O'Donnell, who also contributed to this book. Our special thanks to Tatiana Chowdhury for her work in the preparation of the list of movies and the bibliography. Our special gratitude to Peter Manning for his very important suggestions, and to Richard Koffler, whose advice greatly improved this work.

We also extend our thanks to the members of our private movie club in East Lansing—Bob and Rosalyn Solo, Bernie Finifter, Daniel and Adelaide Suits, Gloria Blatt, Herbert and Zione Bisno, Albert and Beatrice Rabin, Paul and Betty Strassman, and Louise Carlson. The discussion of movies in this club was extremely useful and helped us to understand the radical distinction between American and Soviet cinema.

Parts II, III, and IV were written mostly by Dmitry Shlapentokh and Parts I and V by Vladimir Shlapentokh.

I

Theoretical and Historical Introduction

Before moving to the dramatic history of the Soviet movie industry, we first elucidate our methodological approach and the major fundamentals of the ideological mechanisms that the Soviet state used to control cinematography.

1

Social Reality and Ideology in Interaction

Two concepts crucial for this book, social reality and ideology, are discussed in the following sections. Let us start with the first.

SOVIET MOVIES AND THE OBJECTIVIST-CONSTRUCTIONIST CONTROVERSY ABOUT REALITIES

Whatever the intentions of filmmakers, they present in their movies their vision of some aspects of their larger social reality, even if they do so in the most allegorical ways.

For this discussion, it is important to distinguish between filmmakers best considered realists and those best considered nonrealists or formalists. These two groups are also referred to as objectivists and constructionists, respectively, since the first group objectivizes (i.e., recognizes and conforms to) ontological reality, whereas the second group *constructs* reality.

The distinction between realist and formalist movies is, of course, anything but clear, and numerous movies combine both approaches [see such Russian movies as Iurii Mamin's *Fountain* (1988), or Sergei Soloviev's *Assa* (1988)]. This combined approach is particularly prominent in comedies [see, for example, G. Bazhanov and A. Eidel'man's *Most Charming and Attractive* (1985) or El'dar Riazanov's *An Office Romance* (1977)].

The distinction between realist and formalist approaches in no way implies that one approach is preferable or inherently "more artistic" than the other, as some have argued (Kracauer 1960). Artists and artistic works have many goals, most of which are independent of whether realism is attained (about distinctions between filmmakers and their attitudes toward reality, see Ogle 1985; Dyer 1985; Mitry 1963; Monaco 1981, pp. 344–49; and Braudy 1976).

3

Realists are those who approach film as a medium for reflecting "real life," either as it objectively exists or as it is reflected in the minds of the film's heroes (Italian neorealist movies of the 1940s are perhaps the best examples of realist movies). Creators of representational movies, with their emphasis on the crucial role of the authors' perceptions of the world, are slightly further away from the goal of total realism than are the realists.

Formalists, by comparison, try to present the world in a manner free of the constraints of objective reality, although they do so under different rubrics (e.g., entertainment, surrealism, expressionism, escapism, and propaganda).[1] Included in the formalist category are advocates of "pure" social realism in Soviet films and the creators of the prescriptive "political films" found in the Third World and in Western countries. Although films by formalists always reflect the objective world to a certain extent, decoding these films is often, although not always, an unfulfilling exercise (see, for instance, the analysis of utopian and realistic elements in Richard Dyer's article about American entertainment movies; Dyer 1985).[2]

The idea of reality on which the analysis in this book is based is now in disfavor among social scientists. Contemporary American social literature generally avoids the concept of objective reality, attacking it from the standpoint of relativism.

The trend toward cognitive relativism emerged as a reaction against naive materialism and under the impact of various social and intellectual trends in Western society after the Second World War. This relativism was nurtured by very disparate intellectual schools of thought, such as existentialism, with its focus on the individual's choices, and Marxism, with its preoccupation with the impact of social environment on the human mind and the altering of reality through revolutionary praxis.

American radical ideology, as it was shaped in the 1960s, also encouraged relativism. It focused on the rights of minorities, multicultural diversity, the sovereignty of the individual, and everyone's right to claim to possess the truth and highly developed values.

Phenomenology in philosophy, psychology, sociology, and ethnomethodology was also important in the promotion of relativism in the perception of reality. It blurred the borders between "hard reality" and "subjective reality," contending that people themselves construct the world in which they live and interact with other people. The trend toward relativism in sociology and psychology reflects a broader trend in the social sciences, the arts, and other areas of society toward the relativization of beliefs and values.

It is noteworthy that the postmodernist trend in epistemology is nearly identical to the Marxist class approach in social science, literature, and the arts that the Soviet political elite enforced with the full power of the Soviet state's oppressive apparatus. The class approach resolutely rejected the possibility of a single objective picture of the world: There were both "bourgeois" and "socialist" visions. Adherents of the class approach found terms such as *objectivity* and *objectivism* as naive and misguided as do contemporary postmodernists [compare the Soviet definition of objectivism in Prokhorov (1983, p. 911) with that of Anderson (1990, pp. 60–64)]. Given the centrality of the class approach to Marxism, it is no surprise that the rejection of relativism and of values imposed by the class approach was one of Gorbachev's major achievements during the *glasnost* era.

Two fashionable intellectual trends—structuralism and deconstructionism—made their own special contributions to cognitive relativism. Structuralism suggests that different structures—material or mental—produce different visions of the world, each of which can claim validity. For example, Kuhn (1970) did this with his theory of scientific paradigms. In its turn, deconstruction, with its attacks against "essentialism" [e.g., the idea of truth, the illusions of objectivity, the privileged reading (the dominant interpretation of novels or movies imposed by power relations)], posits that artistic and literary works send different messages whose interpretation depends on individuals and the social context in which they find themselves (Foucault 1977; Derrida 1981; Ellis 1989, pp. 67–96).

As relativistic views gained favor, social phenomena and the social construction of reality by laypeople and scholars became the major preoccupation of those interested in epistemological issues. Terms such as *reality, objective reality,* and *the objective world* disappeared from publications in social science, and no such terms appear in the indexes of recent prestigious publications (see, for example, Coleman 1990; Smelser 1989; see also Lindzey and Aronson 1985). However, in emphasizing the numerous social factors that influence human perception, many modern authors of epistemological publications have disregarded purely cognitive processes, that is, those cognitive skills that operate relatively free from the influences of external variables (see, for example, Berger and Luckmann 1966).

Yet, in everyday life, as well as in the arts and sciences, most people implicitly follow some concept of reality and objectivity: Comparing available information with objective reality is an inherent aspect of human activity. Such comparisons are made when an individual contrasts the reality of goods or services as they are portrayed in the mass media to the way the goods and services are actually delivered in real life—in the individual's objective reality. Comparing the various realities presented by the prosecution and the defense with objective reality is the core duty of a jury. Psychiatrists and psychologists attempt to help their patients differentiate between their own personal realities and objective reality.

Similarly, movie and literature critics, as well as laypeople, spend considerable time comparing what they have seen or read to objective reality. For example, Norman Denzin, in his analysis of alcoholism in American cinema (despite his flirtation with deconstruction), contends that "alcoholism films do not faithfully reproduce reality," and agreeing with R. Steudler he suggests that "a film 'screens' and frames reality to fit particular ideological, or distorted images of 'real' social relationship." He also claims that "sociological analysis must uncover the ideological distortions that are embedded within any film's text." Furthermore, he (using deconstruction terminology) opposes his "realistic reading" to Hall's "hegemonic and negotiated readings," even if he is ready to use "subversive reading" as an alternative interpretation of the text (Denzin 1991, pp. 9–10; see also Hall 1980; Steudler 1987, p. 46; Grossberg 1988, p. 67). Similar debates have raged about the objectivity of recent movies such as Oliver Stone's *JFK* (1992) and Spike Lee's *Jungle Fever* (1991). (See also Gore Vidal's book [*Screening History* 1992] about the reflection of history in American movies.)

Objective reality is also used as a benchmark when historians assess the value of a particular source of information—whether it is the famous Middle Ages penal code, the so-called Barbarian Laws, or material from contemporary mass media. Quantitative sociologists make judgments regarding objective reality when they evaluate the extent to which the results published by one of their peers accurately reflect life in a given society. And recall the controversy surrounding Coleman's book (1983) on public and private schools, in which he was accused of distorting objective reality.

Finally, when people select sources of information, they trust or distrust these sources depending on how well the sources compare to their conceptions of "mundane reality," a term used by social psychologists (Aronson and Lindzey 1968). Mass media surveys abound with questions asking respondents to evaluate the objectivity of various sources of information, particularly individual sources from the mass media—newspapers, television, etc. (Schuman 1981).

Despite any caveats or protestations to the contrary, all of these examples suggest that people operate with an idea of "what really happened," to borrow the phrase of Leopold Ranke, the nineteenth-century German historian. We will use our idea of what really happened when examining the impact of ideology on Soviet movies, and assessing their importance as a source of information about Soviet society.

THE CONCEPT OF REALITY IN THIS BOOK

In analyzing Soviet movies, we will follow the materialist tradition in epistemology and differentiate between *real* and *subjective* reality in the following ways. *Objective* or *ontological* reality is the objective world faced by all people and institutions. *Subjective* reality is the reflection or representation of objective reality held in the psyches and documents of those same people and institutions.

This approach differs from the concept of objective and subjective reality proposed by Berger and Luckmann, who argue that objective reality is the image of the world accepted in a given social milieu and used as the basis for socialization and resocialization (Berger and Luckmann 1966). Our approach more closely matches that of Quinney, who argues that objective social reality is that with which people are presented, even if they then act to change reality in various ways (Quinney 1982, p. 46).

We maintain that there exists only one ontological, objective reality, the Kantian reality "for itself," which cannot be fully grasped by the human being. This implicit assumption is made, in fact, by all social actors—there exist as many subjective realities as there are individuals and institutions that hold perceptions of the world. As such, it is only by using a typology of social actors and their realities that we can reduce their numbers to a level conducive to analysis. Our approach includes the following five types, or classes, of reality:

1. Ontological, Kantian reality—objectively existing or objective reality.
2. Individual reality—ontological reality as reflected in individual psyches.
3. Institutional reality—reality as created by social institutions (especially the mass media and educational, religious, and political institutions).
4. Artistic reality—reality as it is created in literature and the arts.
5. Scientific reality—reality as it is created through the use of current scientific methods.

All these realities interact with each other at the phenomenological as well as ontological levels. The individual's perception of the world is shaped under the influence of institutional and artistic, especially cinema, realities, not to mention the impact of the perceptions of other individuals. Of course, institutional, artistic, and even scientific realities also bear the impact of other realities. What is more, the interaction between subjective realities directly affects the material world since individuals, groups, and institutions change their behavior under their perceptions of the world.

The interaction between the realities mentioned above is quite extensive, and is of crucial importance for this book. In examining this interaction, it is reasonable to make a distinction between consumers and producers of various subjective realities (about this distinction, see Anderson 1990, p. 9).

Individuals are, for the most part, consumers of realities produced by social institutions, figures in literature and the arts, and, to a limited degree, scholars. Individuals are especially susceptible to the influence of outside, subjective realities in facets of their lives that are beyond the scope of their everyday experience (e.g., subjective realities presented by the mass media regarding events in foreign countries). However, individuals also produce realities for others, especially when they attempt to impress others in order to increase their status or reach specific objectives (Goffmann 1959).

Filmmakers are, of course, producers of subjective realities, while their audiences are the consumers.

MOVIE REALITY AS A SOURCE OF INFORMATION ABOUT SOCIETY

Like novels and other creative works, movies provide an invaluable source of information regarding the society and era in which they are created. This thesis was in the past underscored by orthodox, non-Soviet Marxists like George Lukacs, who at the same time made a preposterous statement about the special devotion of the proletariat and its ideologues to truth (see Lovell 1980; Jarvie 1978).

Like all films, Soviet movies include each of the types of reality mentioned above: subjective reality, as held by the characters in, as well as the viewers of, the movies; institutional reality, which to some degree influences all social actors, whether imaginary or real (e.g., filmmakers of the Stalin era received directives regarding every element of their movies); artistic reality, which is created by every movie; and scientific reality, which is used in assessing a movie's accuracy in reflecting ontological reality.[3]

Of course, no single source of information, whether films or sociological studies, can claim to offer complete and reliable coverage of any given social issue. All investigations, including those declared objective, are vulnerable to the subtle influences of the investigator's own personal ideology (for our concept of ideology see below). Even the most sophisticated quantitative methodology is susceptible to the influence of what

Alvin Gouldner called "the domain of the sociologist," that is, his or her ideology, past experiences, individual tastes, and so on (Gouldner 1979; about the influence of ideologies on Soviet sociologists, see Shlapentokh 1987).

Given their dependence on intuition and imagination, however, novels and movies, especially those of low quality, are even more susceptible to the influence of their creator's personal ideology than are "scientific" sources, and are therefore less likely to provide objective pictures of reality. Similarly, the interpretation of fictional work is more dependent on the views of the examiner than is the interpretation of hard sociological data. In this respect, some ideas advanced by hermeneutics and deconstruction if taken with *cum grano salis* are extremely useful.

Still, despite these "limitations" (in a positivistic sense; see Hughes 1976, pp. 53–54), movies and other visual media permit a more complete, integrated, and multidimensional reconstruction of life than is possible through social science or even literature, both of which are limited by their linear/consecutive, rather than simultaneous mode of reporting. One major difference between movie reality and other realities is the role of gestalt—the overall image created from complex, simultaneous images of the world (about the role of the gestalt approach in movies, see Andrews 1984, pp. 26–27).

Sociological data, by definition, can provide only relatively abstract, composite information regarding the average member of a certain social group or institution (e.g., an average party apparatchik or an average member of the Young Communist League). However, movies (as well as fiction) present concrete, individualized cases that often convey more information to social scientists (as well as to laypeople) than do scientifically collected and processed data.

Although we reject Andre Bazin's statement that films somehow reveal the essential transcendental "truth" of reality (1985; see MacBean 1975, p. 5), we nonetheless suggest that movies provide a unique medium through which to view reality. We further suggest that, when following a multimethod, multisource approach to information gathering, movies can be used as one of many sources of information that, when taken together, may provide a reasonably objective picture of society (see Campbell and Fiske 1959; see also Shlapentokh 1985, 1986).

As intimated earlier, every movie provides a blend of hard and soft facts. That is, a movie reflects not only reality, but also the ideological orientation of its director as well as his or her (often limited) knowledge of the world. This ideological orientation, in turn, is shaped by many factors, including the political situation in the country, public opinion in general, the director's individual beliefs regarding specific ideological issues and, of course, the director's own life experiences. As such, movies reflect both the *overt values* of the ideology being presented and the *covert values* of popular culture in general. Thus, in contrast to the auteur theory, which holds films to be the creations of their directors and thus denies the impact of real life, we consider narrative films to be a valuable source of information about objective reality.

Unfortunately, there exists no instrument to help researchers determine the extent to which a movie is a source of information regarding reality or a source of information regarding the director's ideology and other elements of his or her worldview. We assume that the balance between hard facts and values is determined, in part, by the particular ideology in question. Specifically, as will be discussed later, we assume that directors with ideologies more critical of the existing regime are less likely to allow their mythologies and values to obstruct their portrayals of reality than are directors whose ideologies are more consonant with those of the current regime. Thus, movies created by directors ideologically critical of the current regime are, as a rule, considered by us to be more factually accurate than are movies created by the apologists of the current regime (of course, this is not always the case, as the history of Western movies in the 1960s suggests, see MacBean 1975).

Of course, all movies, including those made under the direct orders of a tyrant, provide rich sources of information regarding the ideologies of their creators. As such, movies like those made under Stalin's direction provide interesting glimpses into the workings of official ideology and the mentality of the dictator.

Movies that reflect ideologies only moderately critical of the current political and social order, as well as movies that are pure "entertainment," tend to reflect the dominant value system (such as those which came out of Hollywood in the 1930s and 1940s, and Soviet comedies before 1985; see Hughes 1976, pp. 65–66). The wrath of Adorno or Marcuse, (as well as other representatives of "critical theory," along with left-wing French and British movie critics in the 1950s to the 1970s) against movies and other products of the American mass culture as bearers of bourgeois ideology make them more valuable for sociologists and historians as a source of information about the dominant values and ideals of the times when the films were made.

Although movies, and in particular documentaries, are increasingly being used as sources of historical and sociological data (see, for instance, Grenville 1971; Smith 1976), movies have yet to be used as a source of data for so-called area studies, i.e., studies of foreign countries. Although American experts on Russia and China cite books and articles published in the countries being studied, they rarely do so with movies or television programs. This avoidance of audiovisual sources is related, in part, to their relative novelty, as well as to the comparative difficulties of nonnative speakers in understanding oral versus written texts.

Authors of publications on any society need be no more concerned that their readers have not seen a particular movie than they are that their readers have not read a particular book or article. In fact, due to videotape technology, movies are as accessible to researchers as are books and articles, and refusals to give credence to arguments buttressed by unfamiliar audiovisual sources (e.g., "I did not see this movie") are as groundless as refusals to accept arguments based on unfamiliar textual sources.

Whatever the reason, a survey of leading Western periodicals devoted to Russia, China, and Africa (and other parts of the world) revealed that the authors of articles published in these journals in 1988–1992 almost totally ignored audiovisual sources of information, including movies.

IDEOLOGY AND THE CONTENT OF MOVIES

The other central concept to this book is that of ideology (or "conceptual machinery"; Berger and Luckmann 1966). An ideology, defined rather broadly, is a more or less coherent set of values and beliefs that influence judgments of the external world and determine the behavior of individuals, groups, institutions, and societies (for similar definitions, see Geertz 1973; Kluckhohn 1951; see also Althusser 1984; McClellan 1986; Barthes 1972; Eagleton 1991; Cormack 1992; about Soviet ideology, see Shlapentokh 1986, 1988, 1990).

Individual or institutional perceptions are influenced to a greater or lesser extent by one or more ideologies, which shape all of the signs and symbols used to describe and maintain images of the world. Among the most important functions of an ideology is control over image management, that is, control over subjective reality.

We dismiss superrelativism, which attempts to equate all ideologies in their influence on the creation of subjective realities (see Bergman and Luckmann 1966, pp. 116–28, for an examination of this approach to ideologies). In this respect we agree with Allan Bloom's attacks against value relativism in social science (see Bloom 1987). We disagree with the concept that ideologies do not differ from each other in their impact on the presentation of real life. In fact, a major thesis of this book is that the official dominant ideology, or the ideology supported by state apparatus, to use Louis Althusser's phrase, distorts reality much more than other ideologies.

Of great importance to this work is the way in which ideologies are institutionally controlled and the extent to which institutions (e.g., state or religious sects) attempt to maintain their monopoly on imposing reality on the people within their sphere of influence. Although social control is sometimes imposed through "therapeutic" devices used to combat deviance (see Berger and Luckmann 1966, pp. 112–13), the primary means of social control have always been coercive. George Orwell in his *1984* was one of the first Western authors to recognize the role of state violence in imposing "necessary reality" on citizens. Habermas (1975, 1984) and Althusser (1984) are two prominent Western scholars who tried to understand theoretically the role of dominant ideology in a society where the ruling elite uses repressive means against its opponents.

We hold that as access to varied sources of information decreases and as institutional control over ideology increases, individuals have fewer opportunities to use their cognitive skills freely and are less able to create subjective realities that relatively accurately reflect ontological reality. Of course, this proposition has clear implications for state control over the movie industry (about ideology and propaganda in movies, see Taylor 1971; Berger 1972; Maynard 1975; Fiske 1982; Nichols 1985; Neale 1985; Turner 1988).

As totalitarian control over ideology decreases (as in democratic societies) and as the variety of available information increases, there is a greater chance that individuals can create subjective realities that more closely resemble ontological reality. Of course, in relatively free societies, radical ideologists on both the left and the right are able to, and often do, distort ontological reality more actively than do apologists of the dominant system (see MacBean 1975).

We maintain that the more an ideology criticizes the institutionalized, dominant beliefs and values of a given society, the more likely it is to spur cognitive activity regarding ontological reality. This approach is related to Karl Mannheim's view regarding the special role of the "free floating" intelligentsia. This group, according to Mannheim, is more able than any other to free itself from the deleterious influence that ideology has on its perceptions of the world (Mannheim 1966).

Our approach is also similar to the old Marxist tradition that considers the dominant ideology to be a false consciousness that impedes cognitive processing. According to this view, the effect of this false consciousness is especially strong during times when ideology is bolstered by mass terror.

Ideologies shape subjective realities primarily through influencing the selection of information and the weight given to single facts and processes (i.e., the degree of correctness and representiveness ascribed to the information). Ideologies also shape subjective realities by affecting the interpretation of cause-effect relationships.

The concept of ideology, as it has been presented here, is central to our recommendation of Soviet films as a source of information regarding Soviet society. In studies of specific cultures and/or time periods, films offer a unique vision of specific ideologies and the ways in which those ideologies influence the reflection of ontological reality.

The vision of the world offered by any ideology is made up of numerous elements, some of which may be understood through works of art and literature. Soviet movies provide countless reflections of the world-views propagated by both the official and unofficial ideologies active in Soviet society.

Analysis of the factors that influence the given picture of reality in movies is one of the most alluring of intellectual exercises. Fortunately, Soviet movies, because of the hostility of the Soviet authorities toward formalism,[4] were mostly films claiming to be realistic. This makes the accomplishment of our task much easier since it allows us to penetrate the mind of a director who deliberately depicts the world in enigmatic symbols.

The Ideological Dimension in the Western Analysis of
Soviet Films

Western authors have also addressed the role of ideology in Soviet films and can be divided into five groups, depending on their viewpoint.

The first group (known as the socialists) accepted the official Soviet view of ideology in Soviet cinema almost at face value, mostly because many of them shared this ideology and were themselves advocates of socialism. They seemingly did not want to join the army of foes of the Soviet Union and become "cold warriors." This group also enthusiastically greeted the films of the Cultural Revolution in China, the movies of the Castro regime in Cuba, as well as any film that claimed to be revolutionary and anti-imperialist (see, for instance, Fitzpatrick 1970, 1974; Schnitzer, Schnitzer, and Martin 1973; Goulding 1989; Taylor and Christie 1988).

The second group of cinema experts, belonging to various schools of postmodernism—mostly followers of auteur theory, structuralism, and deconstruction (we call them relativists; many of them could also be placed in the first group)—assumed that each cinematographer conveys his or her vision of the world, and uses films as messages "capable of producing multiple levels of meaning" while the viewers have "the freedom of decoding" (in Umberto Eco's words). In turn, the viewer "selects the one that holds true for his or her understanding of the social-cultural-historical environment" (Banks 1992, p. 195). These authors, like Banks, used Foucault's relativistic concept of truth, which supposes that truth "is produced by power," and therefore that truths generated by different powers are equal. These authors tend to ignore the direct pressure of ideology and power on cinematographers as well as the role of official cinema in the creation of an intentionally false reality.

Giannetti rebukes the Stalinist regime mostly for its rejection of formalism and elitism. Presenting this regime as the supporter only of realism, as if Stalin and his heirs were interested in the objective portraying of life, he asserted that "most of the best Soviet films are rather neutral politically," ignoring totally the radical impact of ideology on Soviet cinematography (Giannetti 1990, pp. 388–89).

The third group of authors tends not to ignore the detrimental pressure of Soviet ideology on cinema, but usually underestimates its impact on Soviet cinema. However, they present their heroes, people like Sergei Eisenstein, Alexander Dovzhenko, or Vsevolod Pudovkin, as martyrs. In their version of history, these directors made brilliant and veracious films free from ideological pressure, all the while fighting against Stalinism and never yielding their principles or participating in Soviet propaganda. It is evident that this quixotic view is not an accurate portrayal. We call these authors naive romanticists (see, for instance, Marshall 1983; Lawton 1987, 1989; Cook 1990).

The fourth group, the estheticists, is composed of a certain number of authors who intentionally ignored the ideological dimension in their studies. They concentrated only on various artistic trends and on innovations in moviemaking (we call this group the de-ideologists). One of them, Nicholas Galichenko (1991), managed to avoid the role of ideology in Soviet Cinema.

Only a handful of Western authors (the realists), who comprised the fifth group, attempted (mostly in the 1970s) to look at the following important issues: the history of Soviet cinema as an area of feverish ideological struggle, the ideological evolution of artists, and the ideological coercion by the formidable political power of the Soviet state. Behind these topical issues is a number of personal tragedies of great artists who were compelled to betray their convictions and their friends while forced, literally, to lick the boots of their superiors (see Taylor 1971; see also Rimberg 1973; Cohen 1973).[5]

Ideology in Soviet and American Films: The Radical Difference

Of course, ideology plays an extremely important role in any movie industry, including the American. It is easy to see the influence of the current ideological trends in American movies of any era. For example, the anticommunist propaganda in the United States during the cold war clearly influenced a considerable number of American films that generated many false portraits of Russians. Current ideological trends in America, including political correctness among others, have left their imprint on several contemporary films.

However, with the exception of the McCarthy period and with the famous Hollywood Ten, the state has never imposed (directly) its will on American cinematographers. They are, for the most part, free to choose their own ideological position and adjust to the public mood as they wish. Of course, the impetus for a filmmaker's ideological stance can stem from purely idealistic or purely commercial motives. American directors can also manifest their ideological stance by making socially loaded movies, as many did in the 1950s and 1960s (Stanley Kramer, for example), or they can offer the public a flight from reality as George Lucas and Steven Spielberg did in the 1970s and 1980s.

Most American moviegoers are unconcerned with how close a film reflects their version of reality. However, Soviet moviegoers, since 1918, usually compared life on the screen with the developments around them. This phenomenon is quite understandable if we remember that Americans have numerous sources of information about social life. The Soviet people until *glasnost*, however, avidly looked to unorthodox sources of social information like poetry or movies because of the control of the official mass media.

It is remarkable how radical the differences are between Russian and American publications about the lives of film directors that are addressed to the general public. While Russian authors dramatize their texts with stories about the innumerable ideological conflicts of their heroes with the authorities (see, for instance, the recent articles about Andrei Tarkovskii: Freindlikh 1992; Strugatskii 1987; *Komsomolskaia Pravda* 4 April 1992; *Nezavisimaia Gazeta* 8 April 1992; *Izvestia* 3 April 1992, 4 April 1992; *Iskusstvo Kino* February 1989, pp. 94–150) or Sergei Paradzhanov (*Nezavisimaia Gazeta* 16 November 1991; *Koza* 12 October 1991; *Literaturnaia Gazeta* 1 August 1990; *Iskusstvo Kino* July 1990, pp. 48–60, December 1990, pp. 32–71, April 1991, pp. 107–25), their American colleagues achieve the same objective with stories about American directors' drinking habits, sexual adventures, and intrigues against their rivals or superstars [among recent publications see McBride (1992) on Frank Capra, Patrick McGilligan (1991) on George Cukor, Mary Pat Kelly (1991) on Martin Scorsese, and Donaldo Spoto (1992) on Alfred Hitchcock].

The specific and limited role of ideology in the American movie industry probably explains why the ideological analysis of American movies is not a leading issue in the literature on films published in this country. It is remarkable that Louis Giannetti's popular *Understanding Movies* (its fifth edition came out in 1990) almost totally ignores ideological factors in shaping the content of films. (The term *ideology* is not even in his index.) The same indifference to the impact of ideology on movies is seen in Vivian Sobchack's *The Address of the Eye: A Phenomenology of Film Experience* (1992), even though she is absorbed with interpretation of the movie's content. At the same time, in the last two decades the number of publications about the influence of ideology on American movies has increased significantly (see O'Connor and Jackson 1979; Jarvie 1978; Pronay and Spring 1982; Denzin 1991)[6].

The Changing Relations between Ideology and Films
in the Soviet Union

The relationships between ideology and cinema in the Soviet Union were complex and dynamic. In the first period after the revolution (1918–1928), most cinematographers accepted official ideology as their own and served it sincerely and with enthusiasm. During Stalin's time (1929–1953), cinematographers had to obey the official ideology regardless of their personal convictions and ideals. However, after Stalin's death and the liberalization of the regime (1954-1985) film directors were finally able to express (somewhat) their own views on the world. They became involved in a game of trying to outsmart the authorities, while the authorities attempted to continue exploiting film directors for purposes of official propaganda. During the last years of the Soviet system (1985–1991), most Soviet cinematographers were involved in the destruction of official ideology. Films of this period often challenged not only socialist reality but human reality as well.

In our opinion, the central, and in many ways the most interesting period was the Stalinist one. These years serve to highlight how flexible the human mind can be when it is attempting to deal with both sheer coercion and artistic creativity. Films from this period also strayed from reality more than any other. For these reasons Stalin and his iron control over the film industry will be one of the major topics of this book.

Official Ideology as a Point of Reference for
Soviet Cinematographers

No doubt such absorption with dominant ideology in the analysis of films is typical of those who deal with cinema in a nondemocratic society, particularly authors who live in such societies. Such a preoccupation with this duality of ideology and reality reflects the everyday life of a population in a totalitarian state with its repressive apparatus.

Ultimately, the history of Soviet cinema involves the drama and tragedy of many extremely talented people that was played out in the fierce ideological struggle and confrontation between fictional and hard realities. In fact, Soviet cinema is an extremely important part of Soviet history in general. Stalin was able to use it as a serious political instrument (along with the mass media, literature, and education) and duped millions of Soviet people into believing in an imaginary world. Many even thought of themselves, contrary to their personal experience and the hardship of their everyday life, as residents of a socialist paradise. In this book we will attempt to convey at least some of this fascinating segment of Soviet history.

While official ideology is the central issue in this book, there were other ideologies that were supported privately in the Soviet Union by many people, mostly in the 1920s and especially in the post-Stalin period. In the first decade in the aftermath of the revolution there were bourgeois liberal and Trotskyist ideologies, and after 1953 neo-Leninist, neo-Stalinist, liberal socialist, and liberal capitalist ideologies, to name only the most important. All these ideologies seriously affected those film directors who tried to oppose, if mostly only indirectly, the official ideology.

METHODOLOGY

In this book, we attempt to use Soviet movies that reflect several different prevalent ideologies, as a source of information about those ideologies and about the lives of the Soviet people (similar American publications include White and Averson 1972; May 1980; Steven 1985).

In order to best capture the complexity of Soviet life as presented in Soviet movies, the current study uses a relatively unstructured content analysis that uses social groups, as they are presented in Soviet movies, as its major unit. Since our sample of movies is technically unrepresentative of the universe of Soviet movies produced in the last two decades [about six thousand movies—see *Tsentral'noie Statisticheskoie Upravlenie* (TsSu SSR), 1987, p. 572—while we use about four hundred movies in our analysis], we (by and large) avoid presenting any statistics that would also be unrepresentative.

In addition, we use elementary decoding techniques to uncover the meaning of Soviet movies. Because of censorship as well as the tradition of allegorical description of reality, Soviet film directors resorted to using parables, allusions, and historical parallels to convey certain messages. Decoding these movies requires knowledge of the symbolic language widely used by the Soviet intelligentsia (including movie directors) to convey its messages to the audience.

Of course, we concede that our interpretation of specific Soviet movies, especially those that are particularly complex and allegorical, may be assailable in light of modern structuralist semiotics. However, we are confident (and the publications of leading Russian movie experts in the last five years substantiate this claim) that our interpretations are similar to those of the majority of Soviet liberal intellectuals, with whom we share not only a history, but a set of values and beliefs.

The Social Groups in Question

One of the major units of our analysis is various social groups. These are categories of people that have some socially important common features that have been depicted in Russian movies since the revolution. The presentation, as well as the importance, of various groups has varied depending on the climate and time in which the film was made. Therefore, an examination of these differences during different historical periods will prove to be an excellent indicator of the changes that occurred in Russia during the last eight decades.

The social groups that have appeared in movies throughout the last eighty years include the bureaucracy, the intelligentsia (with intellectuals as its core), the masses (both Russian and non-Russian), the youth, as well as various other categories of people. Among them are various political actors in Soviet and Russian history, such as revolutionaries, leaders, the old dominant class, the tsar, enemies of the people, model workers, foreigners, ethnic Russians, Orientals, Jews, the Red Army and its commanders, prominent Russian scholars from the past, outstanding Russian commanders in the past, and progressive foreigners. Other groups, occasionally singled out by directors as their main characters, include criminals, prostitutes, and drunkards.

A few words about these major social groups seem appropriate. By the end of the 1980s, the bureaucracy of the Soviet Union consisted primarily of party apparatchiks, figures in various official public organizations (e.g., the Young Communist League, trade unions, the Union of Soviet Writers), officials in government bodies, and directors of large enterprises. These people made up the *nomenklatura* and were appointed by party committees at various levels. Although estimates of the size of the Soviet bureaucracy during the 1980s vary, a widely accepted number is about eighteen million (for more about the Soviet bureaucracy, see Voslenski 1980).

There are two approaches to defining the intelligentsia and the intellectuals. The first approach, which is normative and therefore somewhat more subjective, supposes that a member of the intelligentsia (or an intellectual) is one who possesses a cluster of intellectual, cultural, and (most importantly) moral virtues such as kindness and altruism. He or she also serves as a model for the rest of society. This approach was dominant in prerevolutionary Russia and continued to be very popular in the Soviet Union (e.g., Pomerants 1982; Solzhenitsyn 1974; Dudintsev 1987; Granin 1987, 1988; see also the discussions in *Literaturnaia Gazeta,* 17 August, 21 September, and 23 November 1988).

The second approach to defining the intelligentsia and the intellectuals uses formal criteria, such as level of education and involvement in creative work (that is, the production of either new ideas or new things). This approach is shared by us with official Soviet statisticians and Soviet sociologists (e.g., Shkaratan 1982; Zaslavskaia 1988a, p. 17).

The masses, as they are presented in Soviet movies, consist primarily of workers and peasants with relatively little education. Soviet movie directors rarely use clerks or technical personnel as representatives of the masses, preferring instead to have their heroes working in factories or on collective farms.

The youth in Soviet movies are generally those under thirty years of age. Special emphasis is placed on characters between the ages of sixteen and twenty-five years old.

The analysis of each of these and other groups will begin with an examination of its "central tendency" (the predominant image of the social group as presented in Soviet movies) and will then examine other trends in the presentation of that group. Thus, any given ideology might figure heavily in the depiction of one social group, but only secondarily in the portrayal of other groups.

NOTES

1. In one of his stories, the famous Czech writer Jaroslav Hasek told about the instigation of a car accident whose single witness was a poet. The police vainly tried to extract some information from this man, who was totally absorbed with his poetic world and seemingly noted nothing else. But one of the smartest investigators asked the poet to show them his most recent poem, which at first glance apparently had nothing to do with the accident. However, after careful decoding, the police found in the exotic sonnet all the information they needed, including the number of the license plate.

2. Even movies that stray widely from "objective reality" contain "real-life" details. Before 1987, the Soviet people were permitted to watch only those American movies that concentrated on the grim side of life in the United States, such as Francis Ford Coppola's *The Godfather* (1972), or William Friedkin's *The French Connection* (1971). Nonetheless, Soviet critics still assessed American life positively, because the movies contained details (such as the number of rooms in an apartment, or the assortment of food available) that suggested that, despite its grisly aspects, life in the United States was still far better than in the Soviet Union.

3. A unique feature of movie reality is its ability to form a basis from which

other artistic realities may emerge. Thus, some literary and film characters spring from previous literary works and films. This is especially true in Russia, where the role of classic literature has always been extensive, and dozens of movies have been made based on novels by Turgenev [Kheifits's *Asia* (1978)], Leo Tolstoy [Shveitser's *Resurrection* (1960–1962); Zarkhi's *Anna Karenina* (1968); Bondarchuk's *War and Peace* (1966)], Fyodor Dostoevsky [Pyriev's *The Brothers Karamazov* (1969) and *The Idiot* (1958)], Anton Chekhov (Kheifits's *The Lady with the Little Dog* (1960); and Annenskii's *The Medal on the Neck* (1954)].

4.   Formalism was relatively strong in the first years of the Soviet movie industry. Vertov or Eisenstein were known for their innovations in the language of film and for their inclination toward various artistic gimmicks. Then in Stalin's time formalism was totally expunged from Soviet films, and only in the 1960s do we see the attempt to restore formalistic movies, mostly in the films of Sergei Paradzhanov and Andrei Tarkovskii.

5.   American Trotskyists in the late 1930s were probably the first to realize the full scale of Stalin's ideological control over Soviet cinema, while most American film critics and historians continued to hail without reservations such Soviet masterpieces as the Vasiliev brothers' *Chapaiev* or Dzigan's *We Are from Kronstadt* (1936). Although Dwight Macdonald, as a left radical himself, recognized their revolutionary spirit, he wrote about "the deformations" in these films imposed by Stalin's propagandists. He also was aware that the greatest figures of Soviet cinema in the 1920s and 1930s including Eisenstein, Pudovkin, and Dovzhenko, "must become political hacks" and noted how Eisenstein's *October* was adjusted to the newest reshuffle in the party leadership (MacDonald 1938, 1939).

6.   It is remarkable that cinema experts in other countries (particularly British) are more often attentive to the ideological dimension of their domestic films (see, for instance, Curran and Porter 1983).

2

State, Ideology, and Film in Soviet History

During its eight decades of existence, the Soviet state created an almost perfect machine to control cinema and to coerce movie people to act as propagandists of Soviet ideology and the current party policy. Even in the final two decades of Soviet history, when cinematographers obtained some freedom, they were able to deviate only very slightly from the orders of the ruling elite. In fact, this machine, which was built in the early 1920s, was dismantled only in 1990–1991, with the collapse of the Soviet Union.

SOVIET MOVIES AS THE MAIN WEAPON OF SOVIET IDEOLOGY

One of the greatest discoveries of Lenin and Stalin was the ability of a powerful state to create a subjective reality that had almost nothing in common with ontological reality. Though the Soviet leaders mobilized all forms of art, literature, science, education, and mass media for the creation of their reality, they realized that movies were the most effective tool for creating and disseminating these false images. Movies, due to their visual presentation, emotional impact, and popularity, were able to influence a wider audience than any other media.[1]

Of course, Lenin's impact on the movie industry is not comparable with that of his heir, whose reign was much longer. However, Lenin did sign the decree nationalizing the movie industry in 1919, proclaiming that "film is the most important of the arts" (Lenin, Collected Works, V. 5, p. 579). He also initiated the regulation of which films were to be shown in theaters.[2] For all intents and purposes, however, the Soviet movie industry was built by Stalin. As might be expected, the peak of this distortion was reached during Stalin's time,[3] which will be discussed at length later.

FICTIONAL REALITY IN MOVIES AND SOVIET LIFE

While life imitates art in any society, this is even more likely to be the case in a totalitarian society. Soviet movies, with their abrasive misrepresentation of reality, spurred the Soviet people to imitate the conduct of the heroes in Soviet films. It was as if Soviet life were not the model for Soviet moviemakers, but rather an object of accommodation to the requirements of ideal reality as it was presented in movies. Soviet people emulated the heroes in movies such as Mark Donskoi's *How Steel Was Tempered* (1942)—a film about the ascetic Pavel Korchagin, an exemplary hero of the civil war—and Alexander Stolper's *The Story of a Real Man* (1948), which was about Alexander Maresiev, a World War II pilot who continued to fly and fight against the Germans even after the amputation of both legs.[4]

The ease with which ordinary people accepted essentially false images of reality was possible because the masses, under the pressure of omnipresent propaganda and out of an Orwellian fear of punishment, believed (against their own personal experience) in the veracity of what they saw on the screen. Of course, their trust was made easier because so many movies were devoted to the past or to foreign countries, both of which existed outside their experience. As Iurii Bogomolov wrote,

> [E]ven for peasants who had experienced the horrors of collectivization, movies like Pyriev's *Swineherd and Shepherd*, *Tractor Drivers*, or *The Rich Bride*, all of which depicted the happy life in the countryside, did not seem to be mocking their real experience. Their own poverty seemed less real. The affluence on the screen was for them evidence of its material existence. (1989, p. 61)

Some authors, believing in escapism as a major function of movies, consider these films both necessary and positive, in that they permitted the people to ignore their harsh everyday life. As an argument in their favor they cite the fact that these movies were very popular. They could just as easily refer to Hollywood comedies, which were extremely popular in America during the Great Depression (Chukhrai 1991a, p. 127).

THE CHOICE OF IDEOLOGY

From the end of 1929, the work of most Soviet filmmakers was controlled by sheer force. In the first decade following the revolution, however, many filmmakers accepted the revolution, and the perspectives it opened for them, with enthusiasm. During this time, such directors as

Sergei Eisenstein, Dziga Vertov, Vsevolod Pudovkin, and Mikhail Romm (and such theater directors as Vsevolod Meierkhold) did appear sincere in their support of communism, world revolution, and the party leadership. Furthermore, this ideology was associated, in the minds of filmmakers (as well as other young artists), with new, so-called leftist trends in arts—vanguardism in the first place. For this reason, revolutionary Marxism was attractive for young people starting their career in a new society with the full support of the new regime.[5]

Of course, during this time movies continued to be censored and regarded as a tool of propaganda. However, young filmmakers did not consider this control as crude coercion, but rather as a manifestation of the party's control over all aspects of life.

This sincere devotion to a new ideology and new forms of art explains why this period witnessed the creation of such masterpieces of cinema (according to most historians) as Vertov's *Movie Eye* (1924), Eisenstein's *Battleship Potemkin* (1925), and Dovzhenko's *Land* (1930). These films, with their anti-individualist emphasis, their focus on the masses, and their lyrical treatment of everyday life, stand in sharp contrast to the accepted view of the cinema community in present-day Russia: that these movies were a sheer distortion of reality.

Along with those who sincerely joined the cause of the revolution, there were a number of filmmakers who simply pretended to be Bolsheviks. Evgenii Gabrilovich, for example, claimed that he was "hostile to the October coup, but only at home, among family members" (Gabrilovich 1992).

With the advent of collectivization and the Great Terror, the psychological situation changed drastically. From the early 1930s, most filmmakers (as well as other intellectuals) viewed official ideology as a merciless power to be obeyed regardless of one's personal views. However, there were some who, following Orwellian logic, tried to love Big Brother and support the changing ideological postulates of the party (especially if their love of the leader and the party was well rewarded).

There is nothing to suggest that Mikhail Chiaureli, the most active filmmaker in the glorification of Stalin, was not sincere in his efforts to complete shooting *The Fall of Berlin* on the seventieth birthday of his beloved leader in 1949. Accounts by participants in this film (which would later prove to be one of the most deceptive movies in Soviet history) reveal that everyone, including the famous actors, was equally sincere.[6]

However, it would be a mistake to look at Soviet filmmakers as a homogeneous community. Gabrilovich, the 1991 recipient of the Nika (the special prize of Russian cinematographers "for honesty and dignity") divided them into three strata: (1) those who glorified reality and ate

salmon and caviar at receptions in the Kremlin; (2) those who denounced reality and were beaten and bloodied; and (3) those who glorified the same reality, but with various reservations and innuendoes.
Gabrilovich put himself in the third group (Gabrilovich 1991, p. 94).
Eisenstein, the famous filmmaker of the 1930s and 1940s, definitely belonged in this category also.[7]

SOVIET MOVIE DIRECTORS AND TRUTH

The relation between Soviet movies and truth, or ontological reality, is
very complex. An historical analysis will help to elucidate the radical
differences in these relationships during different periods of Soviet
history.

During the first period (until the death of Stalin), movie directors were
almost totally unconcerned with truth. As discussed previously, most
filmmakers during this time constructed a reality that pleased the party
leadership. These filmmakers (some of whom would become leading
figures in the liberal movements of the 1960s) eagerly accepted the official rewards (medals, prizes, etc.) for their distorted films.

However, after Stalin's death directors easily, and seemingly without
scruples, changed their old movies, adapting them to a new version of
official history. Thus Romm cut from his *Lenin in October* (1937) and *Lenin
in 1918* (1939) the scenes with Stalin, while leaving the rest intact. Leonid
Lukov replaced a portrait of Stalin with one of Lenin in one scene of his
Great Life (1940–1946) and, like Romm, allowed the Soviet people to see
the new version of the movie.[8]

Only a handful of film directors (and only two decades after the revolution) attempted, using Aesopian allegory, to say something that was at
odds with official ideology. And even fewer dared not accept publicly
the official critique of their movies, as did Eisenstein when he recanted
his flaws in *Bezhin Meadow* (1935–1937)(see Eisenstein 1956, p. 387).[9]

Only with Stalin's death did the idea of truth (however interpreted)
and censorship begin to be important to movie directors, although they
were still strongly divided ideologically. Some film directors, as well as
many other intellectuals, had a sort of liberal subconscious, which, as
soon as it was safe, immediately directed them to the defense of liberal
and democratic ideas. Mikhail Romm is a good example; having made
one of the most dishonest movies (*The Russian Question*, 1948), he drastically changed his behavior as soon as he realized that his life and his
position were no longer in jeopardy. The same can be said about the
legion of other filmmakers who became progressive in the 1960s, including Iosif Kheifits, Evgenii Gabrilovich, Iulii Raizman, and Gleb Panfilov.

It is interesting that, during the 1960s and 1970s, several Western experts were attacking the idea of objective reality in filmmaking while Soviet filmmakers were attacking countless official beliefs and images of Soviet society, both past and present.

With the first signs of liberalization during Khrushchev's thaw, film directors began producing movies that reflected, although rather timidly, several real issues of Soviet life. Some of these movies also contained allusions to the Stalin era and its remnants.

HOW FILMMAKERS WERE CONTROLLED

Soviet bureaucrats often used brutal and corrupt methods to impose official ideology on moviemakers. Regarding the ideological effect of movies on the population as being of primary importance, the same Soviet authorities who in many cases were sensitive to the international recognition of Soviet achievement in endeavors like musical performance and sport, were implacable to ideologically bad movies, even if these movies were acclaimed in the West. As Riazanov mentioned in 1990, "the State Movie Committee did not stand on ceremonies with us, filmmakers, and treated us as serfs" (1990, p. 27).

Two great Soviet intellectuals—the famous film director Sergei Eisenstein, and the brilliant actor Nikolai Cherkasov—kept a transcript of their 1947 meeting with Stalin regarding their film *Ivan the Terrible* (1945). The transcript, published thirty-one years later, shows that the world-famous creator of *Battleship Potemkin* (1925) asked Stalin for directions regarding the length of Ivan's beard, and the actor sought approval for various scenes in the movie (*Moskovskie Novosti*, 7 August 1988).

Official interference in Soviet filmmaking did not stop following Stalin's death. Although Khrushchev allowed the film director Iulii Raizman the freedom to name a new movie (against the wishes of the minister in charge of the movie industry), and he allowed the public presentation of Elem Klimov's first movie (*The Communist; Ogoniok* 2, 1958, p. 16), officials (including Khrushchev) were not always so agreeable.

In 1988 Klimov recounted what he was told by a high-ranking party official who demanded that he remove a scene from a film. After the official had exhausted all of his arguments, he told Klimov, "You argue to no purpose. Under Stalin emerged an all-pervasive system of power which none of the absolute monarchies had. You will never win" (Klimov 1989).

Similarly, the Soviet establishment not only refused, for anti-Semitic reasons, to release Alexander Askol'dov's movie (*Commissar*, 1989)—which sympathetically described the life of Jews during the civil war—but ordered all copies of the film destroyed and punished the film director with many years of poverty (about this incident, see *Novoye Russkoye Slovo*, 21 June 1988).

The history of the Soviet system is illustrated by the number of movies forbidden or radically changed under direct pressure from the authorities (not to mention the large number of scripts and proposals rejected before shooting). During the post-Stalin period, the ratio of rejected or radically changed films and rejected scripts increased significantly because in the past administrative control, as well as self-control, was much stronger than later. Only a few movies were prohibited for public viewing during Stalin's time [for example, the second part of Eisenstein's *Ivan the Terrible* (1945), the second part of Leonid Lukov's *The Great Life* (1940–1946), and Alexander Ivanov's *Star*[10] (1949)], while a large number of movies were prohibited in the post-Stalin period. However, during Stalin's time a number of movies were destroyed during production, as was the case with Eisenstein's *Bezhin Meadow* and *Que Viva Mexico!* (1931).[11]

The relatively small number of movies rejected by Stalin is directly attributable to the fact that "the great leader and teacher of the people," as Shostakovich mockingly referred to him in his memoirs, gave direct orders to moviemakers concerning the type of film he wanted. For instance, he gave very specific directives to the Vasiliev brothers when they were commissioned to make a movie about Vasilii Chapaiev, a hero of the civil war (1934).[12]

The case with Tarkovskii's movies demonstrates a similar atmosphere during Brezhnev's period. The international recognition his movies received [for example, *Andrei Rublev* (1971) or *Mirror* (1975)] did nothing to mitigate the attacks against them in the USSR.[13]

As Tarkovskii wrote in his diary (which he titled "Martyrologue"), "without the permission of the state it is impossible to even begin filming. And attempting to use your own money is even more forbidden. Such an action would be immediately assessed as criminal, ideological diversion, and subversive activity" (Tarkovskii 1992). Tarkovskii described many cases of direct intervention into his work by state bodies.[14] Certain movies of Alexei German, Otar Ioseliani[15], and Kira Muratova were also prohibited.

Publications released following the events of August 1991 revealed even more details about the role of coercion and fear in the life and activity of moviemakers. A document from the party's secret archives describes how the Central Committee directly forbade Vasilii Shukshin to make a movie about Stepan Razin, the leader of a peasant rebellion in the seventeenth century. The script was considered too realistic in its description of the horror of the uprising, and it depicted Razin, an icon in Soviet history, as "hysterical and irrational" (*Literaturnaia Gazeta*, 26 February 1992).

Riazanov told a number of stories concerning his fights with the authorities about his movies. One of them is about his film *Please, Say a Good Word about Poor Hussar* (1981). From the very beginning the authorities did not like that in this movie, devoted to life in tsarist Russia, the secret police were presented in a bad light: They supposed that the viewers would equate the police with the KGB. Director and scriptwriter were forced to make many corrections, which left little of the initial text intact. What is more, the officials themselves made cuts in the movie before showing it on TV.

Another story tells about the attempt of Riazanov to cast Yevgeni Yevtushenko, the famous poet, in the role of Cyrano de Bergerac in the movie of the same title. Mikhail Suslov, the main Soviet ideologue in Brezhnev's time, did not permit it and scuttled the whole project (Riazanov 1990).[16]

The Party Apparatus as Supervisor

The time spent by Stalin controlling the movie industry was certainly the exception for Russian leaders. After his death no Soviet leader was nearly as involved in this sort of activity. Khrushchev, Stalin's immediate successor, exerted some control over movies, and we know very little about Brezhnev's and his successors' involvement.

For the most part, supervision over the movies was performed by the Central Committee (mostly by the Department of Culture), and the State Committee of Cinematography (Goskino). After Stalin's death, regional and republican party committees, which controlled the movie studios on their territories, also had a significant influence on films. However, their intervention in the movie industry occasionally led to conflicts between Moscow and the republican or regional center. These conflicts were, of course, settled by the general secretary.[17]

Party control over films was carried out not only by the Central Committee and Goskino. In fact, each studio had its own party secretary who exerted ideological control over any production from the very beginning, the endorsement of a proposal, to the film's completion. The district party committee on whose territory a film was shot was deeply involved in supervision. Glavlit, the official censorship body, was also a serious barrier to new films, even if they had been endorsed by the other bodies.

Ideological control over movies was also exerted by a number of pressure groups protecting their special interests. These groups, which included the KGB, the army, and various ministries, all had the right to veto the production of any movie that was damaging to them, and to promote those films useful to their agenda.

The KGB was particularly active, especially during the 1970s and early 1980s. This institution employed a number of scriptwriters who knew exactly what their patrons expected from films. One such author was Iulian Semenov, who wrote dozens of scripts glorifying the KGB; some of his more famous scripts include *Seventeen Moments of Spring* (1973), *Tass Is Authorized to Announce* (1986), and *Confrontation* (1985). Furthermore, a leading KGB chief, Semion Tsvigun under the pen name of Dneprov, also wrote a number of scripts for such movies as *Front Line without Front Line* (1978) and *Front Line behind Front Line* (1975). [For more about the administrative control over Soviet cinema, see Golovskoy (1986, pp. 7–37).]

The party apparatus used many devices to undermine an undesirable movie before its creation (usually while it was still a proposal or script). In the 1930s and 1940s, when this activity was at its peak, the major arguments against such movies were not only purely political (such as, for instance, those which Stalin leveled against Dovzhenko's script *Ukraine in Flames*, 1944), but also artistic. For example, some movies were condemned for being of the "wrong" artistic style, such as formalism. In fact, the term *formalism* was basically a code name, not for vanguardism or modernism, but for a high intellectual level not suitable for propaganda purposes.

This tactic was used against Eisenstein's *Bezhin Meadow* in 1937 (*Kino*, 22 and 24 April 1937). Other terms, such as *objectivism, pessimism, distortion of historical truth, hidden Zionism, pacifism, abstract humanism, the denigration of the Soviet people*, and *naturalism* were also used by the party in the post-Stalin period as justification for shelving or preventing the creation of a movie.[18] Such ideological cliches aided the party in obfuscating the real reason for a movie's destruction.

It is remarkable how after 1989 former party apparatchiks began to publish articles and give interviews in order to embellish their behavior as the supervisors of the movie industry and tormentors of cinematographers. These people tried to present themselves as those who protected filmmakers against apparatchiks much worse than they were. They depict themselves as the defenders of various well-known directors, particularly Tarkovskii and Shukshin (see, for instance, the interview with Igor Chernouzan, formerly important in the Central Committee, who was responsible for the arts; *Nezavisimaia Gazeta*, 4 August 1992).

The Role of Fear

With the advent of *glasnost*, Soviet film directors were able for the first time to expose the role of physical fear in their lives and their creative work. This fear was so overwhelming that during Stalin's time, and to a lesser extent later, any act of benevolence on the part of the authorities was perceived by many intellectuals as a sign of "salvation" from arrest or dismissal from one's job. Raizman recounts what happened when his friend Mikhail Romm was awarded a medal in 1937: Romm ran upstairs shouting "I got the Order of Lenin, they will not arrest me now" (*Sovietskaia Kul'tura*, 4 June 1988).

Memoirs of the 1949 anticosmopolitan campaign (which could have been published only during *glasnost*) graphically depicted the fear that plagued intellectuals, as well as the numerous cases of betrayal between friends and colleagues. Sergei Iutkevich recounted how his friend and actor Mark Donskoi ardently attacked him at a public meeting devoted to the denunciation of cosmopolitans (Iutkevich 1988, p. 106).[19]

Speaking about his life during the last five decades, Gabrilovich commented:

As a close witness of those years, I can contend that the Academies of Sciences, Arts, and Marxism, in establishing the moving forces of history, have neglected a crucial, and perhaps even the most important, mainspring: fear. In order to understand so many of the puzzles, secrets, and absurdities of our complicated life, it is necessary to comprehend, most of all, the real significance of fear. (*Sovietskaia Kul'tura*, 17 June 1989)

Omnipresent fear, combined with the pressure of official ideology, forced cinematographers to discuss openly the activity of subversives and spies in the movie industry. When Boris Shumiatskii (the head of Goskino) was arrested in 1937, Pudovkin conferred with S. Dukelskii, the new head of this institution, and provided him with new "evidence" of the criminal activity of the previous leadership. At the same time, as a good friend, he tried to exploit this discussion in favor of his colleagues, by suggesting that they were also the victims of "the enemies of people" who controlled cinematography. In this way he was able to protect both himself and his friends (*Iskusstvo Kino* 12, 1991, pp. 141–49).

This fear subsided only partially after Stalin. Alexei German described how, when his movies started to be shelved in the early 1980s, his circle of friends became smaller and smaller. Ultimately, he had no one to invite to his birthday party (see Kornilov 1988).

Colleagues as Tools of Control

Official ideologues used filmmakers, including those who were well respected and had liberal leanings, to control the ideological purity of Soviet movies. By making cinematographers and the Union of Moviemakers, an organization tightly controlled by the party until 1987, their sycophants, Soviet leaders achieved many goals simultaneously. For one thing, movie people could "supervise" each other much better than bureaucrats could. But perhaps most important was the demoralization of film people brought about by their involvement in the dirty work of political snitching and cooperation with the KGB. During this time (especially in the 1920s), filmmakers began to resemble *capos*—the prisoners appointed by Nazis to be the seniors among their cellmates.

In the 1930s the mutual denunciation of filmmakers continued unabated. At film conferences in Moscow, the party leadership had little trouble pushing young directors like Iutkevich and Trauberg into belittling Eisenstein and Pudovkin, who, for all their obedience, still did not behave with enough servility. Later, Eisenstein's *Bezhin Meadow* was actively chastised by his colleagues and even by a group of filmmakers at a public meeting, a typical occurrence during this period (Freilikh 1990; Iampol'skii 1990, p. 98).

Even after 1953, when the regime was much milder, filmmakers continued to engage in their "police functions." Pyriev was a leading figure in the denunciation of Shveitser's *Tight Knot* (1957). Donskoi and even Romm, the conscience of Soviet cinema in these years, aided the Soviet minister of culture when he lambasted Alov and Naumov's movie *Peace to Those Who Enter* (1961) only because the soldiers and officers at the front did not look clean (*Iskusstvo Kino* 5, 1990, pp. 20–24).

Filmmakers were regularly recruited for the castigation of Tarkovskii's movies. Naumov and Alov, after being the victims of ideological critique themselves, joined with Raizman, Marlen Khutsiev, Chukhrai, and Soloviev (all of whom were directors with strong liberal reputations), in the authority-sponsored campaign against Tarkovskii's film *Mirror*.

Soviet filmmakers were also active in helping the authorities undermine Askol'dov's *Commissar* (1989). One of the most conspicuous detractors was Leonid Trauberg, a famous filmmaker of Jewish origin, who also happened to be Askol'dov's teacher. One day after praising this film, Trauberg reversed his position when he discovered the negative opinion of his superiors. He went on to attack the film because it concentrated on the fate of the Jewish people, a topic that was forbidden at this time due to Israeli aggression against Palestinian Arabs (*Iskusstvo Kino* 1, 1989, pp. 110–21). The list of prominent cinematographers who aided the authorities in their fight against the truth in movies is extensive, and includes such names as Iutkevich, Mikhail Bleiman, and Rostislav Iuren'ev.[20]

The Case of the Anticosmopolitan Campaign

Of all the political plots in which the party pitted cinematographers against each other (a phenomenon well known in Hollywood during the

McCarthy era), the most grievous was, of course, Stalin's 1949–1953 anticosmopolitan campaign. Those targeted were Jewish intellectuals and all potential liberals, who were accused of being unpatriotic and inimical to the Russian people and its culture.

In an atmosphere of terror it was easy for the authorities to force filmmakers to betray their colleagues. Trauberg and Iutkevich, both directors with relatively "clean" ideological records, were selected as the main ideological villains. After Stalin's death, they were permitted to produce ideologically loaded movies again.[21]

The list of those recruited for these purposes was remarkable. It included not only such notorious loyalists as Ivan Pyriev (known for his Russian chauvinism), but several people with high moral status in the movie community—Sergei Vasiliev and especially Pudovkin. One of the most active turncoats was Mark Donskoi, who as a Jew could have easily been the victim of this campaign. The vindictiveness of his speeches against his comrades was probably an attempt to stave off this danger.

During a meeting on 24 February 1949, these four filmmakers attempted to outdo each other in their denunciations of colleagues for ideological vices, apparently understanding that each of these vices could be grounds for arrest and the *Gulag* (the network of concentration camps in the Soviet Union).[22]

Movie People and the KGB

As is now apparent, filmmakers, along with other intellectuals (and the Soviet people in general), were part of the gigantic army of KGB informers. Thus far, because the KGB archives are still mostly sealed, there are no direct data about those who collaborated with the KGB. Currently there is only indirect information about the collaboration of filmmakers, as well as other intellectuals, with the political police.[23]

The weekly *Argumenty i Fakty* could only publish an excerpt from a report of a KGB official who named the aliases of the agents who, on the eve of the fifth congress of cinematographers, informed the KGB about some "negative tendencies" in the movie industry. Readers could only speculate as to the true identities of those hidden behind these nicknames (*Argumenty i Fakty*, April 1992).[24]

THE GRADUAL RELEASE FROM FEAR

Only with the death of Stalin and the disappearance of mass terror were filmmakers (as well as other intellectuals) able to begin to create their own ideological vision of the world. They were finally able to become, on their own initiative, genuine advocates of various ideologies that began to circulate in the country. Of course, a host of film figures continued (even until the late 1980s) to hold the official line as their own view.

Having the freedom to espouse one's own ideology, filmmakers began to advocate their ideology in their movies, often using subtle techniques to get their point across. However, the end of the Stalin era did not mean the end of ideological control. In fact, as soon as a filmmaker began to adhere to a certain ideology, his or her comrades-in-arms would begin to exert pressure so that the filmmaker would not deviate from the mainstream of that ideology. This circumstance explains why in the 1960s and 1970s liberal film directors were not able to deviate from their views (even if this would mean gaining the favor of the state) because others in their milieu would harshly condemn them for doing so.

This was the case with liberal Soviet filmmakers such as Riazanov, who, regardless of political circumstances, tried to make movies according to his own internalized values and beliefs [compare, for instance, *Carnival Night* (1956), made during the Khrushchev era, *Garage* (1980), made during the Brezhnev era, and *Forgotten Melody for Flute and Orchestra* (1987), made during Gorbachev's *glasnost*, each of which reveals the same sympathies and antipathies].

At the same time, a filmmaker may also choose a particular ideology for conformist and opportunistic reasons, and then abandon this ideology as soon as it is convenient to do so. This approach was taken by directors such as Alov and Naumov, whose movies include *Worried Youth* (1955), which followed the dictates of Soviet Marxism, as well as *The Shore* (1984), which was clearly inspired by Russophile ideology. Similarly, Soloviev, who in 1988 made *Assa*, a film denouncing the fundamentals of the Soviet system, was also the director of *One Hundred Days after Childhood* (1975). The latter film, made during the worst days of the Brezhnev era, was loyal to the system and therefore was highly praised by the regime.

CONCLUSION

Reality has been a central issue for the Soviet film industry since its beginning. The Communist party and the Soviet state created a powerful apparatus to impose their ideology on Soviet cinematographers, forcing them to distort reality in numerous ways. Stalin's period was, in this respect, the most interesting and, at the same time, the most painful for Soviet filmmakers.

Stalin was a unique leader who was extremely absorbed with movies and the moviemaking industry. He managed to create a reality on the screen that had very little in common with real life. Soviet filmmakers were under the permanent control of various party bodies and of Goskino. The Soviet state also used filmmakers to supervise each other, making sure that official policy was implemented fully. With Stalin's death, the pressure on filmmakers declined. However, the control of the film industry remained basically intact.

NOTES

1. During the 1950s and 1960s, the average Soviet citizen visited movie theaters at least twice a month. Regular viewers attended movie theaters about thirty-five times a year (Zinin and Dishkin 1985, p. 154). In the 1960s the average individual spent about forty minutes per week on movies, approximately as much as time spent reading newspapers (Dumnov, Ruthaiser, and Shmarov 1984, p. 149).

2. The index of Lenin's fifty-five-volume collected works cites only nine pages in which he refers to cinematography, while in the fourteenth volume of Stalin's sixteen-volume collected works (this volume was not published because of Stalin's death), speeches and letters about movies made up the majority.

3. About the movies in Stalin's time, see Andre Bazin's article "Stalin Myths in Soviet Cinema," in Nichols (1985, pp. 30–40). This article appeared for the first time in 1950, and was the target of vicious attacks by French Communists, who could not tolerate even reserved criticism of movies glorifying Stalin. See also Maynard (1975, pp. 9, 18–20), Ferro (1976, pp. 83–94), Shmyrov (1989, pp. 80–94).

4. About the role of *podvig* (heroic art) in Soviet movies, see Iurii Buida "Voskhozhdenie na materinskuiu grud'," *Nezavisimaia Gazeta* 24 October 1991).

5. As Alexander Matskin wrote, Meierkhold, a forty-four-year-old man, accepted the new revolutionary beliefs without "any internal struggle." Meierkhold believed that theater is the mirror of society, and that it is necessary to build it according to social requirements. He felt that discipline and order were the most important goals of society. And, of course, the theater should serve the ideas of the world revolution (*Nezavisimaia Gazeta* 4 February 1992).

6. Marina Kovaleva, the female lead in the movie, wrote many years later that "at that time we were making the movie with all sincerity and unselfishness" (*Iskusstvo Kino* 8, 1989, p. 85).

7. In the past, filmmakers were often evaluated not so much on the quality of their work and their professional honesty, but on their personal traits, especially their readiness to help their colleagues. Thus Pyriev, one of the pillars of Stalinist cinematography, was warmly praised by Grigorii Chukhrai, who in his article "Personality" ignored many of Pyriev's deeds, for instance, his participation in the anticosmopolitan campaign (Chukhrai 1991b).

8. Romm and Raizman, who would go on to create the first liberal movies during the first thaw, proudly bore five badges of the Stalin laureate (as many as Chiaureli, Stalin's official troubadour in the movies).

9. Dovzhenko is an exception. After Stalin denigrated his script *Ukraine in*

Flames in 1944, Dovzhenko never publicly repented or denounced himself as Eisenstein had.

10.   This movie was met with a special resolution of the Central Committee, which denounced it for distorting socialist reality.

11.   It is now known that Stalin sent a special cable to Upton Sinclair, an ardent supporter of Stalin's regime and the financier of this movie. In this cable the Soviet leader described Eisenstein as a "deserter who broke off with his country." This statement was enough for Sinclair to withdraw his support and end the shooting of the movie in Mexico (Karetnikova 1991).

12.   According to Chapaiev's daughter, Stalin demanded that film directors "present Chapaiev as a legendary red commander, a son of the ordinary people." He also demanded that Anka, a female machine-gunner in Chapaiev's division, should "exemplify a woman fighting for the revolutionary cause" while Pet'ka, Chapaiev's aide, had to be "an ordinary man who learns the meaning of life" (*Megalopolis*, 31 October 1991).

13.   Tarkovskii remarked in his diary: "What kind of a strange country does not want international recognition of its arts, new films or novels? True art frightened them (the people in power)" (1992, p. 5).

14.   With great pain he described how uneducated people like F. Ermash, N. Sizov, and E. Barabash (in Tarkovskii's opinion these people "could probably read only a payroll list") demanded changes in *Soliaris* (1972) and *Mirror*. In fact, many movies that Tarkovskii wanted to make were terminated before shooting began. It is also remarkable how officials tried to force Tarkovskii to shoot movies they regarded as necessary for ideological reasons—for example, about technological progress, about Lenin, etc. (Tarkovskii 1992).

15.   One of his movies, *Song Thrush* (1970), angered the authorities because the main character—a talented loafer—stirred up the sympathy of viewers, while *Pastoral* (1976) was shelved because the collective farm in the movie did not look appealing (*Nezavisimaia Gazeta* 25 January 1992).

16.   During *glasnost*, filmmakers were finally able to discuss the extent to which the authorities had controlled their activities, often shelving movies for years. Among the forbidden movies of the Brezhnev era were Tarkovskii's *Andrei Rublev* (1971), Klimov's *Agony* (1981), Mikhalkov's *The Story of Asya Kliachina, Who Loved But Did Not Marry* (1967). Askol'dov's *Commissar* (1989), German's *Checkpoint* (1987), Panfilov's *Theme* (1986). About these movies, see *Iskusstvo Kino* (9, 1988, p. 67) and *Nezavisimaia Gazeta* (27 August 1992).

The release of movies forbidden in the past and the publication of novels and other literary works prohibited by the authorities were the greatest cultural accomplishments during *glasnost*.

17.   Val Golovskoy recounted the conflict between Filip Ermash, the head of Goskino, and Grigorii Romanov, the first secretary of the Leningrad Regional Party Committee, about Panfilov's movie *May I Have the Floor* (1976). Ermash wanted the movie to be released, while Romanov did not. Ermash mobilized some members of the Politburo and pushed the movie through, but Romanov ousted Panfilov from the Leningrad state movie company (Golovskoy 1986, p. 19).

18.   Ivanov's *Star* (1949) was sent to the archive because the film was "pessimistic," "pacifistic," and "abstractly humanist" (*Iskusstvo Kino* 5, 1990, p. 19). Alov and Naumov's *Peace to Those Who Enter* (1961) was denounced by Ekaterina Furtseva, minister of culture, as a film that denigrated the Soviet people by portraying officers and soldiers during the war as "dirty and greasy

people." Furtseva stated that "in fact, before going to die in a tank battle, the Russian man will always put himself in order, and clean himself before death, [because] he wants to die in a clean shirt" (*Iskusstvo Kino* 5, 1990, p. 22). Pessimism and denigration of Soviet life were the most popular arguments used in the 1960s and 1970s to reject scripts. These arguments silenced scripts written by many prominent writers: V. Tendriakov's *Three, Seven, and Ace*, Vladimir Voinovich's *On the Eve of Holiday* and *We Live Here*, Iurii Chernichenko's *Virgin Land*, Boris Mozhaiev's *Egor Ivanovich*, and Valentin Rasputin's *Dead Line* (*Iskusstvo Kino* 2, 1990, pp. 102–8).

19. The campaign against cosmopolitans (usually the code word for Jews) was started by Stalin in 1949 as part of increasing the ideological pressure on the intelligentsia based on Russian chauvinism. The major targets of this anti-Semitic campaign were Jewish theater and movie figures, as well as writers and scholars. It reached its peak with the arrest in January 1953 of Jewish doctors accused of plotting to kill leading politicians. The campaign ended with Stalin's death in March 1953.

20. Only a few cinematographers (such as Lev Arnstam) were honored by intellectuals in the 1990s as decent and brave individuals who always defended honest scripts and movies (*Iskusstvo Kino* 2, 1990, p. 104).

21. Iutkevich in particular was ideologically active after 1953, creating a series of movies about Lenin—*Stories about Lenin* (1958), *Lenin in Poland* (1966), *Lenin in Paris* (1981)—all of which were despised in Gorbachev's Russia.

22. Pyriev said of the victims, the Jews, that "they do not understand the character and psychology of the Russian people." Vasiliev, who tried to minimize the venom of his speech, nevertheless said that Trauberg and Iutkevich ultimately had become the enemies. Donskoi, who rebuked Vasiliev for his tolerance of both individuals, likened Trauberg to a fascist. Pudovkin went so far as to accuse both defendants of pursuing subversive activities for many years (*Iskusstvo Kino* 2, 1990, pp. 93–101).

23. In his memoirs, Gabrilovich refers to discussions with a writer who described the recruitment of agents among intellectuals (Gabrilovich 1991, pp. 90–91).

24. Certain movie people displayed anxiety about being labeled as KGB agents. *Sovietskaia Rossia* published an interview with Nikita Mikhalkov entitled "Perhaps I Am a KGB Agent." In the interview this famous film director declared that he "is not interested in who was connected with the KGB," because these connections could have a very casual and routine character. He acknowledged that he also received some ideological assignments (to support, for instance, the last decision of a party congress). He then posed the rhetorical question: "Does it mean that I was a KGB agent?" (*Sovietskaia Rossia* 21 May 1992). It is curious that his brother, Andrei Mikhalkov-Konchalovskii, reported that Tarkovskii, who had already defected to the West, suspected him of being a KGB agent.

II

Soviet Movies in the Revolutionary Period (1918–1928):
Cordial Acceptance of Official Ideology

The Soviet state installed ideological control over the movie industry immediately after the Bolshevik revolution. However, in the first ten years it was relatively weak, mostly because the new regime was immediately able to recruit many young enthusiasts in the movie industry who were sincerely devoted to the new cause. At the same time, it was still possible to make movies which went against the grain. The new authorities did not yet feel strong and self-confident enough to impose the meticulous supervision over cinematography that they would ten years later.

3

Soviet Movies in the Aftermath of the October Revolution: The Civil War

THE IDEOLOGICAL CLIMATE

In the aftermath of the Bolshevik Revolution the new regime was absorbed only with its physical survival. The civil war placed Lenin and his comrades-in-arms at the edge of defeat several times. Having eliminated freedom of speech and banned the opposition press, the Bolsheviks were, however, preoccupied with other pressing issues and were probably not yet so dogmatic (as they would become in the future) to put the movie industry into shackles.[1]

The prerevolutionary cinematography industry, despite its nationalization in 1919, seemingly survived the Red Terror and the persecution of the old classes and even continued to produce films with hidden critiques of the new regime. Meanwhile new and young filmmakers who joined the Bolsheviks started to offer true revolutionary movies, glorifying the new regime and its ideology and blasting its enemies.

REVOLUTIONARY IDEOLOGY AND THE MOVIES

In the first years after the revolution, official ideology was not as vigorously imposed on filmmakers and other intellectuals as it would be some years later. Dozens of films that totally ignored the revolution were made in 1918. Lenin and his colleagues still believed in socialist utopia, although with less verve than before the revolution. They also believed that revolutionary intellectuals would defend Marxism on their own initiative, so direct supervision was not necessary. Therefore, the impact of Marxist ideology on movies in the aftermath of the revolution was rather nebulous and took many forms. The early leaders also believed in the enlightening, educational function of cinema (Anatolii Lunacharskii, the first commissar for education, was the best-known spokesman for

39

this idea). This somewhat tempered their desire to exploit movies as pure propaganda.

The leading theme of this period was the liberation of the masses. Combined with utopianism and millenarianism (the belief in a coming ideal society created by revolutionary action), the masses' liberation was presented in early Soviet movies as a cosmic revolution.

There were several reasons why Soviet ideology was presented as such a revolution. First, Marxism itself had millenarian characteristics. Although Marx, or to be more exact Engels, stressed that human beings were similar to other species and would eventually perish, he also stressed that all of human history up to his time was simply prehistory. Real history would begin following the socialist revolution. Marx also stressed that the socialist revolution was to be a global, worldwide process. All of these elements helped give Marxism its millenarian and eschatological overtones.

Second, Soviet ideology had strong roots in the Russian intellectual tradition. It specifically embraced the ideology of revolutionary populism, which endorsed the omnipotence of science. Nikolai Fedorov, an eccentric Russian philosopher who espoused a blend of conservative and radical ideas, was a leader of this line of Russian thought. Fedorov argued that humankind's technological development would eventually allow complete mastery over nature. This mastery would lead to the resurrection of the dead and the spread of humanity throughout the cosmos. Although Fedorov's ideas were little known among the Bolshevik elite, his teachings undoubtedly represented an important ideological trend in Russian thought, including radical thought, which advocated science almost religiously.

Third, the very nature of the revolutionary struggle was millenarian. Indeed, the masses could hardly be mobilized for the ultimate struggle— with all its attendant suffering and bloodshed—if only limited goals were envisioned. Thus, in the context of this ideological paradigm, the Bolshevik Revolution was rife with millenarian thought and was viewed by its participants as a cosmic drama.

GENERAL CHARACTERISTICS OF THE MOVIES

The Masses as Major Figures

Soviet films conveyed this millenarian perception of reality through a special cinematographic technique: Many scenes from movies of that period remind one of an icon or poster. The images were simplified and depersonalized; they actually portrayed symbolic manifestations of good and evil. These graphic, simplified images not only addressed the eschatological mentality, but they conveyed ideas to the masses—the major consumers of the movies.

In Marxist philosophy, workers were singled out to spearhead historical development. In early Soviet movies, however, workers not only lacked individual characteristics, but individual workers blended into workers in general, who in turn blended into all of humankind. Given this blending, workers were often challenged not by other people, but by cosmic evil or by the blind forces of nature—forces with which workers, or rather humankind, were locked in mortal combat.

Such themes are found in Tisse's *The Black Days of Kronstadt* (1921), which portrays events in the city of Kronstadt during the civil war. Kronstadt's proximity to Petrograd made it strategically important, and the film depicts the suffering of its residents from death and malnutrition during the struggle for control of the city. The bleakness of the situation is emphasized by the gray mists that blanket the city in the morning. The hardships and suffering of the population are portrayed as necessary for the bright rebirth of the new society, just as the gray mists give way to the brilliant morning sunshine. Indeed, the triumphant sunlight provides the movie's philosophical and artistic consummation.

Whereas most revolution era movies idealized the masses (with no differentiation between various groups in the population), some occasionally engaged in criticism. These movies still presented the masses as being rather benign, but hinted that they sometimes act against their own interest and forget their messianic mission. This point is made in Lev Kuleshov's *The Dream of Taras* (1919), which tells of a soldier in the Red Army who breaks military discipline by getting drunk and falling asleep. In a dream, he sees himself as a soldier in the prerevolutionary tsarist army. During a visit to a prostitute, he runs into a general, who attacks and then arrests him. The soldier is sentenced to execution, but at the last minute wakes up with the happy realization that he is not actually a soldier under the tsar. This ending implies that Red Army soldiers should fight for the Soviet regime and do their best to prevent a return to the rule of capitalists and landlords, who would exploit the masses.

National Minorities

National minorities, especially the Jews, played an important and positive role in early Soviet movies. This role contrasts sharply with that seen in the Soviet movies of the 1950s through the 1970s, which had blatantly chauvinistic and anti-Semitic overtones.

In line with Marxism, official postrevolutionary ideology discounted the significance of the so-called national problem. According to Marx, one's social position (whether one sided with the bourgeoisie or the proletariat) far outweighed one's national affiliation. Still, the national minorities played a special role in Soviet ideology. This ideology regarded imperial Russia as a "prison of nations," in which all national minorities were suppressed, regardless of their social affiliation. Soviet ideologists tended to de-emphasize social divisions among the minorities, and instead stressed their benign social characteristics.

Within this philosophy, all minority peoples were viewed as being on the side of the revolution and as participating in the creation of the new political order. This theme was central to Feofan Shipulinskii's *Tovarich Abraham* (1919), which dealt with the life of Abraham, a Jewish boy from a provincial hamlet. The story is framed in the context of quasi-religious philosophy: Jews, symbolic of the oppressed masses, are humiliated as was Christ, but these humiliations only emphasize the Jews' righteousness. In the end, Abraham joins the revolution and shakes off the oppressive rule, paving the way for a harmonious society.

Intellectuals: A Target for Reeducation

Revolution era Soviet ideology viewed the world as essentially divided between the two camps of cosmic evil and cosmic good, which were represented by the bourgeoisie and the masses, respectively. In most cases, those representing these forces were not only depersonalized, but archetypified. That is, the forces of evil were actually represented by symbolic monsters rather than by identifiable capitalists.

The single exception to this bifurcated worldview was the position of the intellectual. Characterizations of intellectuals were absent from the films of the revolutionary and civil war periods. Intellectuals were considered not a separate class but merely a "stratum" (*prosloika*) of society—a transitory group without the corporate consciousness necessary to hold political and economic power on its own. It was assumed that part of this layer would identify with the bourgeoisie and join the forces of darkness, while the progressive elements would join the revolutionary movement and be subsumed in the revolutionary tide. Although there were some exceptions to this rule, the prevailing thinking was that any independent grouping of intellectuals was transient since they would eventually drift into one camp or the other.

This theme is best exemplified by Panteleev, Pashkovskii, and Dolinov's *Consolidation* (1918), which examined the problems of the intellectual in revolutionary times.[2] The movie focuses on the so-called consolidation of living quarters during the revolutionary period, when workers were housed in the homes of well-to-do citizens. The motivation for this policy was twofold: first, to ameliorate the severe urban housing shortage, and second, to socialize the population to revolutionary values. The policy graphically demonstrated to the urban populace that the Soviet government was concerned with its welfare and was acting in its interests.

In this movie, Professor Chrustin, a well-to-do intellectual occupying a spacious flat, was selected for consolidation, and a worker named Pul'nikov was chosen to share his apartment. The professor represented the intellectual stratum, in that he lacked a definite social orientation. On the one hand, he was apparently well paid—at least he had been prior to the revolution; on the other hand, he was not portrayed as a useless member of society—a bourgeois parasite living at the expense of the workers. In fact, he appeared to be in a sort of social limbo; he could potentially join either the forces of good or the forces of evil. The uncertainty of his social position is emphasized both by the social inclinations of his family members and by his professional environment. His oldest son runs off to cadet school and becomes strongly anti-Bolshevik (the cadets, or Junkers, were known as implacable enemies of the new political order), and the professor's graduate students are also portrayed as being hostile to the new regime.

At the same time, the professor's younger son exhibits a completely different social orientation by falling in love with a proletarian's daughter. Their affair was not a love affair as it is commonly understood. While completely platonic, it was not simply a manifestation of private feelings. In the apocalyptic world of the Russian Revolution there were no private lives and no individual motivations. Instead, there was only service as a soldier in one of the two diametrically opposed armies fighting their cosmic struggle. Private activity thus became a public act and a political statement. In this context, the young couple's love becomes an integral part of the professor's social position, demonstrating that he is not completely on the side of counterrevolutionary forces.

Thus, the movie portrays the ideological struggle for the professor's soul. One the one hand, his oldest son and his graduate students urge him to join the counterrevolutionary forces. On the other hand, his younger son's passion is a libidinous manifestation of his gravitation toward the correct cause, that is, the revolution.

The intervention of the proletarian state eases the professor's choice: The professor's older son is arrested by the CHEKA (Soviet secret police) and presumably executed as an enemy of the people. Although one might assume that such an event would drive both the professor and his younger son directly into the arms of the counterrevolutionaries (or at least provoke an attitude of fatalistic indifference), the exact opposite occurs. The younger son's love for his proletarian beauty continues undiminished, while the professor's affinity for the regime strengthens. At first these actions seem quite illogical, but they are rational in light of the earlier Soviet ideology of the period, which did not deal with individual personalities as the term is commonly understood in contemporary Western culture.

This was also true about other Soviet movies of the era. In these films, characters were often allegorical representations of one side or another in the class struggle. In *Consolidation*, the professor is not so much a person with his own individual traits, but an amalgam of certain petty bourgeois elements of society (Soviet political scientists sometimes categorized intellectuals as such), who vacillated between the proletariat and the bourgeoisie.

From this perspective one can easily understand why the professor's attachment to the revolutionary cause and his younger son's love for his proletarian woman grew stronger following the loss of their family member. They were being portrayed not as individuals but as social symbols—symbolic figures that represented the petty bourgeoisie. The strength and scope of the revolutionary terror demonstrated the power of the revolution to the petty bourgeois elements and encouraged them to cooperate with the proletariat. This is the only rational explanation for the seemingly cold behavior of the professor and his younger son.

After siding with the proletariat, the professor engages in various revolutionary activities and lectures for the workers. Finally, he participates in workers' demonstrations. In a sense, this is the climax of the movie in that it demonstrates both the professor's break with the forces of reaction and the dissolving of the professor's individual personality into the collective personality of the revolutionary masses.

ANTI-BOLSHEVIK MOVIES

The new Soviet system could not destroy Russia's civil society overnight. Some film-makers not belonging to the new system continued to produce movies, and even they were strongly affected by the storm that swept Russia.

The theme of apocalyptic change could be seen in privately made anti-Bolshevik movies. This movie genre is perhaps best represented by a movie based on Dmitry S. Merezhkovskii's three-volume book, *Christ and Antichrist* (Merezhkovskii was a well-known author of the period). Whereas Bolshevik intellectuals considered the Bolshevik Revolution to be a positive transformation, the enemies of the regime considered it a negative apocalypse. In fact, the anti-Bolsheviks viewed this period as the beginning of Satan's reign.

Bolsheviks as Devils

Merezhkovskii's work succinctly conveyed the idea of the Bolsheviks as Satan incarnate. Many Russian intellectuals insisted that this satanic rule heralded nothing less than the second coming of Christ. In the opinion of these intellectuals, the Bolsheviks' belief that they could create an ideal society and ensure humankind's dominion over nature involved a dangerous degree of hubris. The anti-Bolshevik intellectuals considered these to be tasks for God, not for humanity, and believed that humankind's attempt to attain these goals represented nothing but devilish temptation.

Merezhkovskii developed this subject extensively. *Julian the Apostate* (1918), based on Merezhkovskii's novel of the same name, examines the life of the Roman emperor Julian, who tried to abolish Christianity as the state religion and return to paganism. Julian ultimately failed, and died feeling himself defeated and Christ victorious. According to legend, his last words were, "I drink to you, Galilean."

The movie's director, elaborating on Merezhkovskii's theme, put a global philosophical twist on this struggle between paganism and Christianity by presenting a confrontation not between two religions but between two approaches to life. The emperor's devotion to paganism was interpreted as his belief in the omnipotence of human reason and its ability to create the ideal society. Christianity was symbolic of another weltanschauung, emphasizing the imperfection of earthly life.

Alexander Sanin's *Peter and Alexis* (1918), also based on a Merezhkovskii novel, addresses the same concept, with one difference: Humankind's striving to create the ideal society, as exemplified by Peter the Great, unleashes terror and destruction. Instead of the ideal society, Peter ushered in a reign of the devil. Whereas Peter epitomizes the hubris of the ultimate egoistic outlook, his son Alexis represents Christian philosophy with its emphasis on the impossibility of creating an ideal society on earth—particularly by force. Similar ideas are presented in the movie *King of the Jews*, based on a play by Konstantin Romanov, the tsar's uncle and a liberal writer.

Antiutopian themes (where the Bolshevik Revolution is portrayed as a sort of demonic event) were common in revolution era movies. In these films, Satan is the symbolic, yet implicit, manifestation of the Bolshevik regime. In Sanin's *Girl's Mountains* (1918), for example, Satan wanders through the ages in search of pious virgins (perhaps symbolizing the motherland in her feminine holiness, natural purity, and unspoiled state). During his quest, Satan must face Russian monks, the sanctified defenders of the motherland. Still, Satan finds and seduces a pious virgin, symbolizing the (perhaps temporary) victory of the satanic Bolshevik forces over Holy Russia. At the end of the movie the audience encounters the slogan "Let's Crush the Enemy of Humankind." Similar sentiments were echoed in other popular movies produced around 1918, including Kharitonov's *The Offspring of the Devil* (1917) and Iakov Protazanov's *Satan Triumphant* (1917).

Religion as a Form of Escapism

Another tactic Russian filmmakers used to demonstrate their opposition to revolutionary officialdom was not to directly oppose the regime or indulge in temporary escapist entertainment. Instead, they advocated a complete withdrawal from life itself by using the symbolism of religion as a vehicle. This approach held that not only was the revolution (i.e., the desire to create an ideal society) doomed to failure, but that life itself was so unpleasant in its external manifestations that one should seek to escape it. Even private life and family could not provide sufficient consolation for the individual.

A good example of this film genre is Protazanov's *Father Sergei* (1918), which was based on a story by Tolstoy. This film depicted the life of Kasatkin, a prince possessed with noble aspirations who loves his tsar, Nicholas I, and wants to contribute to society. Society, however, is not structured toward striving for harmony but toward achieving personal ambition. The prince's dream of creating an ideal society is slowly being destroyed, and the last straw—which destroys his dreams and his life— is his fiancee's departure to become the mistress of the tsar. He loses faith not only in the state but in worldly life itself and decides to withdraw and become a monk.

Lovers as Heroes

Although anti-Bolshevik intellectuals often used apocalyptic subject matter to demonstrate their antipathy toward the Bolshevik regime, they also demonstrated their opposition by creating films purely for entertainment that were relatively devoid of political or social messages. These films often dealt with historical subject matter (as in *Favorite of Catherine II* and *The Mystery of the Death of Peter III*) and lacked themes depicting the struggle between the forces of good and evil. Instead, they focused exclusively on the personal and individual events in the private lives of historical persons. In doing so, they denied any historical essence by focusing not on the social implications of each historical episode but on the private lives of the players in the historical drama.

NOTES

1.   In 1923, Leon Trotsky wrote that "the fact that we have not, in nearly six years, taken possession of filmmaking shows how slow and uneducated we are, as well as frankly stupid" (*Pravda*, 12 July 1923).
2.   Anatolii V. Lunacharskii, himself an intellectual, wrote the script for this movie.

4

The Partial Restoration of Capitalism (1921–1929)

These eight years in Soviet society were the most successful for Soviet cinema. It acquired world fame in these years. It was an era when young Soviet film directors felt themselves intimately linked with the new power of the Bolsheviks and eagerly served it with their strongly ideologically loaded films.

THE IDEOLOGICAL CLIMATE AND THE MOVIES

In 1921, the civil war ended and the country entered a new period of development that continued until 1929 (this period was known as the New Economic Policy, NEP). This new policy, implemented by the Bolsheviks under the threat of mass rebellion, restored (to some extent) the market economy and private property in small- and medium-sized businesses. It resulted in an immediate economic recovery and a rise of the standard of living throughout the country.

The masses, for the most part, preferred Russia under the NEP to civil war Russia and the Russia of collectivization and purges. Still, the NEP was not seen as entirely favorably by the masses. A number of Russian workers remained dissatisfied and some even looked back wistfully on the civil war.

There were two reasons for this dissatisfaction. First, a fledgling market economy developed under the NEP and a bourgeoisie developed in both urban and country settings. At the same time, the workers's quality of life improved only marginally, while some workers were unemployed. One side effect of this was the spread of corruption, promiscuity, and drunkenness. Second, the NEP led to the spread of a bureaucracy that workers viewed as a detriment to their well-being. The left opposition, headed by Trotsky, capitalized on the workers's discontent and compared the current political situation with the Thermidor, the reactionary degeneration of the revolutionary regime during the French Revolution.

At the same time, economic liberalization was accompanied by a relative softening of ideological control over intellectual activities. Vasilii Shulgin, the famous monarchist who secretly visited Russia in 1923, was amazed to see his book, with its strong anti-Bolshevik tone, being sold in bookstores along with other books whose authors just years earlier would have been shot by the CHEKA (Shulgin 1991). The authorities tolerated philosophical, economic, and political debates even among those intellectuals who made no secret of where their sympathies lay. Iakov Protazanov, the director, was thus able to return from emigration without fearing for his life.

Still, the official ideology was clearly dominant and was protected and enhanced by the Kremlin. This was ensured through the expulsion of large numbers of prominent intellectuals (such as Berdiaev and Sorokin),[1] and the arrests of thousands of people accused of cooperating with the enemies of the Soviet state.

Despite the horrors of the civil war, the new regime was still enthusiastically supported by many young intellectuals who continued to believe fanatically in the cause of the revolution and the eventual victory of socialism throughout the world. They believed in technological progress and science, and they saw the country's economic and cultural growth as their main responsibility. They also continued to view the Bolshevik Revolution as a cosmic phenomenon and as the beginning of humanity's conquest of nature. Among young film directors who became prominent during this period were Vsevolod Pudovkin, Alexander Dovzhenko, and Fridrikh Ermler. While revolutionary eschatology continued to play a leading role in Soviet ideology, these cinematographers had to take into account that revolutionary optimism was seriously undermined by the sociopolitical processes characteristic of Soviet Russia after the instituting of the NEP. The significant processes of this time were the rebirth of the market and the bourgeoisie.

During this period, the movie industry was already almost totally controlled by revolutionary intellectuals. They openly vowed to serve the regime and educate the people according to the precepts of the official ideology. These intellectuals basked in the support of the regime, whose goals they sincerely shared. Such future masters of Soviet cinematography as Vsevolod Pudovkin, Sergei Eisenstein, and Grigorii Kozintsev (and a few others), in a remarkable address to the party conference in March 1928, expressed the necessity to introduce "a united ideological plan" for the film industry. They also suggested the creation of "an authoritative organ that will plan the production of films, [and will work] directly under the Central Committee's Agitprop Section." In other words, they asked the party to control them as much as possible (Pudovkin 1975, 2, p. 355). It is only natural that the party conference of cinematographers demanded that "cinema must be an instrument of the proletariat in its struggle for hegemony, leadership and influence in relation to other classes, [and] in the hands of the party it must be the most powerful medium of Communist enlightenment and agitation" (Ol'khovyi 1929, p. 429).[2] At only one other period in Soviet history was there such a cordial relationship between cinematographers and the Kremlin—during Gorbachev's *glasnost*.

Those filmmakers who opposed the regime (for instance, from the Trotskyist position) concealed their true attitudes, choosing instead either to adjust to it or to express their genuine feelings and apprehensions indirectly.

MOVIES IN THE EARLY 1920S

Humanization of Postrevolutionary Movies

The growing popularity of the cinema strongly affected film directors, who now tried to make movies more "human" than those created immediately after the revolution. Moreover, the NEP atmosphere, with the initial equanimity of the regime to the new bourgeoisie, encouraged (somewhat) the good life.

Because of this evolution, the movie heroes of the 1920s were more similar to the people. At the same time, however, they were the very engine of the revolutionary process and that process was considered cosmic in its global consequences. In the public's eyes, movie stars took on extraordinary qualities that made them seem like superhumans or revolutionary demigods. Even progressive intellectuals were accorded this reverence, because, at least in their scientific endeavors, they manifested unusual qualities. Still, a movie star's image could become tainted in several ways. First, protagonists had to be juxtaposed to antagonists, their enemies. Second, a positive role model might degenerate and become, if not a conscious enemy of the revolution, at least no longer a leader of the revolutionary process. And third, a movie hero could fall in private life, i.e., could be diverted from public life to family concerns and even sexual relations.

The Masses and Their Leaders

During this time, the image of the populace continued to play an important role in Soviet movies. As in the revolutionary period, the populace was presented as the major revolutionary force—without the masses, the leader could not achieve his goals. Still, there were important changes in the presentation of the populace. First, the relationship between the populace and the leader was different. Second, sometimes the populace was used by reactionary forces to fight against its own interests—against its own class brothers and sisters. Eisenstein became prominent during this period as a director who focused on the masses. In *Strike* (1925) he differentiated between the capitalists (and their servants) and the workers; the capitalists and strikebreakers were all portrayed as anomalous figures, while the working mass was glorified. *October* (1927), inspired by the American author John Reed's *Ten Days That Shook the World* (1926), was about the history of the October Revolution, the events that preceded it, as well as the Bolshevik's seizure of power in Petrograd in October 1917. Again the mass scenes, with thousands of extras, are the center of the movie.

This accent on the heroic masses was necessary because the Soviet ruling elite still did not feel itself the legitimate master of the country. They tried to persuade themselves, as well as the population, that the new power was represented in the masses. This focus was fully in line with official Marxist ideology, with its glorification of the producers of material goods, especially workers.

Also important was the leader's close relationship with the populace. In an attempt to be an ordinary individual, the leader lived among the people and took control only in times of emergency. Still, the leader was essential for the realization of the populace's revolutionary potential. And without the leader's intervention, the masses would suffer from oppression or would even side with the oppressor against members of its own class. The idea of class conflict was thus reconceptualized and became more realistic. The class enemy ceased to be an abstract imperialist monster; instead, he or she was a concrete person and not necessarily a capitalist.

This approach to the revolutionary masses was used in Eisenstein's *Battleship Potemkin* (1925), which centers on a crucial event in the 1905 revolution when the crew of a military ship mutinied. In portraying the revolutionary populace, the director followed the tradition of revolution era movies. The populace is oppressed by the ruling elite, epitomized by the ship's officers. Fat, rude, and indifferent to suffering, the officers treat their sailors like animals. Still, social injustice per se does not compel the sailors to revolt since they accept a certain level of injustice as necessary for political order. Only when the injustice is excessive do the sailors rise up.

This occurs when the sailors find worms in their meat and complain to no avail. They decide to protest, but rather meekly—they simply refuse to eat the rotten meat. The response of the captain is to order the execution of the rebellious sailors with fellow sailors ordered to carry out the executions. This would have taken place, but at the crucial moment the revolutionary leader appeals to the sailors aiming at the rebels, asking, "Whom are you ready to shoot?" At this moment, with the leader's involvement in the protest, the sailors' mutiny becomes a real revolution. It is directed thereafter not only against this specific case of social injustice but against the entire political order. The sailors, united in their hatred of the officers, seize the battleship and become actively involved in the 1905 revolution.

A similar theme appears in Pudovkin's *The End of St. Petersburg* (1927). Although not overtly stated, the point of the movie is that the masses, even the proletariat, can never understand their historical mission on their own. They require a revolutionary leadership dedicated to leading them to their historical destiny.

Instead of stressing the strength of the populace, as was the case with revolution and civil war era movies, this film emphasizes the relative powerlessness of the masses. The tone is set in the opening scene, in which a peasant woman is giving birth. As the child, a peasant boy, develops he is represented as a naive, uneducated, defenseless creature with enormous social vulnerability.

The major protagonist, named Fellow (an obvious symbol of the faceless, personless Russian masses), cannot find employment in his native village and therefore goes to the city. As he enters the city, moviegoers are again deluged with images of his helplessness, which is contrasted with the huge and imposing buildings, the massive bronze statues, and the self-confident, prosperous bureaucrats and businessmen. His powerlessness is accentuated by the squalid misery of his quarters.

Once in the city, Fellow becomes a worker. Still, the fact that he has become a part of the class destined to change the course of history barely affects his general outlook. He remains helplessly naive and defenseless. The authorities easily manipulate him to become a strikebreaker—a traitor to his fellow workers. He finally comes to understand that he has been used to commit some sort of treachery against his class brothers. Even so, his outburst of rage is simply another expression of his ultimate powerlessness; it requires little effort on the part of the authorities to subdue him.

The film ends with the outbreak of the Bolshevik Revolution, in which Fellow participates. Yet even in the throes of revolution he remains a rather uncouth and naive fellow, prosaically consuming potatoes in the splendor of the Winter Palace. Pudovkin makes the explicit point that Fellow could never have thrown off the capitalist yoke without the leadership of the party.

The same ambivalence on the part of the populace can be seen in the science fiction movie *Aelita* (Protazanov, 1924). This film centers on a passive Martian populace that needs the help of Gusev, a Bolshevik who comes from Earth, in order to undertake their uprising.

Newborn Bolsheviks

During this period new heroes emerged—people who, after disappointment and painful reflections, began to believe in the righteousness of the new order.

Protazanov's *The Man from the Restaurant* (1927) is a good example of such a positive transformation. The movie is set in 1917, during the February revolution. The protagonist is a waiter, a humble employee of a restaurant. He is an impeccably honest and good man but is petty bourgeois to the core and has no interests beyond the private concerns of his family and achieving a modest station in life. His greatest wish is that his daughter receive a good education and be happily married. While not explicitly taking sides in the coming struggle between the proletariat and the bourgeoisie, his political passivity implicitly places him on the side of the prevailing political order. His very status as a petty bourgeois is his crime.

However, when a rich customer of the restaurant tries to seduce his daughter, he is compelled to change his mind and become politically involved. The outraged father slaps the scoundrel's face, which symbolizes the fallacy of adopting a neutral position. In a class-stratified society, especially in the case of incipient civil war, there is no possibility of pursuing a private life. Sooner or later, all private persons will be forced to adopt a public stand. Again, this is an important element of the Bolshevist ideology, which was always inimical to political neutrality.

The waiter might have symbolically accepted the existing order by acquiescing to the seduction of his daughter. Instead, his defense of his daughter's honor is actually not a defense of his private dreams but a renunciation of them and an acceptance of the revolutionary position. Thus, by striking the seducer, the waiter has joined ranks with the revolutionaries. By defending his daughter, he has renounced his family for a higher, public stance. As a revolutionary, he can now spare no time for a private life and must put his family in the background while he serves the public cause.

Two movies by Pudovkin—*Mother* (1926) and *The Heir to Genghis Khan* (1928)—also contained the theme of the people's gradual revolutionary enlightenment. *Mother* is a film based on Gorky's famous novel published before the revolution, a book of biblical proportions for Bolsheviks. It depicts how an old woman, who was at first hostile toward the revolutionary activity of her son, becomes an ardent supporter of the revolution and is ready to sacrifice him for the cause.

The Heir to Genghis Khan portrays a poor Mongol hunter living during the civil war. He has little interest in political problems and accepts the existing political order. He is robbed and wounded, however, by a white merchant who represents the white colonial power (presumably England). The attack on the hunter is viewed as part of the oppression of the white administration, and more broadly the European oppression of Asia.

The hunter manages to escape and join a guerrilla movement. In one of the clashes with colonial troops, the hunter is taken prisoner and shot. One of those who shoots him finds among his belongings a document that demonstrates that the hunter is possibly a descendant of Genghis Khan. The colonial administrators decide to use this document for their own benefit. They nurse the ailing hunter back to life and try to establish him as a puppet leader. As part of the West's attempt to harness the East, he is treated well and promoted as the ruler of Mongolia.

But the attempt fails. The hunter soon realizes that he has no real power and is subordinate to Western colonialists. He cannot prevent the colonialists from mistreating his people. He flees the palace, assembles an army of natives, and attacks the colonial troops. The movie ends with a Mongol cavalry charge against the Western troops, which symbolizes the apocalyptic confrontation between East and West.

Revolutionary Leaders as the Main Heroes in Movies

Official propaganda changed its attitudes toward the role of the revolutionary leader after the civil war. By the beginning of the NEP, the state and the leadership had finally taken shape in the revolutionary mentality. The state and the leader were still fairly abstract categories, but they started to acquire some personal characteristics. Thus, the revolution became the job not only of the masses but of the leader and the state as well. The leader and masses became highly interconnected. They functioned as one social body with the leader and the state acting as the head, and the masses as the muscle.

As mentioned above, for the revolution era intellectuals who supported the Bolsheviks, reality was depersonalized. It was nothing but an abstraction. The situation was different during the NEP period, however, due to the peculiar situation of revolutionary power and leadership. The revolution became a springboard for leaders. A dictatorial revolutionary state emerged by the summer of 1918 and it became alienated from the masses because the masses became the principal victims of its revolutionary terror.

Despite this, the concept of the revolutionary machinery and leadership as something different from the masses was not sufficiently ingrained in revolutionary ideology and mass consciousness. The revolution was thought of as the work of the masses, with the state and leaders being only tools in their hands; the leaders were thereby dissolved in the masses. Now the role of leaders in ideology, and subsequently in movies, changed. As stated before, the role of the leader and the state became crucial for the revolutionary process.

Protazanov's *Aelita* (1924) and Kuleshov's *Death Ray* (1925), both based on Aleksei Tolstoy novels, provide good examples of the new Soviet vision of leaders. In *Aelita*, an expedition is arranged to visit Mars. The two-man crew consists of Gusev, a Communist stalwart and presumably a minor party functionary, and Losev, the spacecraft's designer. They land successfully on the planet and discover an elaborate civilization. After their arrival, an uprising takes place among the native populace that is eventually quelled by the ruling elite. The newcomers from Earth participate in the uprising, putting themselves in danger, but they manage to escape and return to Earth.

The movie demonstrates that eschatological and millenarian views continued to be dominant in official, or at least semiofficial Soviet thought. According to these views, the Bolshevik Revolution was considered limitless. The revolution implies the transformation, based on the model of Russian society, not only of all nations on Earth but of the entire universe. The role of the USSR is that of revolutionary cosmic messiah. In this sense, the revolution is not just a social process but actually a biometaphysical transformation involving the conquest of the cosmos and the biological transformation of humanity as a result of its encounter with other sentient species. The love of Losev for the beautiful Martian girl Aelita is symbolic of this future hybridization.

The revolutionary leadership, represented by Gusev, plays an important role in the cosmic transformation. Gusev is a proletarian; he was a soldier during the civil war and seems to have had little or no education. As someone from the masses, he is not above petty indulgences. While on Mars, he collects items to sell back on Earth. Upon his return, he lectures to the public for a fee and becomes well off.

In the movie, however, he is also a leader in the revolutionary uprising on Mars and demonstrates all of the necessary traits of a revolutionary leader. First, he has political vision. He understands that the Martians will not improve their life without violent revolution and without solidarity with their brethren on Earth and on other planets. Second, he has the tactical skill to organize the uprising. He arranges for the seizure of the arsenal and directs a successful military operation against the forces of reaction. Third, he is an optimist, not easily discouraged by temporary defeat. Though the uprising on Mars is routed and Gusev barely escapes, he remains convinced that the liberation of the Martian workers is inevitable. Returning to Earth, he organizes a revolutionary party whose paramount goal is to liberate Mars. Finally, Gusev shows physical courage. He participates in the uprising and is among the first to attack the government's position.

With all of his mental and physical capacities, Gusev embodies the proletarians's best revolutionary qualities. He becomes a sort of demigod and is hero-worshiped by the Martian people. The Martian rulers also understand his importance in the revolutionary struggle. They can see that without his leadership the Martian populace poses no threat to their power. Consequently, they try their best to kill him.

Death Ray, also based on a book by Tolstoy that had cosmic overtones, provides a similar vision of political reality and the importance of leadership in the revolutionary struggle. It portrays Garin, an engineer who invents the hyperboloid, a kind of powerful laser. He dreams of using this machine to enrich himself and eventually become the ruler of the earth. He is opposed by the Communist Shulga, who seizes control of the laser and uses it to hasten the worldwide proletarian revolution. Like Gusev, Shulga possesses the qualities of a revolutionary superman. He has a clear vision of history and is convinced that the revolution is destined to spread throughout the world. Also like Gusev, he is a brilliant tactician who organizes the uprising. And finally, he is a man of physical strength, bravery, and iron will.

In all movies of this genre, although the revolutionary leader is essential to society's cosmic transformation, he cannot act alone. He needs a partner.

The Progressive Intellectuals

This partner is none other than the progressive intellectual. This is interesting because intellectuals still rarely appeared in revolution era movies and they did not play important roles. By the end of the civil war, however, the situation had changed for several reasons. First, the new regime started using intellectuals to rebuild the country's economy. Even those who did not belong to the Bolshevik party (the only legitimate party by this time) were employed in important positions in science and industry. Of course, those who were somewhat sympathetic to the regime were the most welcome. Second, acknowledging the importance of the leader in revolutionary development led movie directors to pay attention to the broader spectrum of personalities that contributed to revolutionary development.

Losev is a good example of the progressive intellectual. His importance in *Aelita* is second only to that of Gusev, and it could be argued that they are equal. The character of Losev was inspired by Konstantin Eduardovich Tsiolkovskii, Fedorov's pupil and a passionate prophet of humanity's cosmic expansion. Losev shares with Gusev the important qualities of bravery and physical strength, but Losev alone possesses the knowledge and technical expertise essential to the success of the enterprise. In a way, he is even more idealistic than Gusev. He is completely preoccupied with his scientific research and completely ignores his material well-being. Unlike Gusev, Losev is not interested in collecting Martian artifacts to sell back on Earth. Rather, he is interested in collecting information about the origins of Martian civilization and Aelita tells him the story of the glorious Martian past.

Yet, despite his positive characteristics, Losev cannot lead. He has no vision of the strategic goal. His desire to fly to Mars is borne of scientific curiosity. He, unlike Gusev, has no vision of the Bolshevik Revolution's cosmic implications or of a future federation of socialist planets. He participates in the Martian revolution reluctantly, only under Gusev's direct pressure. Moreover, Losev shows himself to be politically passive and prone to fatalism. Another character in the film is Losev's Martian alter ego, whose negative characteristics are more exaggerated. The Martian intellectual-revolutionary joins the uprising but lacks real revolutionary stamina and lapses into absolute fatalism following an initial defeat.

Losev's romantic approach to women is another of his shortcomings. In this he also differs from Gusev, who is married and seems to love his wife. Yet he is not completely devoted to her and has a brief affair with a Martian. This change of partners is not meant to show Gusev as promiscuous but to reveal his approach to interpersonal relationships. Gusev's relationships are important only when they are connected with his revolutionary activity. To him, people are easily interchangeable. He is concerned not with relationships but with revolution.

Losev, however, can truly fall in love. His love is more important to him than the revolution or even his scientific research. Aelita, the beautiful Martian woman who is the object of his affection, causes him to forget about everything else. When Losev and Gusev return to Earth, Gusev plans to visit Mars once more in order to incite a new revolution. Losev also wants to return but not because of the revolution or science. He wants to see Aelita again.

The Enemies of the People

The concept of enemies of the revolution and of the people was an essential ingredient of the Bolshevik ideology since its very beginning. It remained so until the collapse of the Soviet system. Young film directors were well aware of this, and almost all movies made from the 1920s until the end of Stalin's regime include enemies of the people in crucial roles.

In the movies of the 1920s the revolutionary superhumans had their counterparts: the enemies of the people—negative superhumans with whom they shared many extraordinary qualities. These villains had strong wills and a clear understanding of their global goal. Contrary to the revolutionary heroes, however, their energies resulted in oppression and evil throughout the cosmos. The dark forces and cosmic evil in revolutionary movies acted through these antiheroes.

But the antiheroes were not abstractions—they were people with complex human traits. Aelita's father is one such character. Similar to the revolutionary heroes, he thinks in terms of centuries or even millennia. However, his energy is used to maintain the workers' submission to the Martian elite (and, by implication, to oppressors everywhere). Gusev embodies the cosmic revolutionary, Aelita's father embodies the cosmic reactionary.

Virtually the same characteristics are found in the major antihero of *Death Ray*. Garin is superficially similar to Losev, and in some ways even exceeds him. His unusual scientific talent enables him to invent a powerful laser and he foresees a new political order in which his invention gives him power over the Earth and absolute rule over its inhabitants. He has great courage and iron will. Like the Martian ruler, he is a prince of darkness, a Satan of modern capitalism. And he is surrounded by minions similar to him in amorality and reactionary intent, but inferior in intelligence.

One of his minions is a capitalist who owns several chemical enterprises. Like the inventor of the death ray, he has a strong will and global vision. In fact, he competes with the inventor but is not his equal. First, his vision is more limited. Whereas the inventor dreams of creating a worldwide fascist dictatorship, the capitalist aspires only to own all of the world's chemical plants. The capitalist is also vulnerable to female charms. Seduced and then spurned by Zoia, his spirit is broken and he ceases to be a rival of the inventor. Instead, he joins the inventor's circle and helps him work toward world domination.

These three characters symbolize infernal forces. The inventor represents brutal violence and the striving to dominate. The capitalist represents obsessive greed. And Zoia represents the deadly sin of lust. She is the femme fatale whose charms no one can resist. She, like the men, seeks power and domination. However, her desire is more limited. She wants sexual domination over her lovers and control over the attendants of her palace and estate.

In *Death Ray*, the leaders of capitalism are characters whose attributes help to emphasize similar attributes in the positive heroes. In other movies, however, these characters are less superlative. They are not manifestations of cosmic forces but are down-to-earth characters.

Degenerated Revolutionaries

The Bolsheviks were quite experienced in the struggle against heresy in their ranks, and against Marxists who were critical of them. They supposed that a revolution could succumb to hostile propaganda, the provocations of class enemies, and moral degeneration and rejection of Bolshevik principles in personal behavior. This phenomenon indeed became typical during NEP, when the new bourgeoisie could subvert apparatchiks and serve as models of the good life.

Sexual relations held special importance for the Bolsheviks during NEP. Russian intellectuals were never known for puritanical mores, and the theories of Alexandra Kollontai, a prominent female Bolshevik leader and feminist theoretician, gained popularity. Kollontai advocated promiscuity and viewed traditional marriage as a bourgeois institution. All of this led to increased promiscuity among the party and state bureaucracy as well as among members of Komsomol, the Young Communist League.

The leaders of the party in the 1920s required party members to be permanently alert to the treason of their comrades. They encouraged spying as well as the merciless punishment of traitors and corrupted Communists. And again young cinematographers responded with enthusiasm to this ideological order. Consequently, the problem of the degeneration of the revolutionary leader became a leading theme in their works.

In dealing with the problem of degeneration, movie directors elaborated on two basic themes. The first theme implied that specialists in a particular field, hired to serve the people, often lost touch with that reality. They started thinking about the people only as exploitable subjects. The party bureaucrats in such cases were corrected by the good party functionaries, who saved the exploited person from the bureaucrats and punished or strongly reprimanded the bureaucrats. This scenario can be found in Protazanov's *Don Diego and Pelageia* (1928), in which a local bureaucrat arrests an old women for minor transgressions. A member of Komsomol has the women released from prison.

The second theme involves significant degeneration not only in the local bureaucracy but among party members themselves. Ermler's *Parisian Cobbler* (1928) elaborates on the mores of youth during the NEP and how these affected the Komsomol members. One Komsomol member seduces a girl and then sullies her name. The behavior of the Komsomol member is juxtaposed with that of the cobbler, a poor handicapped person who protects the girl. This protection appeals to the masses, who then reprimand the degenerate party member.

HEROES IN PRIVATE LIFE AND HEROES AS LOVERS

As in the first years after the revolution, during this period (and up until the 1960s), the official Soviet vision of society left no room for private life. People were fundamentally members of their class. Their private activities (for example, their love interests) were nothing but a manifestation of their political stand. In fact, individuals were dissolved in their class and in human history. Thus, personal life was dissolved in historical time and each action had political significance: It was either a step toward the liberation of all people on Earth from the shackles of oppression and toward humanity's final victory over nature, or a step in the opposite direction. Private life was therefore an oxymoron, since life, by definition, was not private. Those who strove for it, if they did not in fact side with the counterrevolution, were at least not on the side of the progressive forces.

Despite this attitude in Soviet ideology, the concept of a private life found its way onto the screen for several reasons. First of all, the NEP unleashed a desire for private life. The nouveau riche cared little for the struggle between the Soviet powers and the dark forces of capitalism. In addition, a considerable number of intellectuals, workers, and party functionaries were tired of revolutionary fervor and wanted to live privately. That is, they wanted to enjoy their lives and think about their personal welfare. Indeed, life was quite harsh for many workers, who had little time to ponder global problems.

The dangers to the Communist stalwart from indulging in private life are examined in Protazanov's *The Forty-First* (1927). This film focuses on love affairs and their detrimental effect on the revolutionary's social consciousness. These affairs lead him or her close to the betrayal of the revolution. The movie is set during the civil war with a female sniper as the heroine. Belonging to that great social body, the Red Army, she has been completely socialized. She has no individual characteristics, no private time, and her private life has been completely dissolved in the *Weltgeist* of history. Because she has no personal life outside the struggle against capitalism and the White armies, she likewise has no sex life. Not only does the movie provide no hint of her dealings with fellow Red soldiers, but, dressed in a coarse military uniform, even her femininity is concealed.

In fact, she has been transformed. She is neither woman nor man but a peculiar blend of medieval knight and female eunuch. Her self-imposed celibacy, bordering on self-castration, is a type of purification from the tempting desires of sex. Such desires, representing private life, would have caused her to be preoccupied with her personal emotions rather than the revolutionary struggle.

In the movie, she kills the soldiers of the White armies, all of whom are men. These killings are symbolic, in that she kills not only her class enemies, but also potential husbands and lovers who could seduce her into private life and cause her to betray her revolutionary calling. The lines of attacking male soldiers assume a libidinous implication, or, more properly, a sociolibidinous implication. In this setting, a sexual encounter is not a sin but a social transgression since it could lead the woman into the seductive clutches of private life. This potential crime would be even worse because it would not be her fellow Red soldiers, or even a politically neutral person with whom she would fall in love, but her class enemy. For this reason, she doggedly persists in attempting to exterminate the White soldiers and records each killing.

She is quite successful in her endeavors. She avoids temptation while successfully killing forty White soldiers. Yet her perseverance and revolutionary puritanism are not enough to keep her from straying. She is confronted by a handsome White officer, obviously of noble birth, and not only fails to kill him but is left alone with him in a remote area.

For the female warrior, her missed shot was not merely a technical mistake or an unlucky event but a sort of sexually social sin. It demonstrated that she, the upstanding Communist, was not immune to temptation. Of course, the inevitable follows—she falls in love with her would-be victim. This act embodies her betrayal of the revolution.

The treacherous social significance of love affairs was emphasized by the character of her lover, Govorukha Otrok. He was not simply a handsome male who seduced the female sharpshooter by virtue of his purely male characteristics. Had this been the case, the seduction would have been a minor transgression and could have been explained by the prevailing ideology as being caused by the physical desire of a woman too long deprived of male attention. In this context, a love affair intended to satisfy one's basic needs would have been above reproach, as long as it was not too lengthy and the lover was eventually replaced with another of appropriate social and political background (for example, a soldier of the Red Army).

In this respect, the relationship, especially after a proper lover was located, could have benefited revolutionary performance, that is, the decimating of White soldiers. The replacement of the lover would resemble the replacement of a bourgeois specialist with a proletarian specialist (a technically qualified person of proper political and social background) as soon as the latter became available for employment. Thus, such an encounter could be forgivable and even unreproachable if it occurred in the context of a tactical retreat until a proper lover became available.

On the other hand, if the lover possessed certain spiritual attractions, such as intelligence, the affair could lead to an emotional involvement. In this case, the affair would be totally inappropriate for the female revolutionary because it could lead to a temptation to stray into private life and to forsake her revolutionary duties.

Thus, although in theory her behavior could be excused, in reality it was unforgivable. Her actual lover was not merely socially and politically inadequate, he was an avowed enemy of the revolution. This was not merely a descent into private life, but an explicit change of sides. While she was enjoying her lover, the sniper was actually committing overt treachery. Only when the death of her lover frees her from his spell is she able to once again move in the proper direction.[3]

For members of the political elite, private life was regarded as a serious transgression bordering on betrayal of the revolutionary movement. For members of the new Soviet bourgeoisie, however, private life was regarded as regrettable but necessary. Likewise, among intellectuals employed by the state, private life was considered a permissible sin. In these cases, private life was viewed as a tactical retreat; it was an existential manifestation of the market economy and could be temporarily tolerated. For these reasons, private life (e.g., love for its own sake) found its way onto the screen.

The concreteness of the daily life portrayed in Abram Room's *The Third Meshchanskaya* (1927) demonstrates a complete disregard of revolutionary eschatology and political life per se. Although the movie's protagonists are preoccupied with their daily problems, they are not egocentric since they are concerned with the outside world. They show their concern privately, however, rather than publicly (such as through involvement in politics). The film's hero has a friend with no place to live (a reference to the severe housing shortage that affected practically all Soviet citizens at that time). Though the hero and his wife have only one room, they decide to invite his friend to live with them. Of course, the predictable happens—the hero's wife becomes his friend's mistress. Later she abandons them both. This is a personal tragedy for the men since both were emotionally attached to her. This tragedy is seen as private, however, in that it has no social repercussions and affects only the lives of these two men.

Soviet ideologists of the time accepted that party members should not indulge themselves in the good life. However this freedom was rather limited, particularly when it came to amorous adventures. Bourgeois specialists had more opportunities to indulge in these "depraved" activities because their social inferiority at least partially excused their un-couth behavior. Of course, if their behavior became obsessive, as seen in Boris Svetozarov's *In the Intoxication of NEP* (1925), they would begin to endanger society by becoming similar to those representatives of pre-revolutionary Russia who employed their power to sexually harass peas-ant girls.

FIRST HIDDEN CRITICS FROM THE INSIDE

As mentioned earlier, during NEP there remained some hidden dis-sent in social science, literature, and the arts. Furthermore, the internal party struggle continued. While most filmmakers followed the official line of the party headed by Stalin, the influence of Trotsky (who had accused the party leadership of bureaucratism) affected filmmakers by making them somewhat critical of the existing situation in the country.

Some of them, making suprarevolutionary films from time to time, were now able to make movies that were somewhat critical of the new regime. In the next years, however, this opportunity totally disap-peared. Of course, directors had to be extremely cautious when criticiz-ing contemporary events. They could not suggest that certain problems, such as bureaucratic abuse of the masses, stemmed from the nature of the regime. Such abuse could only be depicted as resulting from degen-eration in a particular part of the regime. This device was popular among movie directors not only because it sidestepped the censorship problem, but because it appealed to Trotsky's supporters, a considerable number of party members, and ordinary citizens, all of whom believed that if something was wrong, it was due to the mistakes of the leader-ship (such as the excessive freedom and lenient treatment given to the NEP bourgeoisie). In fact, it is possible that the movie directors them-selves believed in the degeneration concept. It is important to note that although directors exposed the degeneration of minor bureaucrats, they were careful not to criticize those in the highest echelons of power.

In the 1920s audiences were already constantly aware that all art (in-cluding movies) was subject to censorship, and that artists were not completely free to explicitly state their ideas on certain political or philo-sophical matters. Thus, audiences were conditioned to read between the lines, and sometimes discovered meanings or messages totally unin-tended by the artist. All art is plagued by miscommunication between artist and audience, but this problem was magnified in Soviet art.

Three devices were used as a means to convey some skepticism about Soviet life: the denunciation of the degeneration of Communists, the presentation of private life as a positive phenomenon, and the use of history to make allusions to the present times (a trick to which Soviet cinematographers would return in the 1960s). Directors who used the degeneration theme often exposed actions of party officials that bordered on treason. In this way, directors who were critical of Soviet reality could express negative feelings about its implementation by depicting the moral degeneration of a Communist stalwart. These stalwarts, while not perhaps of the elite, were definite candidates for high positions in the future.

PRIVATE LIFE AS A DEVICE

Grigorii Kozintsev and Leonid Trauberg's *Overcoat* (1926) provides another excellent example of a movie brimming with hints of the oppressive nature of the Soviet regime. The very fact that well-known writer Iurii Tynianov wrote the script demonstrated that the movie had an oppositional political viewpoint. Tynianov's dislike of the regime was well known. His writings often dealt with the era of Nicholas I—an era characterized by bureaucratization, regimentation, and brutal repression. During this time, not only was real political protest suppressed but even the most innocent deviation from the prescribed way of thinking was enough to invite disaster.

These characteristics of the reign of Nicholas I were also prevalent during the NEP period. Like the tsarist regime, this was a time of intense bureaucratization of Soviet life. Additionally, as in Nicholas's time, the Soviet government allowed a certain degree of freedom for those engaged in purely economic activity. On the other hand, it was suspicious of intellectuals, especially freethinking writers. Given its parallels with the Soviet NEP period, the reign of Nicholas I provided excellent allegorical material. It was also open to attack because the period was officially designated as having been reactionary.

Overcoat traces the life of Akakii Akakievich Bashmachnikov from the time when, as a young fellow, he arrives in St. Petersburg. The movie contrasts his small size against a backdrop of the huge buildings of the capital. The effigy of the sphinx and a pervasive sense of surrealism give shape to the all-embracing, almost smothering, bureaucratic monster. The hero is spiritually crushed by this oppressive system, while at the same time being absorbed in it by becoming a functionary in the bureaucratic machinery. In one scene he is even buried under a rain of fountain pens. The bureaucratic machine is cast as ubiquitous and forbidding, as well as repressive.

In the film, the only respite from this grim reality is love. The hero's love object—the celestial creature, as he calls her—has a double meaning. On the one hand, she symbolizes the political goal of the ideal society that was to replace the grim bureaucratic reality. On the other hand she represents the pleasures of private life, that is, the personal happiness resulting from two human beings creating a harmonious island amidst imperfect social reality.

To achieve this goal, that is, to win the love of the celestial creature (and build the perfect society, or at least a happy microcosm), the hero becomes somewhat of a revolutionary. He violates the rules of the system and forges some documents. However, his dreams are dashed. He is frustrated not because the celestial creature rejects his advances—in fact it is implied that she could easily have succumbed to his charms. However, she is revealed in two separate dreams to be less than the ideal he thought she was.

In the first dream, the celestial creature is a symbol of an ideal society that could not be attained. The political consummation of the relationship would lead to her degeneration. The ideal society would turn into the same bureaucratic and satanic regime the hero wanted to escape. This symbolizes, in essence, the futility of all political change.

In the second, Bashmachnikov approaches the moment of consummation with his dream girl. The sumptuous scene begins changing before his eyes to resemble the office where he works and he begins to be surrounded by his colleagues, supervisors, and other bureaucrats. The clear message of these two scenes is that not only is the ideal society impossible but the private happiness of two people is equally unachievable.

While his disappointment with the beautiful woman was both allegorical and personal, Bashmachnikov still had one other chance to escape the grim and brutal reality of the bureaucratized society. This was the complete withdrawal of the self into private and family life, which creates an island of beauty in the grim expanse of gray bureaucracy. Yet even the family was not private life in its pure form, for it implied that a union of two individuals is a special manifestation of society rather than a private, individual universe. True private life implied a complete alienation from reality. In this sense, the individual had to sever all contacts not only with political institutions (represented in the film by huge, forbidding buildings) and civic society (represented by Bashmachnikov's colleagues), but also with all human beings, including those of the opposite sex.

In fact, Bashmachnikov had a rather platonic vision of relationships between the sexes. For him, sexual encounters had never been purely physical acts but primarily symbols of the spiritual unity of people. Therefore, as soon as he found out that such a platonic union was impossible because the bureaucratic leviathan was poisoning everything and turning his celestial creature into a cheap whore, he lost all interest

in sex. This complete social alienation resulted in the symbolic emascula-
tion of Bashmachnikov. While in the beginning of the film he is portrayed as a young, idealist brimming with sexuality (or more properly,
sexuality distilled into a desire for spiritual communication at the highest level), the end of the movie finds him a weary old man with no desire
for external communication of any sort.

Our hero's descent into self-absorption is manifested by his desire to
acquire a new overcoat. This overcoat symbolizes a sort of protective
shell against the harshness of reality. However, despite this shell, his
quest to achieve at least a modicum of emotional equilibrium is futile.
The poisonous leviathan, in the form of a robber, appears to take the
coat away from Bashmachnikov. This reinforces not only the harshness
of the social environment but the abject helplessness of the position of
the individual.

Thus the movie *Overcoat* was similar to Gogol's story of the same
name. The use of Gogol's theme was additional protection for Tynianov
and the movie's directors against criticism for portraying the life of a
clerk, who was a petty bourgeois and deserved neither attention nor
sympathy. In the film, the clerk was formerly a part of the state bureaucratic machinery but had become alienated from it and victimized by it.
The leviathan confronting the clerk not only represented the bureaucratic machinery itself, but, together with all aspects of life in the city, represented a cruel and repressive regime. The entire movie was infused with
an air of irrationality that emphasized the omnipresent bureaucratic regime as poisoning society. From this perspective, the movie followed the
familiar anti-Bolshevik theme of the revolutionary period that viewed
the Bolshevik victory as the ultimate victory of the forces of evil.

The director took a very fatalistic approach, implying that any attempt
to change the existing order was doomed and would ultimately result in
the subjugation of the individual and the creation of an all-embracing
bureaucracy. To compound this pessimistic view, the film also implied
that any attempt by the individual to absorb him- or herself in private
life, or seek solace in family ties, was also doomed to failure. It is clear
that the director saw no hope for humanity.

THE HISTORICAL DEVICE

For the most part, movie directors were only able to criticize the Soviet
regime indirectly through the use of allegory and historical analogy.
They could attack the top Soviet leadership only if they cloaked their
criticism in attacks on the oppressive Russian tsars. In this way, they
could suggest to their audiences that the system was rotten to the core

and that it was not the petty bureaucrats but the top echelons who were responsible for the people's mistreatment. Their ambivalent presentations of past events helped them express their nonconformist ideas. These films clearly implied that fighting with the authoritarian government (either Bolshevik or imperial) was impossible.

Iurii Tarich's *The Wings of a Serf* (1926), which dealt with the reign of Ivan the Terrible, is a good example of a movie that mildly critiqued the regime. By the late 1920s, Pokrovskii, the eminent Soviet historian, had become the dean of Russian historiography, and his interpretation of Russian history had become the accepted version. According to Pokrovskii, Ivan the Terrible symbolized both the feudal lords and the emerging bourgeoisie. Although considered somewhat progressive [his purge of the landed aristocracy (the boyars) established the essential conditions for creating a unified Russia], he nevertheless represented the oppressor classes and therefore deserved no accolades. As a result, his regime was considered ghastly for the workers. The slaves (*kholopy*) were among the most unfortunate. They were viewed as chattel, and any exercise of individuality or cleverness was considered somewhat seditious.

The hero of *The Wings of a Serf* is an incredibly intelligent slave who invents wings that enable him to fly. The authorities decide that he must have sold his soul to the devil and he is duly executed. The movie emphasizes the brutality of the regime, as well as several other themes prominent in Pokrovskii's school, such as the importance of merchant capital in the economic and political development of sixteenth-century Russia.

It is unlikely that the director of this movie explicitly set out to attack the Soviet regime. He probably wanted only to expose the oppressive rule of tsardom and to lay bare the miserable conditions of the masses. At the same time, however, his presentation of the cruelty of the regime and the misery of the masses bore an uncanny resemblance to contemporary Soviet reality. Thus, much of the audience may have perceived an invitation to make a rather unfavorable comparison between their situation and that of the time of Ivan the Terrible.

Themes of intellectual confrontation with an authoritarian state can also be found in Kozintsev's *The Club of the Big Deed (S.V.D.)* (1927), which is set in the time of Nicholas I and also suggests comparisons to the contemporary situation. As in *Overcoat*, two major forces are arrayed against each other. On one side is the totalitarian, almost satanic state. It relies not only on powerful repressive machinery and a huge bureaucracy, but also on the base instincts of its citizens to achieve its aims. On the other side is the noble revolutionary, a Decembrist.[4] In this case, the revolutionary is presented not as a cunning plotter who would attempt to undermine the government through subversion and sabotage, but as an idealist who believes in an ideal society and who adheres to high moral standards. In this regard, he is reminiscent of Bashmachnikov in *Overcoat*.

It is not surprising that the director chose a Decembrist for this role. Compared to the revolutionaries who followed them (the Populists and Bolsheviks), the Decembrists were exclusively members of the gentry and adhered to very high standards of personal behavior.

As in *Overcoat*, the protagonist of the movie is doomed from the outset. Not only is the state's repressive machinery all-powerful, but society itself can neither accept the concept of an ideal social organization nor understand the utility of adopting high moral standards. It ends up supporting the repressive forces.

In the film, the Decembrist hero is wounded in a confrontation with tsarist security forces. Bleeding, he runs into a gambling casino. This is certainly a symbol of the society that the Decembrist wanted to liberate and for which he was risking his life. He expects to find people gloomy and depressed because they are deprived of their freedom. He is surprised to find instead that the casino patrons, i.e., the members of society, seem to be quite happy. Even the casino employees, who initially seem sympathetic toward the Decembrist, turn against him. A girl offers him champagne poured into a hat and then throws it in his face as he tries to drink it.

Thus, society is shown to be not only unappreciative but actually hostile to our hero. The problem is that his impeccable moral credentials and sheer nobility constantly remind society of its unworthiness. A victory by the hero would be a disaster because it would imply that society must change and become as good as the hero. Thus, most of society would rather side with the government. The immoral authoritarian establishment has no problems allowing similar behavior on the part of its citizenry. In fact, it might even welcome such behavior.

Thus, it is not surprising that the crowd in the casino begins rejoicing at the Decembrist's desperate condition and slow death. It begins gleefully capering around him, the dancers's distorted features recalling Goya's Capriccios. In the context of the movie, the entire society has become so corrupt that its members have lost their humanity. The alliance between the government and the general populace is emphasized by the fact that an agent provocateur in the service of the secret police is among the casino's patrons. Under the approving giggles of the crowd, he points his pistol at the hero.

Similar criticism of the authoritarian government of Nicholas I (and implicitly the Soviet government with whom Nicholas was associated) can be found in Evgenii Cherviakov's *The Poet and the Tsar* (1927). As in the preceding examples, *The Poet and the Tsar* deals with the reign of

Nicholas I and his repressive bureaucracy, which was extremely hostile toward any independent-minded person and implicitly relied upon a society that was either corrupted or apathetic, or both. Alexander S. Pushkin, the classic Russian writer and the hero of the film, is juxtaposed with the repressive tsardom and the corrupted populace. Pushkin implicitly represents the freethinking intellectual of Soviet Russia who is confronted by a repressive Soviet state and a morally degenerate populace determined to exploit the opportunities of the NEP period (that is, to enrich themselves and promote the baser pleasures of life).

Like the heroes of the previous movies, Pushkin is inspired by a noble desire to change society and he manifests this longing through his poetry. Like that of Bashmachnikov, Pushkin's love affairs have a double meaning. On the one hand, his amorous adventures symbolize the quest for the ideal life. On the other hand, they represent an attempt to escape from an increasingly corrupted society and seek solace in the union of two souls in love. Pushkin's end is similar to those of Bashmachnikov and the Decembrist: He is shot in a duel. Although the poet was an implacable enemy of the establishment, it was not the establishment that killed him. His opponent in the duel was apparently only indirectly connected to the government: He was a part of the society that had become corrupted by the government and had become an ally of, or perhaps even undistinguishable from, that government.

CONCLUSION

More than in any other period, the first decade after the revolution found most film directors collaborating with the authorities willingly and accepting official ideology as their own. Film directors were not overly concerned with portraying an accurate picture of life in their movies. As future historians will find, many of them, including those considered excellent directors, readily distorted the life around them. However, film directors believed that their movies served the noble cause of the revolution and socialism.

This happy marriage between filmmakers and the state would come to an end with Stalin's ascent to power. The next years witnessed the transformation of revolutionary filmmakers into obsequious servants of the supreme leader. At the same time, the twenties was the last period, before Gorbachev's *glasnost*, when directors could afford some hidden criticism of existing social reality. In the next period they would risk their lives if they dared to do even remotely critical work.

NOTES

1. Nikolai Berdiaev (1874–1948) was a prominent Russian philosopher who became known in the West after his immigration. He was a consistent enemy of Marxism and the Bolsheviks. After 1985 he was one of the most cited authors in Russia. Pitirim Sorokin (1889–1968) was a prominent Russian sociologist. From 1930 until his death, he was a professor at Harvard University.

2. Dziga Vertov, the most ideologically active filmmaker, demanded that movies's should "establish a visual link between the workers of the world" (*Pravda*, 16 July 1925). Eisenstein felt similarly. Along with Grigorii Alexandrov, he wrote (in 1928) that "the first basic function of our films is to interpret the theses and decrees, to reveal them and make them infectious through a visual demonstration of their significance in the general cause of socialist construction, thereby incorporating each individual's will in the general will of the workers' and peasants' state as a whole" (*Komsomolskaia Pravda*, 1 April 1928). In several other articles published in the late 1920s and early 1930s Eisenstein presented himself as an ideological zealot (see *Na literaturnom postu*, 4, 1928, pp. 15–18).

3. Three decades later Grigorii Chukhrai made his version of this story, with the same title. His version will be discussed below.

4. The Decembrists attempted an unsuccessful uprising against Tsar Nicholas I in 1825.

III

Movies During Stalin's Time:
Total Submission to the Official Ideology

By 1928–1929, the political situation in the country had changed radically. By this time, Stalin had squelched any opposition to his rule inside the party and practically completed the installation of the totalitarian regime. The collectivization of agriculture and the mass starvation accompanied by increasing repression signaled the end of the revolutionary period. At this point intellectuals, as well as the rest of the population, had no choice but to accept (at least superficially) the dominant ideology and pretend that they supported Stalin and the regime. The time when intellectuals could choose Communist ideology on their own was gone; it was now imposed on them forceably by the totalitarian state. Of course, this had significant ramifications for their work. Until the beginning of Gorbachev's *perestroika*, Soviet cinematographers lived in a totalitarian society that unceremoniously controlled their work and often punished them for violating the rules.

5

Stalin and Soviet Movies

It so happened that the omnipotent founder of the totalitarian system was a great fan of cinema. This rather casual circumstance had an immense impact on the history of the Soviet movies for the following six decades. Stalin built up a mechanism for the supervision of cinema that outlasted him and was abolished finally along with the Soviet Union. Stalin's relations with prominent film directors as well as the influence of his personal tastes on the whole film industry make up one of the most dramatic episodes in the history of world cinema.

STALIN'S INFATUATION WITH CINEMA

Stalin was always extensively involved in movie production, and he considered the control of films to be one of the main goals of the party and state apparatus. Although the reason for his interest is not clear, certainly his love of movies played a role in the importance he gave to them. In fact, his desire to supervise Soviet cinematography bordered on an obsession, and for almost three decades the Soviet movie industry was under his vigilant surveillance.

The following story demonstrates the extent of his obsession. In 1940, with the war already raging in Western Europe, and with Poland already controlled by Hitler, the Soviet Union was on the brink of war with Germany. Researchers in the late 1980s were able to obtain access to Stalin's archives and to the materials that should be included in the fourteenth volume of Stalin's collected works (the publication stopped at the thirteenth volume, which contains Stalin's texts for 1940). To one researcher's great surprise, he discovered that in that year Stalin made only one speech, in which he denounced Stolper and Ivanov's movie *The Law of Life* (1940).[1] He also discovered that Stalin had written letters to Ivan Bol'shakov, then the head of Goskino, about the scripts for two films—Mikhail Doller and Vselovod Pudovkin's *Suvorov* (1941; about a famous Russian commander in the eighteenth century), and Chiaureli's

Georgii Saakadze (1942–1943; about a Georgian leader in the seventeenth century).[2]

Even during the terrible war with Germany, Stalin deemed it important to instruct film directors on how to make specific movies. In January 1944, when the outcome of the war was still unclear, Stalin put Dovzhenko's script on the Politburo's meeting agenda, as if it were a vital issue for the country.[3] In fact, Stalin's obsession with movies occasionally appeared almost pathological. Kozintsev described how Stalin, while watching his film *Maxim's Youth* (1935), expressed his anger and praise as if he were "watching the film not as a pictured story, but as real events, as things really happening before his eyes" (Kozintsev 1992, pp. 343–44).

Another curious episode confirms Kozintsev's observations about Stalin's naive perception of movies as true reality and of his belief in the possibility of manipulating this reality. Before the war, Mikhail Gelovany, a Georgian actor who looked like Stalin and had the same accent, was the only one allowed to play Stalin in the movies. However, after the war when Stalin made Russian chauvinism an essential part of his ideology, he ordered the replacement of Gelovany, his countryman, by a pure Russian actor, Alexei Dikii, as if the spectators watching this actor would forget the Georgian origin of the leader and his strong accent.

Stalin knew all the leading film directors personally, and met with each of them several times, an honor rarely bestowed on other intellectuals. During these meetings he would often give instructions as to the direction certain films should take. This was the case with Alexander Dovzhenko, the Ukrainian film director and writer, who received instructions regarding *Aerograd* (1935), a movie about the development of the Far East, and *Shchors* (1939), which was about the Ukrainian revolutionary commander during the civil war (*Izvestia*, 5 November 1936; *Pravda*, 11 January 1936; *Literaturnaia Gazeta*, 20 March 1935). Sergei Eisenstein also had the honor of being invited to the Kremlin in 1947, where he had to listen humbly to Stalin's suggestions regarding the second part of *Ivan the Terrible* (1945) (*Moskovskie Novosti*, 7 August 1988).

Aside from influencing movies already in production, Stalin often ordered the creation of a particular movie. For example, he assigned Mikhail Romm to shoot *Thirteen* (1937), a movie about the struggle between Soviet border guards and Muslim nationalists in Central Asia (whom the movie presented as mere bandits).

Stalin also wielded great influence by banning movies that he found politically damaging. The story of Kheifits's *My Motherland* (1933) is remarkable in this regard. Kheifits and his friend, scriptwriter and director Alexander Zarkhi, were asked by the Political Section of Goskino to make a film about the military conflict between the Red Army and Chinese troops in Manchuria in the 1930s. In the movie the Red Army, after defeating Chiang Kai-shek's army, retreated from Chinese territory while conquering the hearts of the Chinese people. Among other things, the Red Army opened the food stores of the Kuomintang army to poor people as a farewell gift.

The movie was tailored to current propaganda, with its emphasis on internationalism and the prospect of world revolution. Furthermore, it was accepted with great enthusiasm by the public, as well as by the highest officials. However, Stalin felt that in the film the Red Army did not respond to the Kuomintang army "with triple strikes," which Stalin had promised before the premier of the film. The filmmakers were accused of preaching Tolstoy's credo of nonresistance to evil, and the film was removed from all theaters and destroyed, without, however, any dire consequences to the filmmakers (Kheifits 1987).

Another example of Stalin's intervention occurred with the second part of Lukov's *Great Life* (1946), a film about the life of miners. Initially, the movie was praised by colleagues at the meeting of the Council of the Ministry of Cinematography. But Stalin felt that the film denigrated Soviet life, because it gave a realistic picture of the miner's lives and problems (for example, they drank excessively). Stalin called Lukov and Pavel Nilin, the scriptwriter, to a meeting of the Organizational Bureau of the Central Committee. Later, at a new meeting of the council, they both recanted their mistakes and promised to correct the movie (ultimately Stalin did not accept this idea and the film was scrapped; *Iskusstvo Kino* 9, 1989, pp. 57–66).

Stalin was also able to influence filmmaking in more subtle ways. For example, he was able to reveal his tastes and preferences by deciding what movies deserved the prize that bore his name and which category of the prize to give them—first, second, or third.

Stalin's love of movies is further demonstrated by the fact that he regularly watched movies in his quarters in the Kremlin. The screenings were usually held late at night in the company of the head of Goskino (a very precarious and risky position at that time),[4] members of the Politburo, and often the filmmakers themselves.[5]

Stalin's passion is probably one reason why almost no film directors were ever sent to the *Gulag*, in contrast to writers, scholars, and administrative workers in cinematography (several of whom were arrested in 1949). This was true even when he was furious with a director's work, as was the case with Dovzhenko, whose script *Ukraine in Flames* (1943) was felt to contain many ideological errors (including nationalism, ignorance of the class approach and Lenin, and calumny against the party, the Soviet system, and the Red Army; see *Iskusstvo Kino* 4, 1990, pp. 89–95).[6]

SOVIET CINEMATOGRAPHERS AND STALIN

As was mentioned earlier, the relations between Stalin and film directors were extremely dramatic even if very contradictory. We will dwell on the two with whom Stalin met much most often: Eisenstein and Dovzhenko.

Eisenstein's Case

By the 1930s, several filmmakers attempted to find some humanistic interpretations of crude Soviet propaganda. For the most part, such attempts were rejected by the Soviet leadership, as was the case for Eisenstein's movie *Bezhin Meadow* (1935–1937).

In this movie Eisenstein attempted to address an ideologically important issue: the superiority of class values over humanistic values. In order to please Stalin (and follow the "social order"), the movie was inspired by the story of Pavlik Morozov, a thirteen-year-old boy who became an official hero. Pavlik, a pioneer, reported his father (an adversary of collectivization) to the political police and was then killed by his uncle. Eisenstein attempted to make this horrible story more palatable for intellectuals (and probably for his own conscience) by presenting it as a biblical story (i.e., father sacrificing his son), thereby legitimizing the official version of the story. It is remarkable how Soviet views on this movie, which was never shown publicly, have evolved. Before 1985 the movie was strongly denounced as the director's professional failure. However, by 1986 many felt that in fact the authorities did not understand Eisenstein's good intention to create "a lofty tragedy about the antagonistic struggle of the new forces with the old ones" (Iutkevich 1986, p. 508). Three years later, with the evolution of *glasnost*, authors began to speak more openly about the cruel treatment of movie people by officials, but still presented Eisenstein as a director who had accepted the official version of Pavlik Morozov's life, and said nothing about his failed conformism (Freilikh 1990).

However, the authorities felt that Eisenstein's work was too subtle for propaganda purposes; the director was forced not only to stop work on the movie,[7] but to publish an article repenting for this work. In this article the director confessed that his inclination toward generalization made the killing of a son by his father appear as a typical phenomenon. He stated that since this was not true he had "distorted the reality of class struggle in the countryside." He also accused himself, repeating the official invectives against his movie, of having let "the drama of a son killer eclipse the class hatred of the kulaks" (Freilikh 1990).

Later, Eisenstein made other attempts to reconcile the direct orders of the authorities with "decent" philosophical ideas, thereby rationalizing in his mind his allegiance to Stalin and his role as a purveyor of propaganda. An excellent example of this can found in his making of *Ivan the Terrible*. Having accepted Stalin's command to make this movie (with the intention of glorifying the hero), he rationalized his participation by stating that the film would examine "the alarming tendency of cruelty in human beings" (Freilikh 1990). Of course, this desire to carry out the authorities' wishes in a subtle and refined way could enhance the propagandistic value of a movie, and this was often cheered by the leader.[8] However, this could be dangerous if Stalin decided that the film director had gone too far, or wanted to use his commission to implement ideas hostile to the official ideology.

In fact, this is what occurred with the second part of *Ivan the Terrible*. Having received Stalin's endorsement of the first part (including the Stalin prize of the first order), Eisenstein decided to be more bold, and present the tsar and the times in accordance with his own views. However, Stalin banned the movie and required significant changes. In his meeting with Stalin, Eisenstein (as well as Nikolai Cherkasov) humbly asked Stalin's recommendation for improving the film (interestingly, some of Eisenstein's friends felt that he had no intention of using Stalin's suggestions). However, Eisenstein's death in 1948 ended any speculation as to the fate of the movie (Kozlov 1992).

Debates about the relationship between Eisenstein and Stalin started with Solzhenitsyn's *One Day in the Life of Ivan Denisovich* (1962), in which a *gulag* prisoner noted in connection with *Ivan the Terrible* that "it is the most nasty political attempt to justify personal tyranny. It is the mockery of three generations of Russian intelligentsia."

With *glasnost* these debates intensified. Victor Seleznev, a sophisticated intellectual from Saratov, addressed this issue in a short article entitled "Was Eisenstein a Conformist?" (*Iskusstvo Kino* 4, 1990, p. 58). Seleznev emphasizes the second part of the movie, and insists that Eisenstein "with his death paid for his prophetic film."

Mezhuiev, a Moscow philosopher, included Eisenstein with those filmmakers who molded the totalitarian mentality. He cited Eisenstein's *Alexander Nevskii* (1938), a movie about the Russian prince who defeated German knights and invaded Russia in the thirteenth century, as another example of Eisenstein's glorification of despotic power. However, Naum Kleinman, an expert on Eisenstein, defended the film director. He felt that this movie, made in the context of impending war with Hitler (who wanted to continue Germany's *Drang nach Osten*—the penetration of Russia from the west), instilled optimism (through the powerful figure of the prince) that the German invasion could be beaten (*Isku-sstvo Kino* 2, 1990, pp. 109–17).

Mezhuiev, however, could also point to another episode in the director's life before the mass terror started. In 1927 Eisenstein, when he created the presumably documentary movie about the Bolshevik Revolution, *October*, obediently cut Leon Trotsky (who was only second to Lenin in directing the overthrow of Kerensky's provisional government) out of the first version of his film because by the end of the shooting Trotsky had been proclaimed an enemy of the party.

Dovzhenko's Case

Filmmakers usually responded to Stalin's direction with both respect and admiration. Dovzhenko (one of the masters of Soviet cinematography) is typical in this regard; he frequently expressed, both publicly and in his diary, his devotion to Stalin (see Ogoniok, 1987, 43; *Literaturnaia Gazeta*, February 1989). Even Stalin's scathing and wrongful attack against his script *Ukraine in Flames* did not lead him to question Stalin's genius, although Dovzhenko was bitterly disappointed and despondent (his status quickly declined).

It was only with time (and Stalin's death) that Dovzhenko allowed himself to express his true feelings. In 1955, he remarked with disgust "I licked these boots" (*Sovietskii Ekran* 17, 1955, p. 14), and later said "the right hand of this great man who ruled for almost two decades was the hand of a little villain, sadist, and bore" (*Iskusstvo Kino* 9, 1989, p. 55).

Dovzhenko's initial deference and love for Stalin was shared by many if not all of his colleagues. Vertov, in the opinion of a critic in the 1990s, made his *Lullaby* (1934) "with the sincere and heartfelt belief in Stalin's sainthood and the impossibility of comparison with ordinary people" (Mamatova 1990, p. 104).

NOTES

1. In this film, the secretary of the regional committee of the Komsomol seduces a girl, and is punished by expulsion from the party. Stalin, despite the retribution of the villain, accused the film of fostering "hatred of Bolsheviks." The scriptwriter (like the hero in the movie) was expelled from the party (Mamatova 1990, p. 107).

2. In the letter to Bol'shakov, Stalin demanded that Suvorov be portrayed as the embodiment of all those military virtues that the Soviet leader wanted in his army (*Iskusstvo Kino* 5, 1990, pp. 4–5). *Suvorov* was finally filmed by Doller and Pudovkin in 1941, and they implemented all of Stalin's directives, thereby pushing the film even further from historical reality than the original script (see

Iskusstvo Kino 5, 1990, pp. 7–10). *Georgii Saakadze* was made by Chiaureli in 1942–1943. Stalin liked the script, which served current propaganda by emphasizing the treason threatening the prince—the direct response to the atmosphere of suspicion and spy mania in the country during these years, which praised the cruel treatment of enemies (*Iskusstvo Kino* 11, 1991, pp. 91–93).

3. Stalin's obsession with movies was derogated after his death by Nikita Khrushchev, who contended that Stalin got much of his information about life in the country from such movies as Pyriev's *Kuban Cossacks* (1950), which he saw in the Kremlin (Khrushchev 1956).

4. One of them—Boris Shumitskii, an old Bolshevik—was executed in 1938.

5. Stalin's passion for movies was the major theme in Andrei Mikhalkov-Konchalovskii's film *The Inner Circle* (1991).

6. He made an exception for the scriptwriter Alexei Kapler (among his "masterpieces" were the scripts for *Lenin in October* and *Lenin in 1918*). However, this exception was made simply because the filmmaker, a Jew, was his daughter's lover.

7. When the authorities ordered the destruction of this film, Eisenstein's wife managed to save only a few pieces, which she kept in a box under their bed.

8. Such was the case with the first part of *Ivan the Terrible*, which began with an ideologically risky scene in which the tsar repented the mass murder of people in Novgorod, a freedom-loving city. The tsar stated that it had been done for "the great cause of the state." Eisenstein used all his extraordinary talents to portray, in a psychologically plausible manner, a positive side to the cruel tsar.

6

Industrialization and Collectivization (1929–1934)

This period was the most terrible for much of the country, and for Soviet cinematographers in particular. With the violent collectivization and spreading terror (which would reach its peak in the next period) film-makers realized for the first time that in order to survive (in some cases even physically), they would have to obey orders from the Kremlin and ignore their desire for self-actualization.

THE IDEOLOGICAL CLIMATE

Major political and ideological processes took place during this period. First of all, abandoning the NEP brought dramatic change to the countryside. The state forcibly collectivized peasant lands and almost all real estate. A new passport system, in effect by 1932, made peasant migration to the cities very difficult and practically fixed peasants on the land.

Comparable transformations in urban settings meant that private enterprise was actually eliminated by the early 1930s. The system of resident permits, or *propiski*, also made migration hard for the proletariat and intelligentsia, and city workers became, in effect, bondsmen of the state.

The USSR's entire economy changed from a market system to a highly centralized bureaucratic system. Because the bureaucracy controlled all distribution of goods and all planning for development, it expanded enormously. Bureaucrats' standard of living rose considerably—they became the ruling social elite as the state and party bureaucracies gradually merged.

The bureaucracy incorporated intellectuals of all sorts. In fact, one could not legally publish or film any work without direct government approval. Now the government not only imposed censorship but directly planned all artistic and scholarly endeavors. Henceforth, even art that was neutral vis-à-vis the authorities was not tolerated because it was not useful to them. Political repression, including arrests and forced exile, increased significantly.

Absolute government control over economic, political, and cultural life put enormous power in the hands of the bureaucracy, especially the political leaders. This totalitarian system came to be know as Stalinism, and its basic elements did not change substantially until the Gorbachev era.

With the leader endowed with almost superhuman capacities and privileges, and with the majority of the population in virtual slavery (literal slavery in the case of concentration camp inmates, who were widely used as cheap labor), the Soviet Union of the late 1920s was similar to oriental despotism. Yet it was despotism with an extremely dynamic economy.

Agricultural collectivization and industrialization was part of Stalin's ambitious plan to catch up with and surpass the most advanced industrial countries of the West—to turn agrarian Russia into an industrial giant. Feverish construction began throughout the country. Although one could argue that the actual achievements of the Soviet Union in the Stalin era were far more modest than Stalin's propaganda claimed, the fact remains that the country took a giant leap forward. Industrial and military capacity was upgraded significantly, as reflected in the country's performance in its confrontation with Nazi Germany.

Furthermore, the regime's relationship with the population was not purely "despotic," in the sense that it did not rely exclusively on repression to maintain control. There were also efforts to gain popular support and political legitimacy. The fight against the Right coincided with the struggle against corruption and degeneration within the political apparatus. In leading these efforts, Stalin assumed the egalitarian mantle of "defender of the workers' interests." Although supporting the good life for the bureaucracy (especially the secret police) was one of the regime's main concerns, it also tried to take care of the industrial proletariat to ensure its productivity as well as its political neutrality and possible support. In its early years, Stalin's regime was unaware that repression alone could keep the workers obedient. Thus, the workers' mood was still considered important.

Soviet cinematographers understood that in the late 1920s and the beginning of the 1930s they had entered a new era in which there would be little tolerance for those who deviated even slightly from the official line of the Kremlin and Stalin. In fact, the Central Committee made a special decision about "cinema cadres." Referring to "the intensification of class struggle on the ideological front," the committee demanded (among other things) "the removal from cinema of the old type of dealer whose work was imbued with an alien ideology" (*Pravda*, 3 February 1929).

Interestingly, Soviet cinematographers usually accepted their new role and enthusiastically invited their colleagues to help the cause of the new regime. Pudovkin, for instance, appealed to his colleagues "to participate actively, through specific films, in helping the cause of reinforcing the defense capability of the USSR and the fighting strength of the Red Army" (*Proletarskoie kino* 13/14, 1932, pp. 1–2).

Prominent filmmaker Natan Zarkhi stated in a speech at the First Congress of Soviet Writers in 1934 that "we must tell our artists everything goes, everything that serves the defense of our homeland, its strengthening, and the triumph of Communism and Bolshevik ideas" (*Pervyi Vsesoiuznyi S'ezd Sovetskikh Pisatelei* 1934, pp. 464–66). In the same year all leading cinematographers sent an obsequious public letter to Stalin, promising that their films would present "the ideas of the brilliant Leader of the most outstanding and revolutionary Party: Joseph Vissarionovich Stalin" (*Sovietskoe Kino* 11/12, 1934, pp. 5–6).

During these years of expanding repression, revolutionary filmmakers began to accuse each other of not being "a party man," as Kuleshov said at the All-Union Conference of Cinematographers in January 1935. At the same conference Trauberg, enjoying the official recognition of *Maxim's Youth* (1935), attacked Eisenstein and Dovzhenko for being devoted to formalism and not reflecting socialist reality in their films (*Za bol'shoie kinoiskusstvo*, 1935, pp. 50-57, 179-21).

The times were past when a filmmaker could use various artistic innovations to enhance his or her professional standing in the West and thus protect his or her life. In any case, filmmakers appeared ready to perform the ideological tasks of the new regime, not with revolutionary enthusiasm and belief in a radiant future, but in fear of raw political power. This terror replaced the revolutionary fervor (which filmmakers had lost by that time) as the main leverage used by authorities over filmmakers. Most filmmakers, as revelations in 1987–1992 demonstrated, had embraced the Orwellian strategy of loving big brother in order to ensure their survival. Thus, despite the horrors of collectivization and industrialization, mass repression, and the open intimidation of the intelligentsia, filmmakers continued to appear as ardent supporters of communism and admirers of Stalin.

However, in those years it was still not only the fear of power that directed the mentality of film directors and other intellectuals. Stalin's successes in transforming a backward country into a modern nation was seemingly evident. Cinematographers, like many Western admirers of Stalin's deeds (e.g., Romain Rolland, Theodor Dreiser, George Bernard Shaw, and numerous New York intellectuals), still could find it necessary to accept the terrible costs of building a new society that was paving the way for the whole world. With mass terror already channeled against intellectuals and the party by 1935, these last illusions about Stalin's progressive role could be maintained only with the Orwellian mechanism.

The main objectives of Soviet propaganda during this period included debunking private property and private instincts in the people, praising collectivism, fervently denouncing enemies of the people, and lambasting the West as well as the prerevolutionary past.

Along with these tasks, propaganda had to continue to praise technological and scientific progress as the basis for radical transformation of Soviet life. To some degree this emphasis on technology can also be ascribed to the dimming hope for a worldwide revolution. Connecting technological progress with collectivism, Soviet propaganda suggested that only with collective efforts would people be able to make progress and take control over nature, which was often presented as hostile to them.

Let us now examine how Soviet cinematographers fulfilled these ideological objectives of the Kremlin.

THE PRAISE OF TECHNOLOGY AND COLLECTIVISM

The combined belief in the miracle of technological and social progress can be found in Eisenstein's *The Old and the New* (1929), which provided the official view of collectivization. In the film, poverty covers the countryside and rampant individualism plagues peasant life. According to Marxist ideology, individualism is an essential element of any capitalist society, both in the city and countryside. It undermines the most sacred institution—the family. In the movie, two brothers are so greedy that they are ready to sever their relationship to hold on to their share of the family estate. They cut their ancestral house in two. The physical cleaving of the house is symbolic both of the cleaving of family ties and of the inhuman implications of capitalism's preoccupation with private property.

Finally, having been shown the way by the party, the peasants understand the iniquity of their individualism. The peasant women decide to start a cooperative enterprise to produce milk. Proceeds of the cooperative allow the peasants to pay for a machine that produces butter. In line with Marxist teaching, obtaining a machine raises their productivity drastically, thus demonstrating the superiority of collective ownership of the means of production. There is also a symbolic victory over nature in the image of a machine that separates butter from milk. The peasants surround the machine to wonder at its capacity. The machine starts to work and fountains of milk emerge, which become bigger and bigger until milk fills the entire screen. The abundance of milk is not only symbolic of the increased productivity wrought by collective ownership, but of the revolutionary transformation of the world in which new technology plays an almost mystical role. Such a vision is similar to those spawned by the revolution era ideology. Still, the new emphasis on technology should not be overlooked. The abundance of technology-produced milk on the screen evokes the river of milk of Russian folktales. It ensures not only a society of plenty, but a world where disease and death itself are eradicated by the "water of life." One of the film's characters, Marfa Lapkina, grows into a giant and symbolic figure personifying an entire stage in the development of the Soviet collective farm industry.

Life's triumph is also emphasized by a dream of the movie's major protagonist. In her dream, an enormous bull approaches a herd of cows. The bull is actually a creature from another dimension; it is as high as the sky and transparent. Its arrival implies that the next generation of cows will be as huge as their father and produce an abundance of milk. Moreover, the new generation of cows will be so different from their mothers that they will actually belong to the other dimension and will live according to new, previously unknown laws of nature. The idea of a new dimension where the old laws of nature are superseded is emphasized by a change in coloration; whereas the old life was gray, the new life is seen in bright colors.[1]

Anti-individualistic ideas combined with the glorification of advanced technology are found in several movies. In all of them, a divided populace plagued by selfish individualism is powerless before the forces of nature. A collectivist spirit eventually prevails, allowing dominance over nature. *For the Harvest* (1929), *Rejuvenated Labor* (1930), and *Countryside* (1930—all directed by Ilia Kopalin—all depict terrible conditions and near starvation caused by bad harvests of the noncollectivized peasants. Collectivization and modern technology breathe new life into their situation: Productivity increases markedly and the peasantry begins living in abundance. Another movie that glorified collectivism and its ally, new technology, as well as the party's tutelage was Nikolai Ekk's *A Pass for Life* (1931).

Forced collectivization, during which millions of peasants starved and left behind thousands of orphaned children, gave rise to the *besprisornik*—children who lived in the streets and survived by stealing. Official propaganda suggested that Soviet authorities did their best to return such children to normal lives. Anton S. Makarenko, a prominent Soviet educator, was an official model in the fight for parentless children. He worked to reeducate the street children and set up special colonies where children were assigned productive work as well as given an education.

The story of the children's colony and their educator served for Soviet propaganda as an example of official concern about children. In *A Pass for Life*, the children are from various ethnic backgrounds, as are the Soviet people, and they are all treated equally. They are talented and good-natured, but without supervision they behave irresponsibly and often viciously. Their street life symbolizes the natural conditions in which the populace would live were it not for government supervision. The children steal, exploit others, and generally live miserably, without any prospects for the future. The educator, Sergeiev, acts like Plato's enlightened philosopher-king. He brings the children into the colony against their will, but in their own and society's best interests. The need for supervision is emphasized when the educator leaves town and the children initiate a violent disorder. When they are supervised and under control once again, the children become productive, disciplined, model citizens. Sergeiev is opposed by Zhigan, a gang leader who tries to undermine his efforts to build the railroad. Ultimately, Sergeiev triumphs even though one of his pupils has died. This is a tragic event, but one still permissible in Soviet movies during this time.

THE OLD ENEMIES: THE MEMBERS OF THE OLD CLASSES

The struggle against class enemies remained (as in the previous period) one of the major preoccupations of filmmakers. Enemies of the revolution and socialism were portrayed, sometimes at the direct request of the authorities, as vile creatures. In this period the major focus was on old class enemies, the remnants of the classes liquidated by the new regime—landowners and capitalists. Cinematographers deftly used classic Russian literature for this purpose.

Vladimir Petrov's *Storm* (1934), based on a play by Alexander Ostrovsky, provides a good example. Set in a mid-nineteenth-century Russian provincial city, *Storm* examines the life of money-grubbing merchants whose greed drowns out any human feelings. The city's economy is based on oppression of the poor by the rich. Dikoi, a rich merchant, terrorizes the residents with wild pranks and demands absolute submission to his will. He cannot tolerate open challenges to his authority, or even the threat of any independent, freethinking person. Because his absolute power is maintained by others' absolute ignorance, he is hostile to scientific research: Scientific discoveries might improve the lives of the city residents and raise their expectations. Dikoi is hardly concerned with technological improvement or even basic education, and one can assume that the sole source of his wealth is his merciless exploitation and chicanery.

Kabanikha is Dikoi's female counterpart. She is preoccupied with self-enrichment and her approach to family life parallels Dikoi's approach to society. She demands and receives absolute submission from faceless old women (who actually look quite birdlike). She provides them with meager food, for which they praise her as a pious and virtuous rich woman. Her son, who is completely under her control, seems to have lost any intellectual capacities and has degenerated to the level of an animal.

Kabanikha's son's wife Katherine is the only positive character in the film. She dreams about real love, and her longing for equality, justice, and dignity symbolizes the hopes of the revolutionary masses. She commits infidelity, which represents an act of revolutionary rebellion. When her infidelity is revealed, the act of rebellion is crushed; the pressure of public opinion makes her life intolerable and she commits suicide.

Whereas *Storm* presents capitalists as simply cruel and dictatorial, Alexander Ivanovskii's *Iudushka Golovlev* (1934) emphasizes capitalists' duplicity. This was a major theme in 1930s ideology: that the capitalist enemy could not easily be unmasked, for he or she concealed his or her identity. *Iudushka Golovlev* is based on Saltykov/Shchedrin's classic novel about late-nineteenth-century Russian society. Iudushka, the central figure, belongs to the upper class. He is so obsessed with money that he loves no one, not even his children. He does his best, however, to conceal his true nature and we see just a few incidents where he pretends to be a good brother, father, and plain, good-natured person.

For example, Iudushka visits his brother on his deathbed. Although he tries to present his visit as motivated by love and care for his brother (he comforts the dying man and tries to cheer him up), it is clear that Iudushka is motivated by selfish considerations. At the very time he is comforting his brother, he opens the drawer where his brother's money is kept and counts it. It is as if Iudushka's face, full of attention for his brother, and his hands, counting the money, live separate lives.

In another episode, Iudushka's son comes to visit him. At first, Iudushka is outwardly loving and grateful to his son for favoring him with a visit. However, when the son tells Iudushka that he has squandered state funds and will be sent to prison unless Iudushka can help him repay the money, Iudushka's face changes. He no longer feigns interest in his son, who gets the message that his presence is not wanted. Iudushka watches his son's departure from a window. He crosses out his son's image in the window, continuing to play the role of the loving father. Elsewhere in the movie we learn that Iudushka has not only disowned his elder son, but does not even want to see the baby born to Iudushka's mistress.

In other movies, stereotyped images of vicious, ugly capitalists from the past are blended with images of present-day kulaks (rich peasants) and ex-NEP men, who were not only unsympathetic to Soviet political reality, but were hostile to it and acted to undermine it, as in Alexander Medvedkin's *Happiness* (1935).

The class pathos was, of course, also directed against foreign capitalists, continuing the tradition born almost immediately after the October Revolution. However, it would take almost four decades before Soviet cinematographers, under the influence of Russophile ideology, would make the distinction between Soviet capitalists, viewed positively, and foreign ones, viewed negatively. For example, the main purpose of Romm's *Plump Girl* (1934), based on Emile Zola's story, is to display the negative traits of the French bourgeoisie.

Post-NEP Soviet ideology was prone to attack individualism and any concern with personal interest. The desire for money, the essence of capitalism, was thought to be the social foundation of individualism and all of its associated sins. By contrast, revolutionary idealism was associated with disdain for money. The same ideological paradigm applied to patriotism. The bourgeoisie, preoccupied with its own enjoyment and personal well-being, was unpatriotic. True patriotism implied disregard for personal well-being and readiness to sacrifice.

Plump Girl illustrates this outlook. Set in France, defeated and humiliated at the conclusion of the Franco-Prussian War, the movie opens with a coach carrying mostly bourgeois passengers, except for the plump girl, a prostitute. The others act shocked at the prostitute's appearance. Pretending to be people of high moral standards (and implicitly patriotic), they do their best to show their disdain for her. In fact, they have no principles and are wholly preoccupied with self-interest. The director emphasizes their preoccupation with their bodies and their carnal desires as symbols of a deep-rooted individualism that renders them incapable of self-sacrifice. Their coarse individualism is contrasted with the integrity of the prostitute, who cares little about herself and is ready to sacrifice for others.

A lunch scene clearly characterizes this contrast. The other passengers have ostentatiously demonstrated their aloofness from the prostitute, some by the look of disgust on their face, others by not even deigning to look at her. Then the prostitute opens her basket and prepares to eat her lunch. She politely offers to share her meal with her fellow travelers. The passengers are quickly overwhelmed by their lust for food and easily forget their principle of not associating with the likes of the protagonist. They devour the food with almost indecent zeal. The movie emphasizes the characters's appetite for flesh by focusing attention on their mouths and greasy beards. They gobble up most of the food, leaving the prostitute only a morsel.

The group reaches a hotel and arranges to spend the night. A Prussian officer residing at the hotel takes a liking to the prostitute and wants to make love to her. She refuses him for the obvious reason that he is a representative of the army that has occupied her motherland. Her abstinence from sex is symbolic in other respects as well. While the lust for food demonstrated the bourgeois people's preoccupation with their bodies and therefore their inability to sacrifice, the prostitute's abstinence symbolizes that she not only has control over her bodily appetites, she actually disregards her body. She is presented as being spiritual and therefore patriotic because patriotism, like any other calling, requires sacrifice.

However, the prostitute's reluctance to have sex with the officer makes him quite angry. He is commandant of this hamlet, and no one may leave without his permission. He uses his authority to forbid the coach from traveling on, which infuriates the other passengers. They pressure her and she finally succumbs; however, we see that it is not she who is responsible for betraying the motherland. Clearly, the egotism of the bourgeoisie prevents it from caring that it has betrayed the national interest.

The negative image of both foreign and domestic bourgeoisie ready to destroy the Soviet republic was not new to Soviet culture and especially to its movies. However, this image was now being presented in new ways. The bourgeoisie was presented less abstractly in the movies of the civil war era and the 1920s.

NEW NATIONALISTS

Soviet ideology in the first half of the 1930s continued to hail internationalism, the solidarity of the workers of the world, and the idea of world revolution (though not as strongly as in the 1920s). Stalin was already considering a shift of official ideology toward Russian chauvinism in the early 1930s, but it would be a few years before this new element of propaganda would appear in films. During this period, filmmakers continued to follow old ideological directives and made a number of movies praising internationalism.

However, the country's approach in confronting the capitalist West began to change. During the early 1920s, confrontations with the West were not with a particular culture or state, but simply a manifestation of the class struggle between capitalists and workers. The Soviet Union was the country of the workers. Soviet ideologues acknowledged that capitalism had entered a period of "temporary stabilization" and that socialism that developed in one country might be temporarily isolated.

While there was no sign of incipient revolution in the West, there was some evidence for it in the East since the revolutionary movement continued to develop in China. Despite its split with the Nationalist Chinese party (the Kuomintang), the Communist party remained influential. Anticolonial movements had also started in the British colonies. Soviet ideologues began viewing these movements not so much as struggles against international capitalism (like the international workers' movement) with no territorial affiliation, but as struggles against the West. Capitalism was recast as a predominantly Western phenomenon. This turn to the East for support was manifested by the ideology of the Eurasianists, who pointed out that Russia indeed belonged to the community of oriental nations. This concept was revived in the early 1990s after the collapse of the Soviet Union.[2] In the late 1920s and early 1930s, Eurasianists who were emigrés were actually spokespersons for some members of the elite in the Soviet government.

However, Moscow's attitudes toward the East remained ambivalent. Asian political movements had not always supported the Bolsheviks. There was strong opposition to the new rulers in Central Asia, and Soviet troops had been fighting guerrilla movements (known as *basmachi*) for a long time. This explains why in many Soviet movies dealing with the lives of non-Russian peoples, their traditional customs were strongly condemned and any elements of Western modernization praised. Additionally, several nationalistic movements in non-European, non-Soviet nations had been antithetical to the Bolshevik regime. After a short-lived alliance, the Chinese Nationalists, for example, became the sworn enemies of the Bolsheviks.

Although these considerations provided one reason for Soviet directors to limit their praise of Asiatic peoples, there was a second reason as well. In the view of Soviet ideologists, the Asian masses possessed the same defects as their Russian counterparts. They needed proper leadership and the support of the Russian workers. Deprived of appropriate leadership, the Asiatic masses might become seduced by Western capitalism and be led astray. This theme can be found in Nikolai Shengelaia's *Twenty-Six Commissars* (1933).

The movie is set during the civil war in Baku, the premier city of Azerbaijan. The city is populated by Turkish-speaking people and located on the Black Sea, a region rich in oil and possessing a large proletariat. The proletariat commune that had been established draws no sympathy from the native bourgeoisie, which is ready to invite English troops to Azerbaijan. The reaction of the proletariat to this threat is central. Despite the fact that the English represent both social and geo-political alien forces, the proletariat is seduced by the promises of the bourgeoisie, and joins with the bourgeoisie to extend an invitation to the British. This causes a near catastrophe as the British enter Baku, shoot twenty-six commissars, and destroy the commune. Severed from their proper leadership, and suffering under English rule, the proletarians realize their errors. Unfortunately, they are helpless to change their situation until the well-led Russian troops extend a comradely hand in their direction.

NOTES

1.   Some Soviet movies were so obsessed with technological progress that they almost ignored the social dimension, focusing on technology almost exclu-sively. This was the case with Victor Turin's *Turksib* (1928–1929), a film about the building of the great railroad that was to traverse Central Asia to Siberia. The movie emphasized the immensity of nature and the power of its forces. Audi-ences were engulfed in a contrasting sea of images depicting the deserts of Central Asia and the ice and snow of Siberia, underscoring the harsh conditions facing those who wished to bind them together. At the same time, the railroad's construction confirms humanity's ability to impose its will on nature and the special role that humankind plays in the universe.

2.   The advocates of Eurasianism praised Genghis Khan as the founder of the great Eurasian empire, which, in their view, preceded imperial Russia and the USSR. The attraction of being identified as part of Eurasian culture was not only its opposition to the West, but its antipathy toward individualism and the idea of private property. Oriental despotism hailed the centralized economy as a means to ensure humankind's victory over nature. The Soviet regime could model itself on oriental despotism and expect to be hailed for threatening to dominate West-ern democracies. The West could even be construed as part of the hostile forces of nature.

7

Time of Mass Terror (1934–1941)

These years were the most painful in the life of Soviet cinematographers. In this period they were cynically coerced into making movies praising the Soviet order and describing the happy life of the masses. Paradoxically, several movies made at this time were very appealing to the people and they have managed to keep their special flavor until now (much like Hollywood comedies made during the Great Depression).

IDEOLOGICAL CLIMATE

The period between 1934 and 1941 was characterized by increases in mass terror, continuous economic growth, and growing international tension. It also marked the total consolidation of Stalin's dictatorship. Earlier, his authority had been incomplete; he was not able simply to ignore the views of other members of the elite.

By the mid-1930s, however, Stalin was completely in charge. This was a time of increased tension in society that led up to the great purges, when Stalin resorted to mass terror against members of the party, including the most active supporters of socialism, and the rest of the population. In 1934, Sergei Kirov, the leader of the Leningrad party organization, was assassinated. It is likely that Stalin himself arranged for the murder, for Kirov was quite popular and was viewed as Stalin's possible successor. In any case, Stalin was able to capitalize on this murder, using it as the pretext for starting a political campaign to eliminate the "enemy among us." The terror peaked in the late 1930s, when millions of Soviet citizens were killed or starved to death in political detention camps.

Stalin predicted that the class struggle would become more widespread as the socialist system developed. In previous periods, the enemy had been characterized as not only external to Soviet society but outside humanity itself.

The new emphasis on internal enemies had a significant effect on Soviet ideology. As before, the enemy was associated with capitalism, but now capitalists included Soviet citizens, especially ex-kulaks (rich peasants) and ex-NEP men (whose heyday was the early 1920s). However, the new campaign stressed that the enemy had wormed its way into the party and state apparatus, like Bolsheviks who had betrayed the revolution and socialism. Their crimes were not that they had become domestic capitalists or landlords (as previous Soviet propaganda suggested), but the agents of foreign countries.

Revelations of the moral degeneration and viciousness of traitors justified their extermination. Of course, the attack on them served other ideological goals: the end of the NEP mentality, with its tolerance for accumulating money, as well as a new emphasis on self-sacrifice and disdain for material gain and greed, which were portrayed as capitalist traits and unpatriotic. A new, concrete image of the enemy was needed.[1]

Emergence of Russian Nationalism

Toward the end of the purges, Stalin, understanding the insufficiency of socialist ideology as a way to legitimize his regime, began to espouse Russian Nationalism as an additional means to justify his power. It first emerged in the late 1920s and early 1930s and was initially fairly subdued, but it came to dominate public consciousness by the late 1930s. Nationalism not only competed successfully with internationalist ideology, but often overshadowed it completely.

However, Russian nationalism did not displace but blended with the ideas of socialism and communism in official ideology. Official ideology placed more emphasis on the messianic role of Russia in her socialist setting, which would lead humankind to a radiant future. The ideas of collectivism, public property, central planning, and other elements of socialism continued in this period and were regarded as being perfectly in tune with national traditions. And events in the revolutionary past, especially those which underscored the role of Stalin, continued to be a very important part of Soviet propaganda.

The Rediscovery of National History

One of the most important indicators of the influence of nationalist ideology was the newfound interest in national history. The rediscovery of history marked the serious transformation of millenarian eschatology. Soviet ideology of the civil war period and early 1920s had no place for history in the sense that revolutionary ideology implied a complete break with the past. This revolutionary ideology was oriented totally toward the future. The past (meaning the prerevolutionary past, because the revolution was too recent a phenomenon to be considered history) was viewed negatively as a time of exploitation and misery. The past played a comparatively minor role in public consciousness, as demonstrated by the relatively small number of historical movies produced and their comparatively small role in shaping society's intellectual life.

Deprived of history, the public consciousness was deprived of national feelings. The Bolshevik Revolution was not a phenomenon of national history but of international meaning. It had more relevance to the revolutionary struggle of the world proletariat in the past and present than to Russian history. The Bolshevik Revolution outgrew the confinement of national history in the same way that Christianity outgrew the confinement of Jewish history. Christianity and the Bolshevik Revolution became international in scope.

When the Soviet ideologists of the early 1920s and the civil war period did turn to the past to find the roots of the Bolshevik Revolution, they displayed no nationalism in their preferences. In fact, they often preferred the example of Western European history to that of native Russian history. The Bolsheviks' love for the history of the French revolutions—especially the Great French Revolution—and for the revolutionary movements of Asian peoples was proof of their preference.

The combination of the orientation toward the future and disregard for national history reflected the millenarian expectations of early Soviet ideologists. They regarded the October Revolution as the turning point in the history of mankind. This vision was prompted by the political and international situation faced by the Soviet regime in its first years. The proletarian revolutionary movement shook the West and had strong counterparts in the East, especially in China. All of this implied that the young Soviet republic would soon be plunged into a revolutionary process of global dimensions.

By the late 1930s, however, the situation had changed drastically. The rise of Nazi Germany and militarist Japan not only relegated the prospect of a worldwide proletarian revolution to the indefinite future but posed a clear threat to the Soviet Union's very existence. This was not a case of socialism in peril, but of the motherland itself. Such changes in the international situation had a profound effect on Soviet ideology. The old ideological paradigm of the Soviet Union as the spearhead of revolutionary development and the dream of world revolution were not abandoned completely but they were relegated to the ideological back burner. The Soviet Union's main historical task changed from encouraging humankind's global transformation to transforming the motherland into a mighty state.

Once the October Revolution and the contemporary Soviet government became Russian phenomena, and once the Soviets became bound to their native soil as keepers of the Russian state, a sense of tradition was required. History became important and intellectuals turned to it not so much to denigrate the prerevolutionary past as, on the contrary, to glorify the motherland. This major change in ideology had a profound effect on Soviet cinematography. The proportion of movies devoted to historical themes grew considerably, and movies became important tools in the ideological campaigns of the late 1930s.

The Growth of Xenophobia and the Glorification of the Red Army

The emergence of Russian nationalism as an essential element of Soviet official ideology brought back the term *patriotism*, which in the past had been regarded as incompatible with internationalism. One element that accompanied this rise of patriotism was a sudden increase of xenophobia in propaganda. During this time foreigners (regardless of their social status), especially those who visited the USSR, were treated as enemies of Soviet Russia. They were viewed as potential spies and destroyers of Russia and socialism.

At the same time, the ideology expanded its portrayal of the Red Army as the reliable defender of the motherland, which was surrounded by dangerous capitalists. Soviet propaganda suggested that if a war were launched against the USSR, the army would not only crush the foreign enemies almost immediately, but would continue to destroy the adversary on its own territory. Military propaganda became an essential attribute of Soviet ideological life in this period.

The Glorification of the Leader

The shift of official ideology to history and Russian nationalism, as well as to the preparation for a new war, allowed for the formation of a cult of Stalin, and, as its theoretical underpinning, the creation of a mythology surrounding the national leader.

As Stalin emerged as the major force in the historical arena, the masses themselves lost all ideological significance. Without leadership, the masses, despite their good intentions, became unruly and hopeless. Official Soviet ideology in the late 1930s went so far as to implicitly justify the tsarist government's repression of the revolutionary masses. The populace became a progressive force only when it dissolved itself completely in the personality of the leader and became an extension of his will. The concept of the leader as a ruthless nationalistic demigod fit neatly into the new nationalistic ideology: Now all of Russian history became the history of ruthless and wise leaders who defended and enlarged the country. While ruthlessness, bravery, and cleverness were the leader's essential characteristics, he also possessed such endearing qualities as understanding the needs and feelings of the masses.

The leader was confronted with enemies outside and inside the borders of Russia. Most enemies were exploiters, such as feudal lords and capitalists. Their negative status was due less to their exploitative nature than to the fact that they were "foreigners." The foreigners were not hostile to the country because it represented a progressive political system (in fact, according to revolutionary ideology, prerevolutionary Russia was a reactionary society). Instead, they were hostile to Russia herself. In their fight against Russia, the real foreigners (those who were foreigners by birth) cooperated with the traitors, those who were Russian-born but who decided to cooperate with the enemy.

Stalin Portrays Life as Merry and Happy

On a superficial level, ideology remained future oriented. The perfection of socialism in the USSR, a socialist revolution in the West, and the realization of a true communist society were still goals of the Soviet Union. However, there was a new twist in ideology that was revealed by Stalin's famous slogan, "Life became better, life became more joyful." The slogan implied that a socialist society had already been created, and, if it was not yet a paradise, it was at least a semiparadise for the majority of Soviet citizens. Now the struggle with enemies aimed less at advancing the revolutionary process and more at preserving the ideal world of Stalin's Russia. Since prosperity and happiness were no longer in the future but at hand, the new ideology required that culture, including film, present this ideal Soviet reality.

The influence of propaganda based on fear was so strong that the masses took Stalin's heavily ideologically loaded movies almost at face value, believing that they had actually reached the good life at last. Moscow movie critics pointed out many decades later (in the early 1990s) that, like the Hollywood comedies of the 1930s, these early movies instilled confidence in life: Villains were always punished and good Soviet people were generously rewarded (Shusharina 1992).

SOVIET CINEMATOGRAPHERS IN THE TIME OF TERROR

Like the rest of the population, Soviet filmmakers were terrorized as a result of Kirov's murder. In this period their number one priority was to guess the intentions of Stalin and then to decode his instructions. Some of them, like Eisenstein, occasionally attempted to offer Stalin more than the usually accepted methods of propaganda. Sometimes they succeeded, sometimes not. In general, however, fear led cinematographers to execute any order from the Kremlin.

The degree of fear is exemplified by the extent to which filmmakers groveled, not only before Stalin, but also before Alexei Stakhanov, an uneducated miner whom Stalin proclaimed to be the model for all Soviet workers. Stakhanov, in an article in *Iskusstvo kino* (3, 4/5, 1938), gave some trivial and ludicrous suggestions to movie directors; directors such as Iakov Protazanov quickly sent letters to the editor praising these suggestions.

By 1939, Eisenstein had emphatically expressed his loyalty to Stalin's regime, even though he could no longer ignore the regime's bloody nature. He wrote:

> [T]he great ideas of our Socialist Fatherland endow our art with remarkable fecundity. I have tried to serve these ideas in all the films which I made in the course of nearly fifteen years. . . . The guardian of national dignity, national pride, national independence and true patriotism throughout the world is first of all the Communist party. (*International Literature* 1, 1939, pp. 90–93)

It should be pointed out that, despite his loyalty, Eisenstein was not the greatest ideological zealot among his colleagues in this time.

Historical Figures: Models of Patriotism and Leadership

The ideology that was promoted in these years demanded that films glorify the leader. The leader should, above all, be valiant, a military leader, and a statesman. This image is seen in most of the Soviet movies of this era, regardless of what historical period they depict. Eisenstein's *Alexander Nevskii* (1938) is one of the most famous movies of this time. It depicts a time in Russian medieval history that was among the most crucial for the nation. In the thirteenth century, Russia was attacked from both the east and the north. Mongols devastated it from the east, and incorporated most of the country into their huge empire. Only the northern part of the country, centered around the cities of Novgorod and Pskov, was free from direct Mongol domination. This northern region, however, was attacked by Teutonic knights from the north. Prince Alexander managed to defeat the knights in 1242, saving the region from subjugation.

Eisenstein tackled this period because of its political appropriateness.

As had been the case during the thirteenth century, the country was strategically encircled: by Nazi Germany to the west and militaristic Japan to the east. From the very beginning, the movie implicitly connects thirteenth-century Russia and the contemporary Soviet Union by stressing the mortal danger in which old Russia finds herself. Broken weapons and skulls of fallen Russian warriors symbolize the Mongol devastation. To the north, the "dog knights" are ready to engulf the rest of semi-independent Russia.

The situation requires both political wisdom and military valor. Alexander, the young prince from Vladimir, is elected prince of Novgorod. In the movie he is the sole independent Russian prince, and therefore he has a great responsibility to all of Russia. The movie implies that, despite his youth, the prince is an experienced politician who understands that Russia cannot fight two formidable enemies simultaneously. So he makes a well-calculated decision: He goes to the Mongol headquarters and rather humbly demonstrates his devotion to the khan.

While diplomatic wisdom was seen as an important trait in a national leader, personal courage and military skill were considered even more important. Alexander possessed all of these qualities in abundance. In the movie, Alexander, full of patriotic vigor, rallies the people to defend the motherland against the Germans: "Rise up, Russian people! Rise up, Russian people! Rise up and fight the Germans!" This refrain is repeated throughout the movie. The images of the Orthodox Church and Christ on the banners symbolize that the Russians are on the side of justice. These images not only help create the flavor of that historical period, but are also important philosophical symbols. Russian Orthodoxy symbolizes the humanitarian Christian tradition, whereas the Germans, despite the crosses on their robes and helmets, have nothing to do with this. Indeed, the Germans are seen as exceptionally cruel, even burning children alive.

Thus, the confrontation between Germans and Russians actually becomes a Manichean confrontation between the cosmic forces of good and evil—a philosophy we have already encountered during the civil war and the 1920s. The only difference is the implied scope of the struggle. For ideologists of the early revolutionary period, the confrontation should lead to the liberation of all humanity. In this portrayal of Alexander Nevskii's time, however, the confrontation is limited to the Russians' victory against the invaders.

The major battle between the German knights and the Russian warriors in *Alexander Nevskii* clearly resembles the confrontation between the revolutionary and counterrevolutionary forces as depicted in civil war posters and movies. The knights, in their matching helmets and robes, are faceless. Their battle array implicitly represents some sort of apocalyptic animal, a brutal and formidable machine of destruction. Alexander, who confronts them, is not only the *symbol* of the Russian army, he *is* the army, in the sense that the ordinary soldiers act as extensions of his body. He is on the front line of the battle, personally leading the fight. In the face of Alexander's and his soldiers' courage and determination, the knights are utterly defeated and the victory is represented as an apocalyptic victory of good over evil. The finality of the victory is implied by the extinction of the knights' army. The battle takes place on the ice of a frozen lake and as the defeated knights retreat they fall through the ice. The knights disappear, drowning in the lake, analogous to sinners being consumed by the fires of hell.

The religious analogy is made even more explicit by the speech Alexander gives before the prisoners. He quotes from holy scriptures: "Those who live by the sword shall perish by the sword." Alexander's princely righteousness and nobility are emphasized by his magnanimity: He grants life to the defeated prisoners of war.

Peter the Great was another Russian tsar whom Stalin ordered cinematographers to glorify. During Peter's reign, Russia underwent speedy economic growth and built a modern army that allowed successful military confrontation with the West. Furthermore, he was more attractive than Ivan the Terrible because Peter's merciless terror was guided less by personal whim than by political calculation. Peter's execution of his son fit nicely into the philosophical conception of sacrificing a dear one for the benefit of the state. It was central to Vladimir Petrov's *Peter the First* (1937–1939), based on Aleksei Tolstoy's novel.

The creation of a mighty Russia and the expansion of Russia's territory were Peter's foremost concerns. His personality combined features of several other positive Russian leaders; he had the political wisdom and personal courage of Alexander, together with the mercilessness of Ivan. *Peter the First* deals extensively with Peter's role as the builder of the new Russia. The movie opens with a description of advanced Western technology and military organization. In the first confrontation with Peter's main enemy, the Swedes, the Russian army is badly defeated because of the country's overall backwardness. This is apparently a translation, in the language of cinematographic images, of Stalin's well-known admonition that Russia had always been beaten because of her backwardness and therefore upgrading the nation's economic potential was essential for its very survival.

However, Peter is not discouraged by this initial defeat. With feverish energy he works to create a modern Russian army and navy. Poltava, the site of the decisive battle between Russia and Sweden, is the culmination of Peter's life. Like Alexander, Peter personally leads his troops to a great victory.

Besides Russian princes and tsars, Stalin wanted attention paid to those Russians who had become famous in the past as the defenders of the Russian state. Pudovkin and Doller's *Minin and Pozharsky* (1939) is one such film. It takes place during the so-called time of troubles, in the early seventeenth century, when the Poles had taken advantage of Russia's difficulties (the end of a dynasty, a peasant uprising, and other problems) and had invaded the country with the intention of incorporating Russia into the Polish commonwealth.

The movie shows how Prince Pozharskii and the merchant Minin save the country. They organize and lead an army that drives the Poles out of Russia. The emphasis on their military talents and personal courage implies that Soviet citizens should prepare for the possibility of another confrontation with Poland, which was once again viewed as Russia's potential enemy.

Xenophobia in Stalinist Movies

The patriotic and foreign theme was dominant in a series of films about past Russian commanders and admirals. One of the first movies of this sort was Doller and Pudovkin's *Suvorov* (1941). In the movie we see Tsar Paul enchanted with Prussia. His fascination with foreigners, especially with Germans, hardly makes him an effective ruler. Because criticism of a particular leader was not meant as criticism of bold leadership per se, Paul is juxtaposed to Suvorov, a well-known Russian general and a good leader. In the movie, Suvorov possesses a variety of positive characteristics, the most important of which is his contempt for foreigners and particularly Germans. In this respect, Suvorov is shown to be similar to Peter the Great, whose movie character despises foreign specialists (this portrayal of Peter is in glaring contradiction to the historical truth, for it was Peter more than anyone who used foreign expertise in building a modern Russia).

The xenophobic orientation is also seen in Igor Savchenko's *Bogdan Khmelnitsky* (1941), a film about the Ukrainian commander and politician who annexed Ukraine to Russia in the seventeenth century. The movie describes Polish nobles, Bogdan's main adversaries, in the most degrading way: While they are apparently polite, proud, and brave, they are actually uncouth, devoid of principles, and craven. Although dressed in the most fashionable clothes, these people harbor barbarity and evil deeds in their souls. Bogdan's Polish wife, Hellen, is also depicted as a worthless individual. And, of course, Bogdan's headquarters are teeming with Polish traitors, who are discovered and destroyed.

Lenin as an Icon

As already mentioned, Russian nationalism had a tremendous effect on Soviet cinema after 1934. However, all Soviet cinematographers were still expected to commend the heroes of the revolution and civil war since the legitimacy of the Soviet system remained rooted in communist ideology.

In the mid-1930s, Soviet filmmakers were assigned to create a series of movies with Lenin as the major protagonist. This was unheard of previously because the old Bolsheviks, now mostly in the *Gulag*, were against the deification of their leader.[2] Examples of such films include Romm's *Lenin in October* (1937) and *Lenin in 1918* (1939), and Sergei Iutkevich's *The Man with a Gun* (1938). These films presented Lenin strictly according to the prescriptions of the Kremlin: He was thoughtful, open to ordinary people, optimistic, temperamental, warm, kind, strong-willed, modest, humorous, brave, and cheerful. He was also a man of action and free of doubt (see Zorkaya 1989, pp. 152–53).[3]

Stalin, of course, was also glorified in films. In fact, from 1938 almost every film was expected to include some elements that augmented the cult of Stalin while also denigrating enemies inside the party. Stalin was a featured character in *Lenin in 1918*, as well as in Iutkevich's *Yakov Sverdlov* (1940), about a leading revolutionary who died in 1919. In this as well as in other movies, Stalin was presented as a leader second only to Lenin and as his closest friend. In *Lenin in 1918*, Bukharin was depicted as a foreign agent and the initiator of the plot to kill Lenin. Surprisingly, not until 1942 did Stalin allow movies with himself as the major hero, as in the Vasiliev brothers *Defense of Tsaritsin* (1942). This was followed by dozens of movies about him.

Aside from glorifying Lenin, cinematographers continued to make movies about ordinary people—the heroes of the revolution and the civil war.

Soviet "Ordinary" Leaders and Heroes

Ideologists of the late 1930s recognized only one leader as the ruler of society. In this respect they differed from ideologists of the previous period, who, while emphasizing the importance of leadership, made it clear that the major hero was only one of the many representatives of the party, or more broadly, of collective society. Thus, movies of the 1920s often presented several positive heroes or leaders simultaneously. By contrast, the coexistence of even two equally important leaders was rare in the Soviet movies of the late 1930s. The leader might be surrounded with assistants, some of whom might be important people and be endowed with several fine qualities, but it was clear that they were subordinate and inferior to the main protagonist. Their inferiority was conveyed in certain character traits, such as excessive emotionality or naivete.

The clear superiority of one leader can be seen in the Vasiliev brothers' *Chapaiev* (1934), one of the most popular and well-done Soviet movies of the 1930s. The movie focuses on Vasilii Chapaiev, a popular hero of the civil war who is finally killed in one of the skirmishes. While Chapaiev is certainly one of the movie's major characters, he is not the hero, in the sense that he is dominated by Furmanov, who is a true leader. Chapaiev cannot be a real political figure, despite his fine characteristics. He is simply too emotional. Although that trait may be useful on the battle-field, where Chapaiev always succeeds in inspiring his soldiers to a daring cavalry attack, it is absolutely unacceptable for a political leader whose passions must be tempered by sober calculation.

Even in the military realm, emotionalism may not always be an asset. The movie presents an attack by the Whites quite positively, thereby im-plicitly praising cold bluntness and calculation. In what may be one of the movie's best-known and most effective scenes, we see the White officer's division attack the position of the Reds. The officers, dressed in their best uniforms, march upright and do not hide from the bullets. The directors of the movie apparently appreciated the coldbloodedness of the enemy. It was this coldbloodedness that put the Reds in an uneasy position.

Emotion was even less appropriate in the political realm, and if a person was not only emotional but also naive, this rendered him or her absolutely useless as a leader. Chapaiev demonstrates emotionality and naivete all too often, as in the following example. One of the soldiers in Chapaiev's division, a veterinarian with some knowledge of human medicine, decides that he wants to become a doctor and demands that one of the doctors certify him. The doctor refuses on the grounds of the veterinarian's ignorance of human medicine. The veterinarian is infu-riated because he sees some hidden factors in the doctor's decision; he thinks the doctor has refused out of social prejudice and hatred. He thinks the doctor, a representative of a prestigious and well-paid profes-sion, does not want a veterinarian to join the upper class. Chapaiev does not take time to sort out the matter and takes the veterinarian's com-plaints at face value. He takes his side with no hesitation and is almost ready to kill the doctor. But the doctor has, in fact, made the correct decision not to certify the veterinarian, who otherwise might have jeop-ardized the entire division.

Chapaiev's relations with his soldiers also demonstrate his inability to lead. Chapaiev is a strict disciplinarian and mercilessly shoots those who break discipline on the battlefield. Yet his sense of discipline is limited because he does not understand that soldiers should be controlled off the battlefield as well. Chapaiev is an emotional and unruly person and assumes his soldiers should also have their share of fun. Thus, he does not restrain them from robbing civilians.

Despite his courage and dedication to the revolution, Chapaiev as a non–party member can only serve a secondary role. Furmanov, a party member and political commissar appointed by the party leadership, is the real leader and hero of the movie. He is courageous like Chapaiev, but he is also a man of iron will and cold blood. It is he who represents order and the state. He is not politically naive and he has breadth of vision; therefore, he often clashes with the shortsighted Chapaiev. In their clashes, Furmanov's leading position is asserted and Chapaiev is put in the secondary role of a brilliant tactician and courageous soldier who could hardly be put in charge of the army on a large scale, much less all of society. Their clashes are an oblique reference to the conflict among the party elite, implying that while some of the Politburo members may be useful, the party leader must be unquestionably in charge. Some of Furmanov's characteristics (e.g., his calmness and his pipe-smoking) suggest that his image was influenced by Stalin's.

On several occasions Furmanov confronts Chapaiev when he behaves emotionally and immaturely. When Chapaiev supports the charges of the veterinarian against the doctor, Furmanov takes the doctor's side, arguing that no one can be a doctor without proper training. Chapaiev disagrees and gets so excited that he breaks a chair. Furmanov responds by quoting a line from Gogol's classic play *The Inspector General*: "Alexander of Macedon was definitely a great man, but he never broke a chair." Chapaiev asks Furmanov who Alexander is and Furmanov tells him about the great military leader. This surprises Chapaiev, who acknowledges that he has never heard about Alexander. It is a turning point in the confrontation between the two men. Chapaiev acknowledges his ignorance and understands the importance of education for those who are the elite, and in charge of society as a whole.

Another confrontation occurs due to Chapaiev's permissiveness in letting his soldiers have their way in mistreating the local residents. Furmanov arrests one of the marauders and keeps him in prison despite Chapaiev's stormy protest. As in the previous case, Furmanov succeeds in proving to Chapaiev the immaturity and political inappropriateness of his behavior.

In short, in all of these confrontations between the two main characters, Furmanov asserts his leading position, and that of the party he represents, and he is understood to be the embodiment of the revolution. Symbolically, it is Chapaiev, not Furmanov, who actually perishes at the end of the movie. Chapaiev's death is indeed a tragic episode, but it is a personal tragedy; the revolutionary army will find another talented and daring commander. On the other hand, Furmanov's death would be tantamount to the death of the revolution itself, and therefore he does not share Chapaiev's fate.

Iron discipline and the debunking of revolutionary anarchism were always dear to Stalin, the founder of the powerful totalitarian state. This theme is pervasive in Dovzhenko's *Shchors* (1939). Here Shchors, a dutiful and rational commander, is juxtaposed to Batko Bozhenko, who like a Cossack chieftain, ignores discipline and is ready to act solely on emotion.[4]

Several other movies in this period contributed to the creation of legends—made up of a mixture of facts and total prevarications—about the revolution and the civil war. The Soviet people, under the pressure of propaganda and fear, and without access to noncontrolled sources of information, accepted these movies with genuine enthusiasm, even if they were not as popular as *Chapaiev*.

Chapaiev was rivaled in popularity by the trilogy made by Kozintsev and Trauberg, consisting of: *Maxim's Youth* (1935), *Maxim's Return* (1937) and *The Vyborg Side* (1939). The main character in these films was an ordinary man who managed to outsmart the enemies of the revolution, as well as run a state bank without any formal education.

Among popular movies about the revolutionary past were Efim Dzigan's *We Are from Kronstadt* (1936) and Kheifits and Zarkhi's *Baltic Deputy* (1937). The first was about brave Red sailors from Kronstadt (the naval base close to Leningrad) who accepted death heroically while not yielding to the Whites. The stereotype created in *Chapaiev* and endorsed by Stalin was utilized here. Martynov, a commissar and an old party member, managed through his courage to influence sailors who were prone to anarchy. After his funeral (he was killed in the battle), each member of the regiment joined the party. Propaganda was already so successful at this time that the authorities were not afraid that spectators would remember that the same sailors from Kronstadt had rebelled against the Bolsheviks in 1921 and had only been stopped by an extremely cruel attack ordered from the Kremlin.

The second film was about Professor Polezhaev, a Russian scholar who, unlike intellectuals in Soviet movies of the past, joined the revolution without any doubts. He loved Lenin and was elected to the Soviet (council) of Workers, Peasants, and Soldiers by the same revolutionary sailors of the Baltic fleet. The film evidently was supposed to suggest (in opposition to the truth) that most Russian intellectuals accepted the revolution wholeheartedly.

Ordinary People as Rulers of the Country

After 1936, when Stalin's new constitution was adopted, a major duty of Soviet propaganda was to persuade the Soviet people that they lived in a democratic society. This was a new approach, in that in the past the focus had been on the dictatorship of the proletariat and the revolutionary conscience of the rulers and ruled.

With Kheifits and Zarkhi's *A Member of the Government* (1940) Soviet cinema made a significant contribution to this myth. In this movie Alexandra Sokolova, a victim of spouse abuse and a poor, downtrodden farmhand, becomes chairman of the collective farm and, eventually, deputy of the Supreme Soviet of the USSR.

In *Bright Road* (1940), Alexandrov repeated the theme of the previous film, since it was already endorsed by Stalin. This time success is achieved by a weaver, Tatiana Morozova, who develops from an ordinary worker into an engineer and a member of the Soviet parliament.

The Red Army

Soviet cinematographers enthusiastically promoted the Red Army, thereby performing two important ideological functions: making service in the army seem attractive to Soviet youth and persuading the Soviet people that the Red Army could defeat any enemy. Among the most popular movies about the army was Romm's *Thirteen* (1937), about the successful struggle of the Red Army against Muslim guerrillas in Central Asia. Another film, Dzigan and Lazar Antsi-Polovski's *If There Should Be War Tomorrow* (1938), described the resounding victory of the Red Army over the enemy that dared to cross its borders. Alexei Pankratiev's *Fighter Planes* (1939) is about young pilots who display courage and professionalism, as well as high moral standards. One of them—Kozhukharov—loses his sight while trying to save a boy, and rejects the love of a woman in order not to be a burden, without knowing that a miraculous operation will save his sight.

Domestic Enemies

During this time, the struggle against foreign enemies was inseparable from that against domestic enemies. Ideologically, there was no real distinction between foreign and domestic enemies—because they were all hostile to the Soviet regime and Russia alike, they were all traitors. Stalinist ideology, much like the Nazis', called for the Soviet people to be merciless to enemies even if they were their spouses, parents, or children. Soviet cinematographers did their best to show how genuine patriots were ready to denounce and punish even those close to them if they were regarded as traitors of the motherland.

The ideologists of the 1930s were eager to find other examples of leaders who fought successfully on the battlefield and who also succeeded in eradicating treason inside the country. Ivan the Terrible, a Russian tsar of the sixteenth century, was the ideal role model for this purpose.

Eisenstein directed *Ivan the Terrible* (1945), in which the tsar's struggle with the nobility was an important theme. Contrary to historical evidence, Ivan is portrayed not as a bloody maniac, but as a person with a gentle soul who loves his wife and trusts his retainers. Some of his associates, however, are unfaithful. They plot to get rid of him and finally poison his wife, which comes as a great shock to the autocrat. He loses his trust for the people and is ready to abdicate. The majority of the Russian people, however, urge him to stay on the throne and implicitly offer him a mandate to eradicate the traitors. Ivan's decisiveness not only saves his own life, but apparently makes Russia more prosperous than ever. By the end of the movie, the country is enjoying unprecedented international prestige, as witnessed by Ivan's negotiations with England.

The same theme—the mercilessness of any enemies—was central to Petrov's *Peter the First* (1937–1939). In the film, Peter's attempts to modernize Russia and make it a strong power are met with resistance from the old elite, of which Peter's son is a member.

The image presented of Peter's son Alexis is more complicated than that of the plotters. The plotters are brutal, cunning scoundrels, with well-defined political goals and no scruples whatsoever. Alexis, on the other hand, is a meek and weak-willed person, with no predisposition to politics. He would rather live a private life with his girlfriend than be a politician. The movie also presents the tsar's brutal rule over the Russian populace and his disregard for the country's historical traditions, particularly the church. It is the latter that personally affects the private and devout Alexis and forces him to question Peter's political program. Yet, regardless of his intentions, Alexis's opposition to his father makes him a traitor to his country. In his desire to avoid his father's wrath, Alexis and his mistress go abroad and ask for protection from foreign powers, thus becoming tools in the hands of a government hostile to Russia.

Peter is not presented as a senseless brute or a person whose concern for the interests of the state leave him without human feelings. He urges his son to follow him and participate in building the new Russia. He also forgives Alexis on various occasions. But when he sees his son as a mortal enemy of his plans to make Russia a great country, as a man who is actually helping foreigners to subjugate his motherland, Peter has no choice but to treat him accordingly. Alexis is tried before a court and sentenced to high treason. Peter visits Alexis in the chamber where he will be executed. As a father he still feels compassion for his son and asks Alexis to forgive him. But he judges that in this case the country's needs supersede his paternal feelings, and he personally authorizes the execution.[5]

For the most part, however, Soviet films devoted most of their attention to the present enemies of the people—typically the agents of foreign intelligence services, counterrevolutionaries, and members of the defeated opposition (including Trotsky, Bukharin, Rykov, and their supporters), who had wormed their way to the top levels of government in order to kill the Soviet leaders, restore capitalism, and sell the country to foreign powers. Fridrikh Ermler's two-part film *A Great Citizen* (1938–1939), about the assassination of Kirov, provides a good example.

The film was designed to illustrate Stalin's postulate that the exacerbation of class struggle with the successes of socialism is unavoidable (even thirty years later, Soviet critics still praised this movie for supporting this thesis; see Groshev et al. 1969, pp. 260–61). The film also attempted to support another of Stalin's theses—that opposition in the party, since the very beginning, was at the service of foreign countries. The movie is full of various enemies who use devious methods to destroy the socialist motherland. In order to make the enemy seem realistic, each is endowed with relatively complex psychological characteristics.

The main hero is Shakhov, an indomitable and unbending Bolshevik who became the first in a long line of such Communists in Soviet cinema, culminating in Raizman and Gabrilovich's *Communist* in 1958. Contrary to the miserable portrait of the enemy—people deeply egotistical and greedy—Shakhov is described as a great statesman, an individual with various talents and broad interests. Although confronted with many difficult situations, he always seems to do the correct thing. For the first time in Soviet cinema, the hero is depicted as a real ethnic Russian, with all the positive features typical of his people.

Soviet movies from the mid-1930s on overflowed with enemies of the people. Even comedies were expected to participate in the education of the Soviet people. In Nadezhda Kosheverova and Iurii Muzykant's *Arinka* (1940), a malicious saboteur attempts to destroy trains. However, he is implicitly an agent of a formidable foreign power, who must be confronted by an equally formidable Russian state with a powerful army and secret police, and the movie's heroine, a pretty young girl, gets rid of him rather easily.

As mentioned earlier, Soviet cinematographers took part in propagating the idea that true Soviet people should report on their relatives and friends if they suspected treason. *Defeat* (1931), a movie based on Alexander Fadeiev's novel, presented the same ideas with slight modification. Here the conflict is not between duty to the state and family obligation, but between duty to the state and friendship. A guerrilla unit is fighting in the civil war in the Far East, and when the hero finds out that his best friend is actually a traitor, he kills him without hesitation.

The Masses

Whereas the leader epitomized the party, the government, and the nation, the masses lost almost all significance in the political philosophy of the late 1930s. Official Marxist philosophy continued to preach that the proletariat was the major engine of history and that the Soviet Union was run by its people, but these ideological paradigms did not find their way onto the Soviet screen, which says a great deal about the real situation of the Soviet people and the rules of their relationships.

Movies did not totally disregard the populace, and some notion of its greatness was maintained. For instance, in *Alexander Nevskii* (1938) we see the Russian townsfolk and peasants easily crush the enemy knights with simple clubs. The same heroes are seen in *Peter the First*, when the Russian soldiers crush the Swedes. All of these Russians were supermen in a sense, but only when inspired and led by the leader. That is, they were great only as they carried out the wishes of the real superman, the leader. Again, they were merely extensions of his body and will.

Occasionally the leader did turn to the people. Peter went to the common people to receive instruction, but the people were not the source of the tsar's projects. Instead, they were primitive elements, which, left on their own, would never accomplish anything. Thus, Peter might study some craft in the workshop of a poor craftsman or ship-building in foreign shipyards. He would be attentive to the instruction and would even be willing to accept criticism from these craftsmen. But that did not mean that the simple craftsmen inspired Peter to create modern industry in Russia or to build a fleet. The techniques and ideas provided by the craftsmen were so transformed in Peter's mind that they became Peter's own, and had little relationship to the original source.

In fact, the leader rarely turned to the populace for real advice. When he did appear to appeal to the people, it was clearly only to confirm a decision he had already made. A leader such as Peter might treat the people in a democratic way by talking with them, apparently on equal footing. But the democracy was illusory, because the leader never took the populace seriously. His democratic approach was not the approach of equal to equal, but similar to a father's treatment of his children. He might engage them in ostensibly serious conversation, and even ask them to advise him, but he rarely if ever took this advice into account. In fact, he believed that in most cases the childlike common people were naive, helpless, and did not understand their own long-term interests. They might also occasionally be dangerous and vicious.

The image of a helpless and naive populace, which could not survive without paternal guidance, can be found in many movies of the late 1930s. In *Ivan the Terrible*, the Russian populace is alarmed by the prospect of Ivan's abdication, and a huge crowd gathers and begs him to return to the throne of his forefathers. In *Lenin in October*, a little girl tells Lenin the horrible story of her mother's starvation. It is implied that the girl represents the Russian people asking Lenin for protection against the speculators. Many Soviet people believed that, deprived of Lenin's protection, they would be absolutely helpless, and therefore they wanted to lynch Lenin's would-be assassin on the spot.

Though Soviet ideologists viewed the populace as a potentially reactionary force (a view that was, to some extent, reflected in the movies), this differed substantially from previous views on this subject. As has been discussed, movies of the late 1920s already depicted the occasionally misguided behavior of the masses, such as the fact that they could sometimes side with the counterrevolutionaries against members of their own class and against their own best interests. In most cases, however, it was implied that such behavior did not result from a conscious decision. This was the lesson in Eisenstein's *Battleship Potemkin*, where soldiers fulfilled their duty to the tsar by acting against the revolutionary populace. The soldiers had lost their identity, apparently through indoctrination, and had become like machines, devoid of human feelings. A similar moral can be found in Ermler's *A Fragment of the Empire* (1929), where Russian soldiers in the First World War kill their class brothers in the opposing trenches because the soldiers on both sides have been duped by their ruling elite. The movie implies that the soldier hero would have defected from the front if he had understood the social absurdity of his action. The feeling of absurdity is conveyed by the image of the German soldier, who looks exactly like his Russian counterpart. Thus, when shooting at German soldiers, the Russian soldier is in effect shooting at himself—at his social alter ego.

In *Chapaiev* one of the movie's protagonists is a poor peasant who serves in the White army, but who is actually a victim of the White movement. His brother is beaten to death and he himself suffers because of his commander, a White officer. Finally, he understands that he has been serving the wrong cause, and defects to the other side, and he even brings his former commander to the Reds as a prisoner of war. The lesson is that the masses take the side of the counterrevolution only when they are duped and indoctrinated; when they participate in reactionary activities, they do so only as senseless and stupid machines.

However, the situation changed in the movies of the late 1930s. The new twist was that the common citizen could consciously be a reactionary, and could even be exceptionally canny in his or her counterrevolutionary activity. Ivan Pyriev's *Party Card* (1936) provides a good example of this new image of the populace.

The movie centers around the career of Kuganov, an individual with a dubious social background. Apparently, he is a kulak (read capitalist) who comes to the city and finds work in a factory. According to Soviet political theory, working in the factory should change his outlook and he should be transformed into a benign proletarian. But he does not change. Of course, his hostility to Soviet power and his negative personal traits could at least partially be blamed on his kulak background. But this cannot explain everything, for Kuganov has been under the influence of the seemingly benign proletarian ideology while working in the factory. The movie implies that the counterrevolutionary element can rear its head among the rank and file workers. A benign social milieu (i.e., belonging to the workers) does not guarantee one's loyalty to the state, and those who join the counterrevolution are not necessarily brainwashed, naive people who can easily be brought back into the fold by proper instruction. Among the benign proletariat there may be cunning counterrevolutionaries, and for this reason the state must be vigilant in dealing with even the seemingly trustworthy social groups.

Another point of the new ideological approach was that the revolutionary movement itself might take a reactionary turn. By the same token, sometimes the reaction's suppression of the revolutionary movement had a progressive outcome. The reason for such a strange ideological twist was as follows: On the one hand, Soviet ideologists of the late 1930s still maintained a Marxist-Leninist approach to political reality in both the past and the future. This approach declared that the class struggle, initiated by the oppressed social group, had always been a progressive phenomenon of history. History, like any other process in the world, developed on the basis of interaction between thesis and antithesis. In the case of human history, opposing social groups represented the thesis and antithesis. Through class struggle, the level of exploitation was reduced as the oppressed developed "productive forces," and this new advanced state of affairs was the synthesis. On the other hand, however, the class struggle created problems for progressive rulers such as Peter the Great. *Peter the First* clearly shows that the social protest was in reaction to the merciless exploitation of the masses by Peter's imperial government. Movie directors were apparently perplexed about having these two "positive" heroes confront each other: the progressive reformist tsar Peter, and the common citizen, who was progressive in his or her resistance to landlords and bureaucrats. Filmmakers were clearly inclined, however, to sacrifice the class struggle to the glory of the state. They frankly acknowledge the tsar's merciless exploitation of the populace and see plenty of reasons for the populace to rebel. But the final historical truth is on Peter's side, and therefore they condone not only Peter's terror against the pure reactionaries (the enemies of reform, centered around Alexis), but also his suppression of popular discontent. In this context, the popular progressive revolutionary movement is not openly reactionary, but is seen as ambivalent. Peter, on the other hand, is seen as a purely progressive person, the Stalin of the eighteenth century.

Soviet People as Happy Individuals

Unlike the early 1930s, official propaganda after 1935 contended that socialism had already been attained in the country, implying that people should be happy and even wealthy. For the promotion of this idea, Soviet cinematographers, under the direct influence of Hollywood, resorted to comedies, the number of which increased significantly in the second half of the 1930s. This explains why the films of the late 1930s are so rich in comedy: Comedy was that era's way of putting on the face of a happy society with no serious contradictions.

Most of the comedies of the 1930s revealed no serious social problems. Evil characters [most often remnants of the past, like Nepman in Alexandrov's *Joyful Fellows* (1934); people with prejudices against blacks, as in his *The Circus* (1936); or ignorant bureaucrats, as in his *Volga-Volga* (1938)] were usually depicted as too weak to be a real threat. The point of these comedies was not the struggle with the bureaucrats, but a demonstration of the happy life of Soviet citizens. In this context, the citizens' only problems were personal ones, which no regime could eliminate.

In Andrei Bulinskii's *The Girl Hurries for Her Date* (1936), as in the earlier movie *Joyful Fellows*, the setting is a pleasant resort, with resort life representing the happy life in the country in general. The movie's protagonists experience no lack of clothing or food. In fact, they have an overabundance of food; scores of fat people spend considerable effort trying to get rid of their excess weight. In Konstantin Iudin's *The Girl with a Temper* (1939), life outside the resort is presented as hardly different from that inside the resort. The heroine of the movie, a young girl, tries her hand at various trades, several of which, such as working in a factory, involve hard physical labor. In the movie, however, this hard work is seen as nothing but play. And, of course, it guarantees the girl a good standard of living. In many movies, the happy, harmonious nature of Soviet society is also emphasized by the ease of social mobility. In this respect these movies resembled comedies of the previous period. In *Joyful Fellows*, a milkmaid easily makes the transition to opera star. Similarly, in Semien Timoshenko's *Goalie* (1936), simple workers who unload watermelons become famous soccer players. The only problems portrayed in such movies are those of a personal nature, such as unrequited love.

The music for most of these comedies (as well as other movies in the

1930s) was composed by some of the best Soviet musicians, such as Isaak Dunaievskii, the Pokrass brothers, and Matvei Blanter. Even Shostakovich and Prokofiev, two of the greatest composers of the twentieth century, were active in composing music for Soviet films. Music (and song) was important to create an atmosphere of levity and merriment in Soviet comedies. Surprisingly, Soviet composers were able to compose such appealing and sincerely merry music while confronted with mass terror and personal fear. In fact, in later years, when the terror had decreased, Soviet composers would not be able to match the popularity of the songs written in the 1930s, many of which are still well-known today.

NOTES

1. By the mid-1930s, the ideological search for an enemy had lost its eschatological underpinnings. In revolutionary times, ideology implied that the destruction of the enemy—the cosmic forces of capitalism—through a worldwide or even cosmic socialist revolution would lead to the creation of a harmonious society, or even to a physical change in humanity. In the 1920s, both the struggle with the West and especially technological progress were viewed as the beginning of humankind's conquest of nature, including its own. By the 1930s, however, such struggles had lost their fascination.

2. The appearance of a "living Lenin" on the screen caused a sensation. As Neiy Zorkaya contends, "spectators applauded and jumped to their feet whenever Shchukin (who performed the role of Lenin in Romm's movies), made-up like Lenin, entered the screen with the gait and manner of speech characteristic of the leader" (Zorkaya 1989, p. 151).

3. Soviet filmmakers continued to produce films glorifying Lenin, mostly based on Shatrov's plays [Iulii Karasik's *The Sixth of July* (1968) was among them], until the early 1980s. The last major movie about Lenin was Sergei Bondarchuk's *Red Bells* (1982). During *glasnost*, *Leniniana* (the series of movies about Lenin) became the target of merciless criticism as a typical product of Stalinism and the falsification of history.

4. After 1985, Soviet intellectuals were able to examine how this and other movies misconstrued history, by comparing them with documents they could now access. Dovzhenko's *Shchors* was one victim of these investigations; it became evident that the filmmaker, in order to oblige Stalin, had created a decidedly false image of the Ukrainian commander (see *Iskusstvo Kino* 9, 1990, pp. 109–20).

5. A few years later, during the war with Hitler, Stalin followed the examples of both Russian potentates, whom he admired for their cruelty and devotion to state interests: He refused to exchange his son Vasilii, who was captured by the Germans, for a German general, suggesting, as in Iurii Ozerov's movie *Liberation* (1970–1972), that it is not proper to swap a junior officer for a general.

8

The Great Patriotic War

World War II ushered in a new period of political and cultural development in the USSR, beginning in 1941 and lasting until victory in 1945. It was a unique period in Soviet history, when the Soviet people genuinely supported Stalin as the national leader.

At the same time, during the war control over cinema did not soften the slightest bit. However, never was Soviet cinematography so close to its Western counterparts. Soviet war movies did not often differ from American or British movies that praised the war efforts of their citizens, officers, soldiers, and leaders (about the war period in American and British movies see Shipman 1984; Izod 1988; Cook 1990; Curran and Porter 1983).

WAR IDEOLOGY: THE FOCUS ON RUSSIAN NATIONALISM

Official ideology and propaganda changed radically in the first year of the war. Russian nationalism became the main focus, and Stalin temporarily removed all socialist and Marxist phraseology and propaganda. Slogans such as "Proletarians of the world, unite" disappeared from the mass media, and were replaced by slogans celebrating the Russian heroic past as well as the Russian national character.

At the same time, Soviet propaganda did not stop glorifying Stalin as the great leader. But at this point Stalin's cult acquired an additional and powerful justification: It was necessary to maintain the leader's high prestige as the commander-in-chief. The glorification of Stalin was also, however, a result of the continuity of the political system, which had been shaped during the late 1930s.

Like the ideology of the previous period, ideology during the war with Germany (despite constraints on the use of socialist terminology) continued to glorify the state and the party as the defenders of the nation and the organizers of victory over the foreign enemy.

Soviet cinematographers and the majority of the Soviet people considered the war against Hitler's Germany their sacred duty. Never would the level of unity between the Kremlin and the people be as high as in 1941–1945. Therefore, filmmakers considered their work (even though still severely controlled) as genuinely patriotic and necessary. Stalin, despite his role as the commander-in-chief, continued to focus on the movie industry, reprimanding and encouraging film directors in their work.

During this time there was a significant increase in documentary movies, and many filmmakers went to the front lines, several of them losing their lives. Cinematographers worked feverishly on these war films and were able to release the first of them by the end of the first year of the war.

THE UNITY OF PEOPLE IN THE WAR

The major goal of Soviet movies (as well as many American movies) during the war was the mobilization of the people for war efforts. This was achieved in two ways: by demonstrating patriotic behavior, and by depicting German atrocities.

Pyriev's *Secretary of the District Committee* (1942) was the first feature war film. The hero, Stepan Kochet, is the ideal party leader who organizes the partisan movement in his district. Courageous and intelligent, he outsmarts Makenau, a German colonel filled with stereotypes about the Russians. The film implied that Russia possessed a host of people able to head the mortal struggle against Nazi Germany.

While Pyriev's film advanced a party leader as the hero, Ermler's *She Defends Her Country* (1943) demonstrated that ordinary people were also important in the defense of the motherland. This film especially highlighted Nazi atrocities during the war.

The hero, Pasha Lukianova, is a happy woman with a loving family and work that she enjoys. However, Germans kill her husband, and her son is crushed to death before her eyes by a German tank. She finds an axe someone has dropped and starts to kill Germans, thereby becoming one of the people's "avengers."

Mark Donskoi's *Rainbow* (1944) depicted German cruelty even further. The movie concentrated on the life of peasants in a Ukrainian village occupied by German soldiers, who sadistically torture residents, including children.

The idea of unity during the war allowed filmmakers to introduce into their films personages that they could not have before the war. The main character in Abram Room's *Invasion* (1945) is Fiodor Talanov, who, returning from prison, finds himself in a city occupied by Nazis. His arrogance angers the local partisans, and they do not trust him. However, Talanov proves himself by sacrificing his life in order to save Kolesnikov, the partisans' leader. In other films, directors depicted traitors as members of the old dominant classes, demonstrating that the tradition of class conflict was still strong.

THE GLORIFICATION OF GREAT RUSSIANS FROM THE PAST

The war helped to strengthen a trend that had already become prevalent before the outbreak of fighting—the commendation of great personages from the Russian past, in particular military men.

Petrov's *Kutuzov* (1944) is a good example of a historical movie with a military leader as the hero. *Kutuzov* is set during the War of 1812, when the Russians confronted a formidable army led by Napoleon. The situation was analogous to contemporary wartime events, and is clearly why this subject was chosen. Kutuzov, the commander of the Russian army, is presented as a great strategist, able to defeat Napoleon. But Kutuzov is not only equal to Napoleon, he surpasses him. By glamorizing Kutuzov, the movie ignores the historical facts that might explain Napoleon's defeat as due to bad accidents, weather, guerrilla attacks, and other issues. In the movie, Napoleon is driven from Russia by the regular army and is actually defeated on the battlefield.

Soviet filmmakers, like their colleagues in other nations, would continue to address the war for many years. The politics and ideology of each period, of course, affected these movies in various ways, and we will return to them in the following chapters.

9

Stalin's Postwar Years

The last years of Stalin's regime were no less painful for Soviet cinema than previous periods and definitely much worse than the war years. Stalin, against expectations of a softening of the regime, turned the ideological screws even tighter than before. Soviet cinema continued to produce false, although entertaining, movies about Soviet life.

THE IDEOLOGICAL CLIMATE

The end of the war with Germany opened up a new period in Soviet history that continued up to Stalin's death in 1953. Politically, this period was characterized by the Soviet Union's transformation into a super-power. The victory over Germany and the expansion of the Soviet empire in East Europe meant the final legitimization of the Soviet regime, which since the revolution had always feared foreign intervention. The victory greatly enhanced Stalin's cult; he was now deified as a living god.

Stalin's ideological policy in the postwar period was directed mostly to the prevention of any dissent in the country. This was all the more necessary because of some hopes for liberalization of the regime, which emerged in the aftermath of the victory. However, at this point the major cudgel for scaring people was not the class struggle, as in the mid-1930s, but Russian nationalism, which, as was pointed out, entered Soviet ideology in the late 1930s and was the basis for war propaganda.

While promoting Russian nationalism, Stalin did not want to totally abandon socialist elements of his ideology, and he restored to some extent their role after their oblivion during the war. By connecting Russian nationalism and socialism, Stalin introduced the concept of Soviet patriotism, which now became the core element of the new propaganda. This concept was used extensively for anti-Western purposes, which now became more important than before or even during the war.

At the same time, Soviet ideology continued to suggest that the Soviet peqple were leading happy lives, and therefore glad to be living in Russia and the Soviet Union. Soviet cinematographers were relatively quick in adjusting to this new propaganda.

Patriotic Movies

The commendation of patriotism and the condemnation of traitors was the theme of several movies. The most notorious of them was Abram Room's *The Court of Honor* (1945). The plot revolves around two Soviet scholars who, neglecting their patriotic duty, attempt to hand a scientific discovery over to their Western colleagues. Needless to say, they are sternly condemned by their patriotic Soviet colleagues.

Between 1945 and 1953, filmmakers also made a large number of movies with ideal Soviet people as heroes who worked selflessly for the sake of the motherland. Alexander Stolper's *Far Away from Moscow* (1950), based on Vasilii Azhaev's ostensibly documentary novel, was about the building of oil pipelines. Batmanov, the construction chief, was an ideal Communist leader who combined competence, organizational skill, and will, along with kindness and sympathy for his subordinates. It only became known many years later that the pipeline in Azhaiev's novel was built by prisoners of the *Gulag*.

Other films about ordinary heroes include Raizman's *The Cavalier of the Gold Star* (1951), in which the hero is the chairman of a prosperous farm, while Mark Donskoi created the image of the ideal teacher in *A Village Teacher* (1947), and Sergei Gerasimov created an ideal physician in *Rural Doctor* (1952).

Xenophobic Movies during the Postwar Years

With the start of the cold war, Soviet film directors began to create anti-Western movies as never before. Romm was the champion of these films, which misrepresented the present and the past in glaring ways. One example is his *The Russian Question* (1948), based on the play of Konstantin Simonov, Stalin's pet writer. It was the first film that portrayed the United States as the major enemy of peace-loving Russia.

This film centers on the struggle between Garry Smith, an honest American journalist, and McPherson, his boss and a typical capitalist shark, who demands that Smith write a slanderous book about Russia. Enlightened by a visit to Moscow, he refuses to write the book and decides to fight for the preservation of peace, which the American elite wants to destroy through a new world war. The end of the film finds Smith coming to the bitter realization that all American freedoms are fake. He also experiences a personal tragedy because his beloved Jessie (portrayed as a typical American) is ready to forget conscience and honor for the sake of a trivial concept of happiness (a house with a white picket fence).[1]

With each passing month the campaign against the United States increased, and Romm's next film, *Secret Mission* (1950), accused the Americans of plotting with Nazi generals against the Soviet Union. Romm continued his crusade against the West even after Stalin's death, with *The Murder on Dante Street* (1956), after which Romm stopped making films for six years.

Several other brilliant directors, who would later be known for their liberal movies, also created propagandistic films about the West. For instance, Alexandrov, in his *Meeting on the Elbe* (1949), presented Moscow as eager to help defeated Germany in building a true democratic society, while Washington had the opposite plan. Mikhail Kalatozov's *The Conspiracy of the Doomed* (1950) is about a plot by Western intelligence services to start a new world war.

The Glorification of Russian Celebrities from the Past

In order to develop his idea of Soviet patriotism—the blend of Russian nationalism and socialism—Stalin started (in 1948) the so-called anti-cosmopolitan campaign. This campaign elaborated on the cultural and military superiority of not only the Soviet Union, but also of Russia in the past, over the rest of the world.

The best Soviet filmmakers were enrolled in the production of films that, often blatantly distorting historical facts, attempted to prove Russian superiority in all areas of science and the arts. These movies not only commended their heroes, but downgraded the role of their Western counterparts, and falsified their political views and attitudes toward religion.

Grigorii Roshal's *Academician Ivan Pavlov* (1949), about the eminent physiologist, presented Pavlov as a great materialist with Marxist tendencies. In truth, Pavlov was a deeply religious person. The film also shows how Pavlov changed his view on the party—again a well-known falsity, because Pavlov had always been inimical to the Soviet regime. Alexander Dovzhenko's *Michurin* (1949) was an extremely distorted portrait, which overestimated Michurin's role in the world of science, as well as his influence on Soviet agriculture.

Roshal's *Musorgskii* (1950), a film about the Russian composer, was also used for propaganda purposes. In the movie, the musician and his friends have to fight against foreign influence on Russian music in order to defend genuine art, which gets its inspiration from the masses. Their opponents are depicted as idiots or villains.

Movies about World War II

After the war, Stalin needed movies about the war not for mobilizing the people for the fight against Germany, but as another means to persuade the population that the country had won the war thanks to the party, the Soviet system, and his leadership.

Sergei Gerasimov's *The Young Guard* (1948), based on Alexander Fadeiev's novel, is about the anti-German underground organization of young people in Krasnodon, a city in Donbass. Fadeiev (especially in the second version of his novel) and Gerasimov, adjusting facts to fit the ideological scheme, depicted young partisans as deeply devoted Soviet patriots whose activity was directed by Communists, in the person of Prozenko, secretary of the regional party committee.[2]

Between 1945 and 1953 a number of other movies about the war praised the Communist party and Stalin. Among them was Alexander Stopler's *The Story of a Real Man* (1948). This film was about Mares'ev, a real-life pilot who continued to fly combat against German planes after having lost both legs in a battle. However, of equal importance in the movie is Party Commissar Vorobiev, to whom Mares'ev, of course, owed his courage and perseverance.

Movies about Stalin

One of the first war movies venerating Stalin was Igor Savchenko's *The Third Strike* (1948); this was followed by Vladimir Petrov's *The Battle of Stalingrad* (1949) and then Mikhail Chiaureli's *The Fall of Berlin* (1950). Each director wanted to surpass his colleagues in the veneration of the great leader, who appeared almost God-like in these films. Not surprisingly, all of these movies were awarded Stalin's prizes.

Movies about Happy Life

As mentioned earlier, in the 1930s the ideal life was presented mostly through comedies, the very nature of which implies a certain detachment from reality. However, in postwar era movies the ideal life was also presented in serious movies that purported to accurately reflect real life.

Pyriev's *Kuban Cossacks* (1950), which would become the epitome of the falsification of Soviet reality, depicted prosperity and happy life in the Soviet countryside, focusing attention on the abundance of food and other commodities. Similar images of life in the difficult postwar years can be seen in Pyriev's *The Story of Siberian Land* (1948), about the happy life of people in Siberia, and in Lukov's *Donbass Miners* (1951), which depicts miners living in luxurious apartments, with excellent food and entertainment facilities.

CONCLUSION

In many ways, Stalin's period in the history of Soviet cinema was the most interesting. At no other time was the movie industry so tightly controlled, for so long, by the leader himself. In this period a group of brilliant, highly talented cinematographers submitted completely to Stalin, and made films with one purpose—to please the leader. Furthermore, it appears that all of them admired and loved the leader, even though these feelings coexisted with the all-embracing fear of Stalin and his political police.

During these twenty-five years Soviet directors created a new social reality that had little in common with the true reality of Stalinist Russia, even if a number of Soviet people tried to imitate the heroes of the Stalinist films.

NOTES

1. As recently as 1980, two Soviet movie historians recounted the plot of this film in all seriousness, as if it reflected real life in the United States during the first years of the war (Vorontsov and Rachuk 1980, pp. 237–39).

2. Later, after Stalin's death, and especially during *glasnost*, several articles were published about the Krasnodon Young Guard that all denounced Fadeiev for distorting fundamental facts.

IV

The Game with Official Ideology

If in the 1920s the majority of Soviet filmmakers enthusiastically worked for the official ideology and accepted it as their own, in the next period they felt themselves slaves of this ideology. However, beginning in the late 1950s they started to release themselves from the ever-present fear of state power and made attempts to outsmart the authorities. For the first time since the revolutionary period Soviet filmmakers began to implement their own ideas and express their own ideological orientations. However, they were forced to do this in mostly indirect ways, trying not to antagonize their patrons, who continued to have full control over the professional life of cinematographers.

10

Movies during the First Thaw (1954–1968):
Timid Challenges to Official Ideology

With Stalin's death in 1953, the country entered a new stage of its development. Mass terror ceased to be the central factor in social life. The leading elite began to divide into various factions, which differed in their views of social problems and espoused different versions of socialist ideology.

A NEW IDEOLOGICAL ATMOSPHERE

With the gradual diminution of fear and growing dissension inside the political elite, cinematographers began to reassess their ideological convictions and elaborate their own views of the world. In addition, they were finally able to look for support among those members of the ruling circles whose views were similar to theirs.

Of course, the dominant ideology as it was shaped after the revolution continued to influence filmmakers, as it would until the demise of the Soviet Union. However, they did not feel as controlled by it as in the past. Around 1954 cinematographers began playing a complicated game with the authorities and official ideology, in which they attempted to convey ideas disparate from the official line.

Like other intellectuals—writers, theater directors, journalists, and social scientists—cinematographers felt it their civic duty to describe truthfully some aspects of their society. They also wanted to send moral messages that ordinary people could not find in official mass media or education. Involvement in politics increased, even if indirectly, and made Soviet cinematographers quite different than their Western counterparts.

Of course, up to 1989 Soviet filmmakers continued to be censored, or at least influenced greatly. Those who followed the Kremlin's lead received various privileges, while those who deviated from the official line were castigated and often lost work. Even the bravest film directors could only hint at the full truth. However, they were now allowed in several cases to choose issues and subjects that could help them minimize the distortion of truth.

CODING AND DECODING WORKS OF
LITERATURE AND ART

The emergence of this limited freedom allowed cinematographers, as well as writers, to express their genuine views to some extent. However, in order to really communicate what they wanted to, it became necessary for them to create a set of devices to help them outsmart party supervisors and develop their own channels of communication with their public.

Obviously, works that challenge the ruling political ideology must do so in subtle and intricate ways. Because of the barriers to creative expression inherent in censorship, writers and film directors are compelled to code their work with various allusions, associations, and hints. Thus, any high-quality Soviet literary or artistic work is to some degree allegorical and requires special decoding efforts.

A number of Soviet writers and film directors have gained notoriety for their ability to encode various messages addressed to educated audiences. Andrei Tarkovskii was particularly skilled at such encoding, and his films, like *Andrei Rublev* (1971), *Mirror* (1975), and *Soliaris* (1972), aroused considerable debate as viewers sought to interpret the hidden messages. [In 1975, Batkin spent two hours at a special seminar analyzing *Mirror* and explaining all its metaphors. He published this analysis in 1988 (*Iskusstvo Kino*, November 1988)]. Other directors have produced films that yielded highly disparate interpretations. Gleb Panfilov's *May I Have the Floor* (1976), which concerned the life of a female mayor in a Soviet city, was such a film. Some viewers saw the work as a trivial apology for Soviet officials, while others saw it as a scathing attack on them.

As in theater, film directors used classic works to convey liberal ideas. Grigorii Kozintsev's *Hamlet* (1964), based on the play by Shakespeare, provides a good example. Although the hero's confrontation with the cynical and cruel life of the court might be interpreted as an oblique criticism of Stalin's or even Khrushchev's government (though Khrushchev liberated many people from Stalin's labor camps, he neither abolished the secret police nor ended the repression of dissidents), the movie also has a more general, existential interpretation. Specifically,

Hamlet's alienation from his state symbolizes the alienation of any honest person from the state and from history; honesty and history thus become incompatible. In order to be good, a person must escape history and retreat into private life.

The post-Stalin and pre-Gorbachev years fall into two periods: Khrushchev's thaw and Brezhnev's stagnation.

THE FIRST THAW

The decade of the first post-Stalin thaw, 1954–1968, found the new leader, having debunked Stalin, attempting to resurrect true socialism as he understood it. This included essentially the same political and economic order but added increased openness to the world, more modernization, and technological progress. He also employed less mass repression and diminished the widespread fear. Developments such as the economic progress of the late 1950s and early 1960s, and the fascinating successes of the Soviet space program, laid the groundwork for the official belief in the future of socialist society and communism. This period is actually a few years longer than Khrushchev's rule since Brezhnev continued the thaw for almost four years—until the invasion of Czechoslovakia in 1968.

Although Khrushchev maintained the regime's political structure as essentially totalitarian, his revelations about Stalin's crimes shook the foundations of the old Soviet ideology. This facilitated the emergence of new ideological trends, which had a significant impact on cinematographers.

This ideological atmosphere differed radically from Stalin's uniformity. However, the official ideology continued to emphasize the important role of the Communist party, collectivism, the class approach, all essential elements of socialist economy (public property and central planning), animosity to the West, and the acceptance of Soviet history (in its Stalinist version, which included praise of the October Revolution and collectivization).

However, intellectuals opposed to this ideology began to create their own version of socialism. It was liberal in its essence and focused on the individual in opposition to collectivism, the crucial role of the intelligentsia in society instead of the glorification of the workers, universal values as opposed to the class approach, and the importance of public opinion versus believing in the omniscience of the leadership. Finally, intellectuals exposed the existence of various social conflicts and flaws in Soviet life which official ideology tried to ignore.

IDEOLOGICALLY LOYAL MOVIES

During Khrushchev's time cinematographers continued to make films in line with current ideological policy. These films suggested that even with the dissolution of Stalin's terror there were still many devoted Communists and conformists able to push society ahead toward a radiant future. However, since official ideology demanded that even loyal cinematographers follow the new spirit, personages in these films were not as one dimensional and primitive as those in Stalin era movies. Directors were even permitted to introduce some minor social conflicts. But despite all these modifications, the official nature of these films remained evident to the public.

Iosif Kheifits's *The Big Family* (1954), based on the novel by Vladimir Kochetov, a conservative writer, continued the tradition of portraying Soviet workers—Zhurbin's family in the movie—as conscientious patriots, devoted to their plant and the collective.

However, the first movie to reflect the official optimism of Khrushchev's leadership was Raizman and Gabrilovich's *Communist* (1958). In this film, demobilized soldier and Communist Vasilii Gubanov puts all his effort into peaceful socialist labor by constructing the first Soviet power station. Unlike older movies about the revolutionary years, this film is more realistic and did not contend that all workers were enthusiasts of the revolutionary cause. This is in part an allusion to the present time and underscores that each period needs its own Gubanov able to lead the masses to victory. Several other movies also continued to hail the revolution and its heroes, with some slight modifications as allowed by the thaw. [See Alov and Naumov's *Pavel Korchagin* (1957), after Ostrovskii's novel *How Steel Was Tempered*, and *The Wind* (1959).]

However, more important for official ideology were such movies as Alexei Saltykov's *The Chairman* (1964), which focuses on this new type of hero—effective, yet noble. Set in a rural background, *The Chairman* depicts the life of a retired soldier, Egor Trubnikov, who has become chairman of his kolkhoz (collective farm). He is a strong believer in collectivism and socialism and vehemently argues with Semen, his brother, who has lost confidence in both. Instead of being a superman (like the heroes in earlier movies), he is physically handicapped. He is not especially kind to the peasants, whom he encourages to work hard, but his prodding is quite different than the pressure exerted by heroes in earlier movies. The leader had demanded that his people make an enormous sacrifice in order to build up a powerful new Russia. By contrast, the chairman thinks his people should work in order to be happy. In fact, he has strong reservations about the power of the state. He actually protests a case where state representatives deprive the peasants of their fair share of grain. Several other movies produced during Khrushchev's thaw also praise this new type of manager [for example, Dmitrii Meskhiev and Veniamin Levitin's *Please Meet Baluiev* (1963)].

In the 1960s Soviet cinema continued to produce canonic movies about Lenin [like Sergei Iutkevich's *Stories about Lenin* (1958)], as well as about the war [Sergei Bondarchuk's *The Destiny of Man* (1959)]. However, these movies, strongly hailed by official bodies, were more subtle in the implementation of the official line than films made during Stalin's time. In the latter movie, for instance, the main positive hero, Andrei Sokolov—a true Russian—was a prisoner of war. This was a challenge to Stalinist propaganda, which described all those who found themselves in German POW camps as traitors.

THE PRAISE OF INTELLECTUALS

As soon as they were able, Soviet cinematographers created films with intellectuals as the heroes and main hope for the country. Revelations about Stalin's crimes helped some Soviet intellectuals renew their faith in the Soviet system and the fundamentals of Soviet ideology. Those who had remained true believers, however, started reconsidering the idea that their vision of the nation and revolution provided the ultimate moral justification for virtually any action. Messianic and nationalistic Machiavellianism, which prevailed in Soviet ideology up to Stalin's death and justified any action deemed necessary to promote the cause of the revolution and the national interest (which were rarely distinguished), came into question. Intellectuals began implying that there was actually no contradiction between general moral norms and the interests of the revolution and nation when properly understood. Stalin's crimes, according to this view, were both immoral and harmful for socialism and Russia. The first post-Stalin films depicted intellectuals as true socialists and patriots who need both the trust of the government and some freedom for their scientific pursuits.

Mikhail Romm's *Nine Days of One Year* (1962) was typical in this respect. It was a true ode to the Soviet intelligentsia and a message addressed to the ruling elite. It warned them to heed the advice of intellectuals, who were the most competent and, at the same time, devoted socialists.

The heroes in this movie are physicists, professionals who were in fashion at this time due to their ability to shape the future of the country with their research. They are depicted not only as important scientists but also ready to brave severe risk to their lives (as did Gusev, a young atomic physicist) for the good of science and, thereby, the country.

Raizman's *Your Contemporary* (1968) is about a prominent scholar and consultant of a big construction firm. The hero, for the first time in Soviet cinema, audaciously defies officials and stands by his opinions.

SOCIAL CONFLICTS AND FLAWS IN SOVIET LIFE

In movies of the previous era the Soviet Union had been depicted as a perfect country practically without social conflict. Movies, as well as mass media, could not even hint at issues such as class differentiation, ethnic conflicts (anti-Semitism, for example), technological backwardness, the low standard of living, corruption, the incompetence of bureaucrats, the privileges of the *nomenklatura* and several other traits of Soviet society. However, the most serious taboo was any critique of the state and party. With the liberalization of the regime, however, filmmakers began to test the waters and include some rather mild conflict with low-level state bodies.

After 1953 liberal film directors felt it their duty to tell the Soviet population some truth about their lives. Kheifits's *Rumyantsev's Case* (1956) was a sensation in the first post-Stalin years. The movie has two main characters, Samokhin, a captain in the militia, and Alexander Rumiantsev, an innocent man unjustly jailed by Samokhin. Samokhin embodies public life and the state. Rumiantsev, unjustly accused, wants to restore justice. Of course, Kheifits could not even mention the KGB, the *Gulag*, or the persecution of millions of people. But the simple fact that the captain was bad, even if he was a mere policeman, and that the prisoner was good was a significant step toward undoing old distortions.

In this same year Riazanov made his first popular film, *Carnival Night* (1956). It was hailed, among other things, for the heroism of the filmmaker for including a scene in which clowns mock the director of the local club, who obviously represent the whole Soviet system. For this reason people also praised Klimov's first movie *Welcome, or No Admittance!* (1964), where the director of the pioneer camp, also a symbol of the Soviet administration, is the target of mocking.

Mikhail Kalatozov's *The First Echelon* (1956) is about Khrushchev's famous Virgin Lands Program—a program designed to place large tracts of remote land under cultivation. The movie presents this idea as involving worthy social goals that, under earlier ideologies, would have provided everything necessary to make the participants happy. However, the characters' encounters usually involve the consumption of vodka and end in brawls. Their sexual relationships are very casual, consisting mostly of one-night stands.

Since 1956, the majority of film directors, even those who were very close to the Central Committee, have inserted some social conflicts or depicted social flaws in their movies. This was actually in line with the current official ideology, which tried to divorce itself from the rigid and discredited Stalinist propaganda. However, there was great variance among cinematographers in their desire to depict social problems. Stanislav Rostotskii's *We'll Get By Till Monday* (1968) described some minor problems in Soviet schools (i.e., all pupils and teachers are not really good and some revolutionary traditions have been forgotten). However, in general no major problems with Soviet youth are addressed.

In Saltykov's *The Chairman* (1964) Soviet spectators got their first taste of the truth about Soviet agriculture in the aftermath of the war. Gerasimov's *The Journalist* (1967) also made a modest attempt to depict the unseemly side of the Soviet local administration.

However, the peak of social criticism was achieved by Romm, who after *Nine Days of One Year* suddenly became, despite his Stalinist record up to 1956, the most liberal movie director. His documentary and very personal *Ordinary Fascism* (1966) made direct allusions to the similarity of Nazi Germany and the Soviet Union. Such a comparison amounted to heresy at that time. In fact, it would be almost a quarter of a century before Hitler and Stalin would be treated as analogous in the Russian media.

THE LEGITIMIZATION OF THE INDIVIDUAL AND HIS OR HER PRIVATE LIFE

It would be incorrect to say that the heroes of Stalinist films did not have a private life. However, the main characters considered their private life to be much less important than their public life, which included work and any struggle for the sake of society. Furthermore, these heroes were almost all very happy in their relations with other people, even including those with the opposite sex.

With the thaw, Soviet cinematographers with liberal tendencies were able to substantially redefine the place of public and private life in society. They started to make films about ordinary people absorbed with their own problems. The appearance of such characters was a revolution in Soviet cinema, a challenge to the old official ideology. However, this revolution did find some sympathy among liberal party apparatchiks who helped shoot such films. Finally, movie directors began to make movies about unhappy private lives, failed romantic love, and even despair.

Some of the first depictions of private life came in movies about World War II. This was a great contrast to Stalinist films, in which people were consumed only with fighting against Nazi Germany. The theme of "happy consciousness" becoming "unhappy consciousness" (that is, the tragedy of the person who, while helping build a new society, becomes quite unhappy in his or her private life) actually originated with films like Pudovkin's *The Return of Vasilia Bortnikova* (1953). It is set during the immediate aftermath of the Great Patriotic War. Soldiers are returning from the front—soldiers of the victorious Red Army who had not only crushed their mortal enemy but spread Soviet domination and socialism throughout Europe. From the point of view of the ideology of the previous period, the hero should be happy since he has furthered the progressive forces of socialism. Yet, as he enters his home expecting his wife to greet him, he finds another man in his bed.

Although he forgives his wife, his marriage is ruined. He throws himself into his work and tries to convince himself that his personal problems are insignificant. He becomes chairman of the local collective farm and treats his people harshly. He wants them to engage wholeheartedly in the work of the state and forget about their families and personal lives—he wants them to become public rather than private persons. However, he fails in this task. His own unhappiness over his private woes remains unshaken and the desire of his workers to escape the grim reality of the prevailing *Weltgeist* are not fulfilled.

Pudovkin's film was only the first cautious step in the introduction of private life into Soviet films. The real breakthrough was Kalatozov's *Cranes Are Flying* (1957). The film's heroes are all patriots who dream about victory in the war. However, they are also immersed in their own personal life and complicated relationships. In addition, they are ready to defend their private lives (family, friends, etc.) and eternal moral values. They are therefore not supermen but ordinary people.

In one of the most touching scenes the soldiers are shown parting with their dear ones before going to the front. We see the father parting with his family, the intellectual bidding farewell to his wife and colleagues, and the hero Boris waiting among the crowd to bid his fiancée Veronica farewell. It is she whom he, as a volunteer, wants to defend, or more precisely the motherland embodied in her image. Unfortunately, they are unable to meet. This unconsummated farewell is a harbinger of future tragedy and stresses the importance of private life in the scheme of things. This failed rendezvous indicates that the hero will probably be killed. The Soviet Union's victory will not lessen the tragedy of an individual's death or the collapse of his dream of a happy private life with the woman he passionately loves.

Despite the destruction of the hero's private life, his death is given meaning because it helps protect the private life of others. His death is depicted on a very personal level by focusing on the feelings of the mortally wounded hero. His dying thoughts are not of Stalin and social-ism. They are of his marriage and symbolize the magnitude of the trag-edy, the death of an individual, and the higher meaning of his death and of Russia's victory. Russia is saved so that other people may enjoy their personal, private happiness (which might not directly correspond to the greatness of the state). The eventual marriage of the hero's fiancée to Marc, another young man who has managed to stay away from the front, is presented to accentuate not only the tragedy (the most deserv-ing young people were not able to enjoy the pleasures of life) but the ultimate meaning of the hero's death and victory in the war with Nazi Germany.

Lev Kulidzhanov and Iakov Segel's *The House I Live In* (1957) was another film about the private life of the Soviet people. It begins in an intimate, familylike environment. The representation of the state is re-duced to a house and not a huge city. Public life, which was the focus of so many previous movies, is reduced to the study of the lives of individ-ual people. This emphasis on intimacy enhances the presentation of these people and in many ways we can see that their private lives are far from ideal. The rooms are cheaply and tastelessly decorated. The family members, friends, and lovers quarrel constantly and cheat on one an-other. The people in the film pay little attention to the public life of state and society.

One of the protagonists, a minor managerial functionary, frequently visits other cities on business. No information is given, however, regard-ing the official reasons for his trips or their intended positive social consequences. The focus is instead on the fact that the man takes these trips because they are part of his job and he needs the job to support his family.

The scene in which the hero/manager is going off to the front is also very characteristic. In parting with his family (perhaps seeing them for the last time), his concerns are not for his social accomplishments or responsibilities, but for his family. His last words with his wife all con-cern practical, private matters, such as how to get his salary from the state and how to water the flowers. It is not his political and social achievement but his family that gives meaning and purpose to his life. As he goes off, the camera focuses on his wedding picture hanging on the wall, underscoring the fact that he is going off to fight for his family's private lives. Even though they are flawed in actuality, private lives are ideal in the sense that they enshrine the eternal laws of nature. Victory at the end of the war is not symbolized by huge parades and spectacles. Instead, the great victory is represented by the simple, intimate home-coming of individual soldiers who are too tired even to take their clothes off before falling into bed. Thus, the hero is portrayed as a simple, flawed man whose grimy uniform contrasts with the whiteness of his bedsheets and emphasizes the difference in his life between the real and the ideal.

Soviet moviegoers were also inundated with unusual flashbacks to prewar times. However, it was not the recollection of brilliant social achievements of the past but the paraphernalia of everyday private life that was emphasized. This can also be considered a significant step in the fight against Stalinist ideology.

However, *The House I Live In* film is set in the 1930s, during the great purges. These events should have greatly influenced the members of the household, especially the manager, who is very vulnerable. Yet the film utterly ignores this subject.

Vladimir Basov's *Silence* (1964) was the first movie where one of the main characters was someone who had been arrested in Stalin's time. Even a hint at the fact that the country had jailed millions of victims produced nervous excitement in movie theaters. However, the theme of Stalin's terror would have to wait another two decades before coming to the screen.[1]

While implicitly an ethnic Russian, Alesha, the hero in Grigorii Chukhrai's *Ballad of a Soldier* (1959), behaves in much the same fashion as the hero of *Cranes Are Flying*. He defends his private life, his girlfriend, and his family, but he does not defend the state. This is emphasized by the nature of the hero's military exploits, which differ significantly from those seen in Stalin era movies. In these movies, not only the leaders but even the simple soldiers were tightly incorporated into the state, in that they were depicted as functioning as an extension of the state. Since the state was a mighty, superhuman organization, all members of the armed forces were superhumans who displayed no trace of human weakness (such as fear of death). As soon as movies separated soldiers from the state, and treated them as private persons, soldiers began to display human qualities such as weakness.

Such is the case with the hero of *Ballad of a Soldier*, which begins with the hero's confrontation with a German tank. The entire scene is designed to underscore the hero's private character, especially his puny size compared to that of the metal monster. Not only does he not look superhuman, he looks quite helpless in the face of an enemy ready to crush him under its treads. The enemy tank is a good representation of a faceless, public machine. It is cruel and remorseless. It expresses no fear, as opposed to the hero, who finds himself in a desperate situation. Nonetheless, the hero manages to grab an antitank gun and destroy the tank.

This scene is rife with symbolism. Whereas in Stalinist battle scenes there was always an objective (a strong point, fort, etc.) to symbolize the state's goal of defeating the enemy, this scene depicts only the hero against the tank. Our hero's valor is exclusively private—it serves to protect him and nothing else.

The hero's disregard for public life is seen elsewhere in the movie. After his victory over the tank, the hero is introduced to the army commander and is promised a decoration for his heroic deed. This prospect does not excite the hero very much and he immediately decides to exchange the decoration for a trip home. His disregard for the state honor and his desire to visit his girlfriend clearly show what he has been fighting for. In essence, he is not only a patriot, but a man with a private life.

The fate of the hero is similar to that of other characters in Khrushchev era war movies. The hero is killed, and, as in *Cranes Are Flying*, his death signifies the tragedy of war and, in perhaps a larger sense, the tragedy of life. The major implication is that the success of the public ideal—a historical development that would lead to a better future—could not eliminate the tragedy of personal loss. Another implication is that a person could not be disposed of simply for the right cause, as was the case in Stalin era movies.

THE FIRST MOVIES ABOUT LOVE

With the liberalization of the regime, film directors began to produce movies almost totally devoted to love. This was an impossibility only a few years before, when such ideas would have been condemned as bourgeois. In Stalinist movies, love between two young people was not based on mutual attraction or emotional kinship but on social factors. Such a factor was whether or not they were good workers and therefore good citizens of the socialist state. Of course, lovers in movies made during the thaw were still involved in their professional and social work. However, their relationships and not their work were now central themes.

Marlen Khutsiev and Felix Mironer's *Spring in Zarechnaia Street* (1956) depicts young steelworkers who fall in love with a new schoolteacher. And Raizman's *And What If It Is Love* (1962) challenged the hypocrisy of official morals even with its title. The film questioned the right of superiors (teachers or parents) to judge the feelings between two teenagers.

Another breakthrough in Soviet films during this period was the recognition of the complexity of human relationships, especially sexual ones. In Stalinist movies love was described in an extremely primitive way. It was usually a sudden romantic attraction between two individuals who would get married and remain faithful under any circumstances. Any deviation from this model was treated as a concession to bourgeois immorality. Extramarital relations in the ideological atmosphere of the 1930s took place only in the West.

For this reason Vasilii Ordynskii's *Man Was Born* (1956) created quite a stir. In the film a woman who has borne a child out of wedlock is depicted as a decent person deceived by a villain. In *Cranes Are Flying* Veronika, betrothed to Boris, succumbs to the courtship of a deserter while volunteering at the front line. However, the scriptwriter condones her behavior, and viewers end up sympathizing with her plight.

With time Soviet directors began to make movies about unrequited and unhappy love. Panfilov told a sad story in *The Beginning* (1970) about a young woman who falls in love with a man. She comes to believe that she is married and has a happy family only to be confronted by the harsh reality that the object of her admiration does not want to commit himself to her. In Mikhalkov-Konchalovskii's *A Lover's Romance* (1974) a woman, having learned about the death of her betrothed whom she loved passionately, marries another man only to find her first lover alive and still in love with her.

A NEW TYPE OF HERO—TRUE RUSSIANS

The introduction of private life in the Soviet cinema led to a radical change in the character of the ordinary man or woman as the main hero in Soviet films. Of course, the Communist hero devoted to public life and the struggle for a new society still made up the majority of positive figures in Soviet films. However, along with them emerged new types of heroes who represented not so much socialist society but Russia. By the late 1950s Russophilism, keeping its distance from Stalinism with its blend of new Marxism and Russian chauvinism, with the presence of religion (which would become the dominant ideology of the intelligentsia in Brezhnev's time) was already taking its first steps into the movie industry. Movies with disguised Russophilism were somewhat oppositional to the dominant ideology. It was not so much their praise of intellectuals and individualism, as in *Nine Days of One Year*, but their challenge of Marxist ideology with their spiritual values and lofty emotions.

Chukhrai's *Ballad of a Soldier* was the first movie of this type. There is no direct reference made to the Russianness of the hero, as would have occurred in the Brezhnev era. There is also no reference to the benign influence of religion on the formation of the hero's soul—the hero is not a holy fool from a Russian folktale (also a popular device in Brezhnev era movies). Still, elements of Russophilism are discernible in the movie.

First, the hero Alesha is not a cosmopolitan urbanite, as was the case in *Cranes Are Flying*. Most of the scenes are shot aboard a train with the countryside as a backdrop. Through the train's windows, moviegoers see small towns and villages, implying that they, and not big cities, constitute the country's foundation.

The hero's apparent lack of education, and his combination of peasant simplicity and practicality, suggest his humble origins. His external appearance is classically Slavic, as is that of his girlfriend. There is no doubt in the viewer's mind that the hero is not a member of a Russian-speaking minority but a true ethnic Russian. *Ballad of a Soldier* does not fully explore the theme of the holy fool, in which a village simpleton, the bearer of humanistic Russian traditions, is surrounded by villains who sometimes constitute the majority of the village residents (the villainy is necessary to highlight the fool's basic goodness). Still, the openhearted and somewhat naive hero possesses some characteristics of a holy fool. His opponent, a cunning and repulsive creature, only serves to highlight the hero's good qualities.

The movie also highlights the Russian people's essential goodness and willingness to sacrifice their lives for the happiness of others. Although the film contains no explicit religious references, it is understood that Russianness is inseparable from religion. Insofar as the hero's death represents the deaths of millions of Russian soldiers, it also represents an act of martyrdom as a symbolic ordeal for Christian Russia. All of this misfortune is both a tragedy and a blessing for the Russians—through their suffering they can reveal the best part of their character.

The next movie with Russophile tendencies was Tarkovskii's *Ivan's Childhood* (1962). The film is set exclusively in the countryside and rural images dominate the screen. The symbolism of the birch trees represents not only Mother Russia but the peasant character of the country. The birch trees also serve as a reminder that, despite the dramatic and painful changes imposed by Soviet rule, peasants succeeded in preserving the essence of their national culture. It remained as it had been for centuries.

For Russophiles, not only is Christianity the basis for the nation's political and cultural life, but Russians are the only true Christian people. Following this logic, the entire country becomes the collective embodiment of Christ. Since meekness and chastity are traits of a true Christian, they obviously must be essential traits of Russian national character. Russia's confrontations with her enemies are transformed into Christ's confrontations with his persecutors. They attempt to humiliate and chastise him, assuming that they can break his will. They miscalculate, however, because Christ (and therefore Russia) is made of different fiber—the torment only makes him stronger. Thus, victory results not from physical strength but from a spiritual force that miraculously transforms the enemy and ensures its utter defeat. This theme is easily discernible in *Ivan's Childhood*, mostly because a child, the epitome of sincerity and purity, is the major protagonist.

The child participates in several military operations as a spy for the Soviet army. This activity has little military implication, however, because he carries no weapon and does not engage in combat. He definitely hates the Germans but it is his love for Mother Russia, epitomized by the image of his mother, that drives his actions. He is reminiscent of the New Testament, where Christ said: "Unless . . . you become like children, you will never enter the kingdom of heaven" (Matthew 18:2–4).

The movie's other major protagonists, the Soviet soldiers, also behave in a Christian manner. As such, they differ sharply from the soldiers in Stalin era movies. In most Stalin era films, the soldiers, as extensions of the state, were always armed, did not hesitate to use their weapons, and were usually successful. Neither Alexander Nevskii nor the simple woman from the collective harbored any doubts about their moral superiority over their enemy. In some cases (such as in *Alexander Nevskii*) there was a Christian underpinning to these beliefs. The prince and the woman from the Russian countryside had no compunction about using their weapons against their enemies. Indeed, the movies generally depicted them doing so with gusto.

This tendency to solve problems by exterminating whatever stood in one's path began fading from movies in the Khrushchev era. In *Cranes Are Flying*, the hero dies without killing any of the enemy, perhaps without even firing a shot in anger. Yet, he and his comrades were still bearing arms. The implication was that contact with the enemy was imminent and losses on both sides were anticipated.

The situation in *Ivan's Childhood* is different. Not only does the hero not bear arms but the offensive capabilities of his comrades are rather vague. The characters in the movie, both Russian soldiers and civilians, are presented exclusively as sufferers at the hands of the enemy.

In one scene, Ivan is crossing a river separating the German and Russian forces. On the German side he sees the corpses of Red Army scouts hanged by the Germans. A sign affixed to their bodies reads WELCOME. In another scene, he recalls the brutal killing of his mother by the enemy. However, throughout the movie, he not only avoids offensive military action but he remains unarmed. These images all contribute to the idea of the essential Christianity and morality of the Russian nation, which, despite its suffering, turns the other cheek and brings no suffering to her enemies. The Soviet victory over Germany is portrayed as a mystical act where personal sacrifice plays a major role. It resembles the mystical symbolism of the resurrection of Christ, which the rational, Euclidean mindset of the West (which worships force and egoism) cannot understand. These motifs emerged during the Khrushchev era and became a major trend in the movies of the Brezhnev era.

The attitude that regarded meekness and humanitarianism as essential elements of Russian culture led Russian intellectuals, including most movie directors, to view the revolution quite differently than their predecessors. While most movies continued glorifying the revolutionary period, movies directed by adherents to Russophilism began approaching this subject differently. In their view, the terror and violence of the revolution were essentially foreign to the humanitarian nature of the Russian people. The essential goodness of the Russian people precluded them from killing even their worst enemies (such as the fascists). How, therefore, could they have inflicted such pain and suffering on themselves?

The only possible answer was that Bolshevism was a non- Russian phenomenon imposed from above. One could argue endlessly about the source of the malady but its essential non-Russian character was beyond question. As soon as Russians could be liberated from these forces, their benign characteristics would naturally come to the fore.

This theme is clearly seen in Chukhrai's *The Forty-First* (1956). The movie is essentially a remake of an earlier film with the same name. As in the first movie, the story is set during the civil war and the major protagonist is a female sniper who falls in love with a White officer. Still, although the external canvas of the new movie is similar, its essential message is completely different. In the new *Forty-First*, private relationships, even with a class enemy, are understandable if reprehensible. In the older *Forty-First*, the protagonist is a sort of ferociously belligerent Red Amazon. She is a member of the exploited class attempting to participate in the class struggle on an equal footing with men. In the newer version, her revolutionary sanguinity is an artificial cover for her real essence: passionate femininity requiring love and caring. This implicit criticism of the heroine's military involvement was, of course, due in part to the Russophiles' rather negative view of the emerging role of women in society. Most Russophiles strongly believed that women should fill only traditional roles and that serving in the army was both aberrant and unsuitable for a woman. Still, sexism alone cannot explain everything. The heroine's behavior must be placed in the context of the Russophile (or more precisely proto-Slavophile, since Russophilism would be fully developed only later) ideology.

For Russophiles, as noted above, Russia is the only true Christian country. It is the collective embodiment of Christ himself, characterized by meekness and abhorrence of violence. At the same time, Russia "herself" is considered an essentially female concept (the idea of the essential femininity of the Russian soul has its roots in nineteenth-century Russian religious and Slavophile philosophy), implying kindness and aversion to violence. In this sense, the image of Christ is more properly represented by the Virgin Mary. She, in a sense, is more Christian than Christ, because whereas Christ was at times ferocious toward his enemies, Mary never acted with anything but kindness and compassion.

Therefore, the sharpshooter, as a Russian woman and to a certain extent the embodiment of the Russian spirit, must be kind and loving. The movie implicitly paints her role as that of a miscast wife and mother. This could be characterized as "positive sexism," in that, although women should play a much different role in society than men, they are in no way inferior to men and, in fact, possess a certain superiority over them. Only a woman can beget new life. This implies that, as a woman, the mother is tender, kind, and ready to sacrifice and comfort. In essence, a female's characteristics are perfectly Russian (and therefore perfectly Christian). Because men cannot give birth, they are more predisposed to cruelty and egotism. From this perspective, the sharpshooter's departure from the traditional female role to the male role of a soldier is not a sign of emancipation (as would be the case in an American movie) but an act of degeneration.

Russophilism did not totally discard the notion that the Russian male could embody Christian characteristics and be kind and loving. However, he could go astray much more easily than could a Russian woman. Even Christ himself strayed somewhat from his forgiving mode, for example, consigning heretics to the flames of hell. However, it was Mary's intercession that saved these unfortunate people. Thus, man, with his additional propensity for cruelty and egotism, was more inclined to fall prey to Western influences (Western culture in this case representing cruelty and egotism).

In this context, the brutality of both the Red and White armies is presented as something foreign to the hero's national character—as a disease that overwhelmed Russia. The gravity of the disease and its utter alienness to Russia's very essence is symbolized by the transformation of the Russian female (that most lovable creature designed to bring life and caring) into a viciously masculinized parody. Whereas in the older *Forty-First* the transformation of the woman into a sort of politically active female eunuch is viewed as an elevation and purification, the new version portrays this transformation as the greatest of perversions. Consequently, the move from the public, politically oriented life of a sniper into the private, internally oriented life of a lover was viewed as an act of regeneration.

The woman's purification from man's essentially anti-Russian characteristics is symbolized by her bullet missing her forty-first victim. Whereas in the older *Forty-First*, the act of missing was portrayed as a weakness, the new movie portrayed it completely differently: as the subconscious revolt of her femininity (her Russian Christian kindness) against the characteristics of the foreign male brutality that had overcome her. Thus, the reassertion of her femininity was nothing less than the reassertion of her Russianness.

The isolation of the sharpshooter and her intended victim from the Red and White armies is significant in that both armies symbolize the artificial political milieu that transformed the two Russians into cruel monsters. Their detachment from the army and their location in an uninhabited area helps them become liberated from the pressures of the army and foreign values (read: the class struggle) and allows them to reassert their essential Russian characteristics.

NOTES

1.   With the installation of Brezhnev's regime the theme of Stalin's repressions was totally taboo for several years. For this reason, the clear allusions in *Silence* to past unfair persecution of one of its heros were totally ignored by the Soviet authors who wrote about Soviet cinema in this period (see Groshev et al.1969 p. 456). Some authors preferred not to speak about this movie, which was quite popular when it was screened at all (see Vorontsov and Rachuk 1980 or Zorkaya 1989).

11

Movies in the Period of Conservatism (1968–1985): The Use of Diversified Official Ideology for Social Critique

The 1970s and the first half of the 1980s were labeled the period of stagnation by Gorbachev's ideologues. To some extent, this tag was correct because it reflects the orientation of the Brezhnevian dominant elite toward stability as the major goal in politics. The regime avoided political and social innovations but was at the same time against a return to Stalinist repression.

In this specific political climate, Soviet cinematographers were forced to abandon their cherished hopes of the sixties about the liberalization of society. However, they still were able to produce relatively honest movies mostly about private life and even some minor social problems, especially if they gave credit to a Russophilism supported by some factions in the Kremlin. In addition, even in these times there were a few film directors like Alexander Askol'dov and Andrei Tarkovskii who dared to challenge the regime with movies that were still loyal to official ideology but contained some elements that irritated officials.

THE POLITICAL AND IDEOLOGICAL SITUATION IN 1968

The October 1964 coup removed Khrushchev from office and eliminated his liberal policies. Afterward, the country gradually entered a period of political reaction. In the aftermath of the coup, the ruling elite still pretended to be friendly toward the intelligentsia, and the period 1964–1968 continued, to some extent, Khrushchev's thaw. With the Soviet invasion of Czechoslovakia in 1968, however, the new regime began eliminating any form of opposition from public life.

Although the policies of the new leadership did not involve the expected sweeping restoration of Stalinist repression, they nevertheless brought significant hardship to intellectual and artistic life. This included increasingly strict control over the movie industry.

The Brezhnev regime and its policies initially faced strong resistance from intellectuals. They responded to the ruling elite's reactionary actions with demonstrations, *samizdat* (self-published underground) publications, public protest letters, the publication of literary works abroad, and even the creation of independent political organizations. This opposition was gradually stifled, however, by the party leadership and the KGB, who carried out a campaign of arrests, exile, forced silence (through blackmail), and corruption. The regime successfully bought the cooperation of many prominent intellectuals, including filmmakers, with promotions, foreign travel, and material goods.

Still, despite the repression and corruption, the Brezhnev regime could not eliminate the intense ideological struggle engulfing Soviet society. The political establishment continued to be disunited. Various factions espoused different ideologies even though they all accepted socialism as the core. The existence of some ideological diversity permitted intellectuals and filmmakers to find scattered supporters for movies with alternative ideological orientations. They were also able to continue their limited critique of Soviet society and its official ideology. The views espoused by intellectuals, with the exception of those following party lines, provided the opportunity for social analysis of Soviet life. Of course, they could not begin to touch its fundamentals until Gorbachev's ascendance to power.

Four major ideologies of the political elite, which can be regarded as various versions of the core official ideology, found their way into Soviet films between 1970 and 1985: the official Brezhnevian ideology, neo-Stalinist ideology, neo-Leninist (or liberal socialist) ideology, and Russophile ideology. The most important ideological battle during this period was between the last two ideologies.

These four ideologies differed from one other in their central values, their attitudes toward the importance of change in Soviet society, their explanation of the causes of stagnation and decline, and the social programs they offered to rejuvenate society. The central value for the bureaucratic (Brezhnevian) and neo-Stalinist ideologies was the might of the state. Social progress, and to some degree individual freedom, was central to the neo-Leninist ideology. The Russophiles regarded national traditions and national religion as sacred.

Except for the bureaucratic ideology, which was strongly conservative, all of the ideologies demanded the radical transformation of Soviet society. Of course, these dynamic ideologies offered different explanations for the Soviet malaise. Neo-Stalinist ideology identified the causes as the demoralization and low labor ethics of the masses, while Neo-Leninists blamed bureaucratization and the current system's lack of public influence. Russian nationalistic ideology blamed the pernicious influence of the West and alien elements in the country as well as the concomitant abandonment of national traditions. Of course, non-Russian nationalistic ideologies blamed Russification and the Soviet system.

Each ideology also had its own vision of a better future. Neo-Stalinists saw a radical strengthening of discipline, firm centralization of the economy, and restoration of order as the key to the country's recovery. Neo-Leninists favored the active participation of the masses in economic and political activity while under the control of bureaucracy. Russian nationalists regarded the main goal as combating Western influence and restoring the old values.

The democratic ideology, with its Western values, was totally absent from public life and from Soviet cinema. Censorship did not allow even hints of it in films. (About the ideological struggle in Russia in the 1970s, see Shlapentokh 1988, 1990.)

THE POLITICAL BEHAVIOR OF FILMMAKERS

In the 1960s and 1970s, most filmmakers were dissident in thought but conformist in behavior. Only Andrei Tarkovskii and Alexander Askol'dov publicly maintained their dissident positions. As a result, Tarkovskii defected to the West and Askol'dov abandoned the movie industry altogether. Other filmmakers tried to play to those factions of the political establishment that best suited their views.[1]

In terms of civic courage, cinematographers lagged far behind writers and painters, not to mention scholars, from whose ranks emerged numerous dissidents. Not until 1985 and 1986, when Mikhail Gorbachev called on intellectuals to help him in his struggle against the old ideology, did filmmakers begin to contribute significantly to the political struggle. Given Gorbachev's blessing, however, their undertakings were far less risky.

Most filmmakers gravitated toward neo-Leninist ideology, which was the most liberal of the four. This ideology, purporting to claim to be loyal to the regime, criticized some elements of social life. Neo-Leninist filmmakers included Mikhail Romm, El'dar Riazanov, Rolan Bykov, Vadim Abdrashitov, and Nikolai Gubenko. Other cinematographers, including Andrei Tarkovskii, Nikita Mikhalkov, and Vasilii Shukshin, were influenced by Russophile ideology. This ideology, which had common elements with the Brezhnevian ideology, also allowed for some opposition to Soviet life.

By contrast, few filmmakers consistently supported neo-Stalinist ideology. Among those who strongly adopted this ideology were Iulian Semenov and Tatiana Lianozova, with their TV serial *Seventeen Moments of Spring* (1973), and *Confrontation* (1985).

The conflicts between various ideologies in Brezhnev's period as revealed in movies demonstrated an especially dramatic and conflicting relationship: both collusion and outright fighting between bureaucrats and intellectuals. Also important was the presentation of the masses, especially ethnic Russians, since Russophilism became so important toward the end of Brezhnev's regime. Each ideology, in fact, incorporated some aspects of Russophilism into their ideological space.

THE MAJOR ACTORS IN MOVIES OF BREZHNEV'S TIME

The Bureaucracy

During this time, party bosses or state officials were the focus of the majority of Soviet movies, regardless of the movie's ideological orientation. With the exception of a few films reflecting official Brezhnev era ideology,[2] Soviet movies of the 1970s and 1980s were generally hostile to bureaucrats (although this hostility pales compared to that seen in movies after 1985). Of the various ideologies, neo-Leninism was the most preoccupied with the bureaucracy. However, movies reflecting Russophile and democratic ideologies tended to portray Soviet bureaucrats in the same light as did neo-Leninist movies.

Two images of the bureaucracy were developed in Soviet movies. Although both denounced bureaucrats as those most responsible for the defects of Soviet life, the images differ in their respective theories regarding the origins of existing problems.

The first theory, referred to as the extermination theory, suggested that the Soviet Union's current problems were rooted in the Stalin era, when the best apparatchiks were exterminated. The second theory, referred to as the degeneration theory, saw the present bureaucracy as a product of the degeneration of the party apparatus that started almost immediately after the civil war of 1917–1921.

The extermination theory, which emerged during Khrushchev's time, clearly distinguishes between the revolutionary regime (which extended from the beginning of the Bolshevik Revolution to the time of the great purges) and the Stalin era. Those who participated in the revolution and the civil war are presented as honest and unselfish people devoted to the cause of communism. Conversely, those who followed these events are portrayed as cynical, despotic, and totally lacking concern for the public good. The Stalinists' ascendance to power is seen as a conspiracy, and any fundamental continuity between the Lenin and Stalin regimes is denied. The distinction between the two regimes is supported by the fact that Lenin's old guard, the generation of the revolution, was physically exterminated by the Stalinists.

Alexei German's film *My Friend Lapshin* (1984) provides a clear example of these perceived discontinuities between the regimes of Lenin and Stalin. The movie portrays life in 1935, when the mass terror had just begun. Lapshin, the film's protagonist, is the chief of the criminal investigation department in a small provincial town. He is endowed with positive characteristics that clearly distinguish him from others in the bureaucracy. He and his friends have no interest in careers or material goods and live in a small, crowded apartment. He is democratically oriented and intensely dedicated to his job of defending the people.

It is clear that the director wants to present Lapshin, his friends, and colleagues as ideal personalities. Interestingly, the film ignores the repressions against peasants and other enemies of the people in which Lapshin had to participate. Only once is the word *Solovki*—the name of a notorious concentration camp created in the 1920s—mentioned, and even then it comes up in a rather facetious way. Although we are told that Lapshin was wounded in the civil war and that he still suffers, we hear nothing about the sufferings of others, e.g., the class enemies, who are depicted as criminals and cruel, rural bandits.

Similar idealization of the purged party apparatus is seen in Tengiz Abuladze's *Repentance* (1984). Those sent to their deaths by Varlam, the head of the city, are depicted as noble and devoted party members. Parallel themes are also apparent in Piotr Todorovskii's *Wartime Romance* (1984).

Viewers of Iaropolk Lapshin's *Prolong the Enchantment* (1984) are presented with the same basic victim image, but with a few variations. In modern society, replete with cynicism and consumerism, the hero, an old party member who spent time in prison or in a camp, is unable to receive moral support even from his children and grandchildren.

Other films reflect a somewhat different vision of Soviet bureaucrats and apparatchiks, mostly sharing the theory of the degeneration of party bureaucrats almost immediately after the revolution. Nikolai Gubenko's *And Life, and Tears, and Love* (1983), Andrei Mikhalkov-Konchalovskii's *Siberiade* (1979), and Ilia Averbakh's *Declaration of Love* (1978) are good examples of such films.

The director of *And Life, and Tears, and Love*, like that of *Lapshin*, juxtaposes different generations of apparatchiks. Unlike the director of *Lapshin*, however, he sees basic continuity between the bureaucrats of the first period and those of the second. *And Life, and Tears, and Love* presents revolutionary heroes in a generally positive light and even with some irony, despite their occasional cruelty in fighting for their ideals (the script compares the terrors of the Russian Revolution with those of the French Revolution). The bureaucrats of the 1930s, however, are presented as cruel, unprincipled brutes. The 1930s bureaucrats—now residents of the nursing home in which the film unfolds—are the most negative characters in the film. One of them, an old lady, is portrayed as a fanatic who admires power even when it is used for the persecution of honest people. Such was the case in the period of the purges. The woman excitedly tells of her infatuation with a political scoundrel who was active in the mass repressions. Although not denying differences between the apparatchiks of the 1920s and 1930s, the film suggests that both were created by the same political system. Even the old revolutionary song "We Boldly Will March Forward Fighting for Soviet Power and We Will All Die Fighting for It" is used in a clearly ironic way, by implying that the revolution devours its children.

By presenting Soviet history from the early 1920s through the 1970s, *Siberiade*, even more than *And Life, and Tears, and Love*, emphasized the continuity between different generations of Soviet bureaucrats and the gradual degeneration of the Bolshevik Revolution's ideals and institutions. The film begins its portrayal of Russian history with a picture of those who were involved in revolutionary activities in Russia at the beginning of the century. The devotion and selflessness of the revolutionaries of this period are beyond reproach, although the film shows that they were ready to use violence to implement their noble, utopian ideas. The filmmaker tries to give the impression that the utopian vision of the future, as well as the revolution it inspired, elevated the human spirit, pushed revolutionaries to self-sacrifice, and brought them closer to the ordinary people. These lofty ideals are presented as vindicating the revolution's violence, especially when it was directed against its enemies.

Using one family as the unit of observation, the director portrays the gradual degeneration of the Soviet bureaucracy. The first generation of bureaucrats, born of the revolution, is depicted as hardworking, unselfish, modest, and inspired by great goals. In the 1930s, however, this generation begins to lose its morale and broadens the scope of its repression to include even loyal individuals. High ideals disappear from the minds of officials as they are increasingly absorbed with material concerns. The film goes on to show the officials' children completely turning their backs on the ideals of communism.

According to *Siberiade*, the 1950s and 1960s marked a new phase in the degeneration of Soviet society and bureaucracy. This degeneration is represented in the character of a general who becomes the first secretary of the regional party committee after the war. However, the character is not totally without merit since it is clear that his professional work is extremely important to him. Unlike his visionary predecessors, how-ever, he pursues the narrow, parochial interests of his region with little concern for the country. Moviegoers see the regional party secretary, already distanced from the ordinary people, surrounded by obsequious assistants and lacking regular contact with the masses. Flying about his region like a demigod, he descends to earth for occasional conversations with the common people, who are insincere with him. Only a few very old people, by taking the role of court jesters, can speak freely with him. His own boss, a secretary of the Central Committee, is still more arro-gant and does not even invite him to sit down when speaking with him in his Moscow office.

Declaration of Love provides a subtle, veiled portrayal (this was, of course, the Brezhnev era) of all postrevolution bureaucrats as schemers and seekers of privilege who are deeply inimical to the masses and to the interests of the country. Even though the first apparatchik presented in the film, an official in CHEKA, spares the life of the main hero (a future writer), he is depicted as a gloomy individual who sends dozens of people from the cellars of the secret police to the firing squad. The next apparatchik depicted in the film is the party editor of a 1920s magazine who mercilessly demands that his authors adjust their material to fit official slogans. Although the film does not elaborate on the life of the writer during the postwar period, we learn that it was only near the end of his life, in the mid-1970s, that he was able to overcome the obstruction of bureaucrats and publish his first book.

Although bureaucrats in some neo-Leninist-oriented films, such as *Siberiade*, seem to care about their professional obligations, bureau-crats in other films are portrayed as almost entirely devoid of any genu-ine sense of responsibility toward society. Films such as Alexander Gel'man's *We, the Undersigned* (1981) and Sergei Mikaelian's *Fell in Love at My Own Request* (1982) are particularly interesting in this regard. Bureau-crats in these films are concerned primarily with their privileges and are not above semicriminal or even criminal activity if it can improve their well-being (see, for example, *We, the Undersigned*). Striving to preserve their privileges and their prestigious jobs, these bureaucrats become quite cynical, resourceful, and cunning. The films provide detailed de-scriptions of the methods used by Soviet bureaucrats to survive and to satisfy their own ambitions. Two of the methods, accommodation and demagoguery, are discussed below.

Accommodation

In their portrayal of the Soviet bureaucracy as the main culprit behind Soviet problems, neo-Leninist films criticize the apparatchiks' abilities to adjust to new policies and trends without forfeiting their positions or their privileges.

V. Popov's *Encounter with My Youth* (1982) shows how easily a bureaucrat can undermine a positive policy (in this case, the expansion of worker participation in management) by only pretending to implement it. In the film, a shrewd but corrupt bureaucrat advises his old friend, the director of a large plant, how to adapt to the new campaign without relinquishing his old, paternalistic style of management.

In Isaak Friedberg's *My Dear Edison* (1986), the director of a research institute is forced to adapt to a campaign promoting modest life-styles. The director is building a resort house for the institute replete with special rooms sumptuously decorated for himself and his guests—big shots from the capital who come to inspect the institute's activities. In the middle of the campaign against corruption, the director decides that to keep these rooms would be dangerous. With no qualms whatsoever, he orders everything that bespeaks of luxury destroyed in order to hide his intentions. *My Dear Edison*, like other films, portrays bureaucrats as interdependent, mutually supportive criminals able to adapt their behavior to almost any political situation. As *My Dear Edison* suggests, any attempt to remove corrupt and indifferent bureaucrats through the use of bureaucratic means is futile.

Demagoguery

Soviet films are especially attentive to the use of sophistry, obfuscation, and propaganda by bureaucrats in defense of their position and privileges. Along with directly distorting the truth, bureaucrats are often depicted as recognizing various problems and demonstrating a certain level of objectivity and sensitivity to human needs only to forget their promises the next moment. This depiction is central to Iosif and Victor Olshanskiis' *Director of a Children's Home* (1984).

Bureaucrats are portrayed as having developed a complex system of arguments to justify their unlawful behavior and their failures. Among these arguments is Russian chauvinism. This argument—"we are all Russians"—is used in *We, the Undersigned* to persuade the chief of the commission to sign fake papers regarding a construction project. Nationalistic justifications are also used by the journalists in A. Sirenko's *The Top Guy* (1986), (a film influenced by Gorbachev) who prepare an inaccurate report on life in the village.

A similar vision of the bureaucracy is presented in Gubenko's *The Life of Vacationers* (1981), which revolves around life in a vacation home. In the film, the wife of an important bureaucrat castigates the West for its promiscuity while remaining open to romantic liaisons with every man she meets.

Neo-Leninist films accuse bureaucrats of behaving even more duplic-
itously with foreigners than with their own subjects. A bureaucrat in
Leonid Bykov's *Leveret* (1985), a disgusting man servile to his boss and
tough to his subordinates, shows no desire to improve the life of the
people. He even obstructs the attempts of a youngster to plant a
garden—the only place where the children of the suburb can play.
When this bureaucrat is approached by foreigners, however, he behaves quite differently by demonstrating exceptional concern for other
people.

Positive Images of the Bureaucracy

As mentioned earlier, negative presentations of bureaucrats are central to most Soviet movies. In neo-Stalinist-oriented movies, however,
bureaucrats, especially those active in the repressive apparatus (i.e., the
KGB, the police, and the army), are treated differently.

Like neo-Leninism, neo-Stalinism appeared as a response to the economic stagnation and corruption of the Brezhnev era. Although similar
to neo-Leninism in its critique of bureaucracy, neo-Stalinism favors a
different approach to change. While neo-Leninist movies assume that
the bureaucracy should be controlled from below, neo-Stalinist movies
trust neither the intellectuals nor the masses. considering them, like the
bureaucracy, to be in need of control from above. Because the neo-
Stalinist political design implies a strong central power, neo-Stalinist
movies approach the state mechanism more conservatively than do neo-
Leninist movies. As a result, neo-Stalinists have failed to elaborate a
strongly negative image of bureaucracy similar to that presented by the
neo-Leninists. They concentrate their attention instead on portraying
positive images of Russia's rulers (such as representatives of security
forces, the militia, and the army), whom they view as central to the
country's rejuvenation. The rulers' positive qualities are emphasized,
thereby distinguishing them from members of Brezhnev's bureaucracy.

Perhaps the most positive image of a party apparatchik was presented
by Semenov and Lianozova, who transformed Semenov's novel into the
famous TV serial *Seventeen Moments of Spring*. In the serial, the Soviet
Communist Isaeiv, posing as the SS man Schtirlitz, penetrates the highest echelons of power in wartime Berlin and outsmarts the most perspi-
cacious intelligence officers in the Nazi capital.

In Semonov and Lianozova's *Confrontation*, a police (read KGB) major
is presented as a national hero and as a potential savior of society.
Because neo-Stalinists wish to preserve the authority of the state, they
are less openly critical of the bureaucracy. Although the film's hero is
clearly displeased with the bureaucracy, he rarely directly criticizes party

officials. During the segments of the film concerned with the pursuit of a traitor, a party bureaucrat appears only once. He is portrayed as a negative character who actually obstructs the search. The hero appeals to practically every sector of Soviet society for assistance in his search but fails to solicit help from the party apparatus.

Confrontation clearly emphasizes the positive characteristics of KGB members. According to the film, KGB agents oppose criminal and semi-criminal activity and are thus quite different from the corrupt, Brezhnev-type party bureaucrats. The secret police, particularly those at the top, are never portrayed as using their positions to obtain privileges. One of the film's heroes, a Georgian KGB man who, due to his nationality, is especially open to being portrayed as prone to semilegal activities, points out that the meat he purchased for a party was obtained absolutely legally.

Another of the film's heroes is a high-ranking KGB officer who stays in a hotel along with ordinary people. His apartment is modest and a lower-ranking provincial KGB man is heard bragging that he enjoys a better apartment than his superior. The hero's clothes are not flashy and a tailor contemptuously remarks about his unstylish manner of dress. He is not seen shopping at any special stores. The canteen where he entertains a female journalist apparently contains no special products or reduced prices. While in the provinces, he dines at a colleague's apartment.

The KGB officer is also portrayed as a good family man. He calls his wife regularly and rejects the sexual advances of a young woman. He exhibits great physical courage and appears to have no nationalist prejudices. Although a Jew in the film is presented as a negative character, the hero is heard referring to another Jew in glowing terms. The fact that the traitor being tracked is a Russian further demonstrates that *Confrontation*'s creator's had no intention of catering to Russian chauvinism.

Neo-Stalinist films such as *Confrontation* also portray bureaucrats as very well-educated and respectful of intellectuals. *Confrontation*'s main hero, for example, demonstrates his respect through his knowledge of and regard for Mandel'shtam, the famous elitist Russian poet. KGB men also demonstrate their appreciation for intellectuals through their free-thinking. Our hero clashes with party officials who try to stop a journalist's activity on the grounds that her publications will provide fuel for bourgeois propaganda. He also demonstrates his appreciation for Vladimir Vysotskii, the famous semiofficial bard of the Brezhnev era. His affinity for intellectuals is further highlighted by its contrast with the main villain's disdain for literature.

Unlike classical Stalinism, neo-Stalinist films portray Soviet apparatchiks as humane and compassionate toward ordinary people. However, direct comparisons are sometimes made between the two groups of Stalinists. In *Confrontation*, for example, the hero often disagrees with those who idealize Stalin's era and complain about the excessive humanism of the present regime. He is also seen being extremely polite to a suspected criminal who complains that the Stalin era has returned. Since this suspect is clearly a negative character, it is evident that his complaints are baseless. The hero points out that the neo-Stalinist ruling elite will not repeat the Stalin era practice of spying on its citizens. He even states that he does not care about citizens' correspondence with foreign countries—including Israel.

Because the army and the militia are also included in the repressive apparatus, they enjoy treatment similar to that given the KGB in neo-Stalinist films. In films with sympathy for some elements of neo-Stalinism such as V. Maksakov's *I Took Control of the City* (1979), Riazanov's *A Train Station for Two* (1983), Veniamin Dorman's *Night Accident* (1981), Alexander Gordon's *Passing Twice* (1979), Mikhail Ptashuk's *Black Castle* (1980), and Vadim Zlobin's *Sunday at Six-Thirty* (1988), militia members are presented as honest and courageous.

In S. Puchinian's *From the Life of the Head of the Prosecutors' Office* (1983), for instance, a prosecutor who happens to live in the same communal apartment as a former criminal becomes involved in the criminal's family life in order to save it from collapse. Although the prosecutor's involvement is unceremonious, and clearly violates the privacy of others, it is clear that his motives are noble.

In *Uneasy Sunday* (1983), V. Georgiev's *Close to the Edge of Danger* (1983), Pavel Liubimov's *Second Time in Crimea* (1984), and E. Orashchenko's *Three Percent Risk* (1984), members of the armed forces are presented in much the same way as are members of the KGB and the militia. Since members of the armed forces do not belong to the upper echelons of power, however, they are presented as somewhat less impeccable than members of the KGB and the militia. For example, personal friction develops among those in the army and some of them are rude to their subordinates (e.g., in *Uneasy Sunday*).

Movies with neo-Stalinist motives also present managers as part of the ruling group [see, for example, Ilia Gurin's *Old Debts* (1980), Riazanov's *An Office Romance* (1977), Victor Sadovskii's *Female Rivals* (1980), and Popov's *Encounter with My Youth* (1982)]. As members of the ruling elite, managers are praised for their strong will and dedication to work. At the same time, however, managers are depicted as even less qualified for admission into the highest echelons of Soviet society than are representatives of the militia and the army. Managers, such as the hero of *Old Debts*, who is seen in romantic liaisons with women, are presented as being less puritanical and disinterested than are KGB people. In addition, managers are often shown treating people rather roughly.

The Intellectuals

Intellectuals are presented dualistically in Soviet movies of this period. On one hand, most Soviet movies depict members of the intellectual community as devoted to their professional work and social ideals. Filmmakers try, albeit inconsistently, to defend the intellectuals. On the other hand, Soviet movies also tend to denounce the depravity of intellectuals. They are presented as equally corrupt as apparatchiks. The tenor in portraying intellectuals was set, once again, by the neo-Leninists. This tenor was supported by the neo-Stalinists and later, in Gorbachev's times, by democrats, but was given only partial support by the Russophiles.

The dominant representations of Soviet intellectuals are discussed separately below.

The Positive Portrayal of Intellectuals

True intellectuals appear as the only valuable heroes in Neo-Leninist movies. Great emphasis is placed on their creative nature and dedication to professional duties—traits that are depicted as lacking in ordinary people.

Praise for creative intellectuals is found in such movies as A. Beck and A. Misharin's *Engineer Berezhkov* (1988). Berezhkov, despite the obstacles created by the Soviet system, continues his activities as an inventor.

Similar treatment of intellectuals is seen in movies such as V. Grigoriev's *The Grasshopper* (1986), in which a young, noble scholar absorbed with his work permits himself to be fooled by a young adventurist. He succumbs to her trap and they marry. When they eventually divorce, he gives her his car and apartment—invaluable assets in Moscow.

In *Kind People* (1980), one sees a historian committed to his job. In Vladimir Bortko's *The Blonde around the Corner* (1984) we meet a similarly dedicated scientist. The image of an honest and sympathetic musician is seen in Riazanov's *A Train Station for Two* (1983). Even apparently corrupt intellectuals can be dedicated to their jobs, as in Riazanov's *Garage* (1980). This commendation of intellectuals as devoted professionals continued in the first years of *perestroika*. R. Goriaev's *The Everyday Life and Holidays of Serafima Gliukina* (1988) describes the selfless activity of a female cultural worker from whom the movie derives its name. In B. Ianshin's *Fast Train* (1988), an intellectual in a remote city risks running a semiprivate theater in order to keep Russian liberal cultural traditions alive.

According to neo-Leninist and neo-Stalinist films, intellectuals also have another positive characteristic: they generally lack any national prejudice. Film producers identify minorities either through their place of origin and accent or through some other identifiable national trait. Residents of the Caucasus, for example, are often presented as temperamental, as in Alla Surikova's *Vanity of Vanities* (1979); as having a patriarchal approach to life, as in Vladimir Rogovoi's *Married Bachelor* (1983); or as being hospitable, as in V. Makarov's *Kidnapping of the Century* (1981). According to neo-Leninist films, the national characteristics of minorities do not cause them problems when dealing with Russian intellectuals. These relationships, as manifested in liaisons and intermarriages between Russian intellectuals and minorities, are presented as being quite harmonious.

Intellectuals as Fighters against Bureaucracy

When portraying the fight against bureaucracy, films with neo-Leninist, liberal tendencies look not toward the masses, and certainly not toward the moral recovery of the apparatchiks, but toward single, brave individuals—usually intellectuals. These heroes in the fight against the bureaucracy are likened to the revolutionaries of the past and they are presented as kind and concerned about others [see the Olshanskiis' *Director of a Children's Home*, Friedberg's *My Dear Edison*, Sirenko's *The Top Guy*, Natalia Troshchenko's *The Long Road to Herself* (1983), Bykov's *Leveret*, Gubenko's *And Life, and Tears, and Love* and Averbach's *Declaration of Love* (1978)]. In many cases, such heroes are quite romantic and have great respect for love [*Valentin and Valentina* (1983, scriptwriter Roshekin), Mikaelian's *Fell in Love at My Own Request*, Riazanov's *A Train Station for Two*, Troshchenko's *The Long Road to Herself*, and Goraiev's *The Everyday Life and Holidays of Serafima Gliukina*).

Often, intellectual heroes first try to improve bad situations by turning to party officials for help. However, they face either open animosity (*My Dear Edison, The Top Guy*) or a bureaucratic response that implies no real action (*Leveret, Director of a Children's Home*). Although such heroes occasionally find positive representatives in the bureaucracy, these bureaucrats usually urge the hero to stop his activity and concentrate on some minor local improvements (*The Top Guy*). Disenchanted with bureaucracy, the hero finally appeals to ordinary people, assuming that they will be eager to support his noble goal.

During the Brezhnev era, when corruption and conformity had reached their peak, movies praised those intellectuals who defied the system. They also praised those who abandoned public activity (which actually benefits the party) in order to pursue private life (where the intellectual could preserve his or her honesty). This was the case with Gushchin, the hero of *Late Date* (1986, director unknown).

Intellectuals in Russophile Movies

Although Russophile movies resemble neo-Leninist and democratic movies in their praise of intellectuals, the characteristics being praised are quite different. Whereas neo-Leninist and democratic movies laud intellectuals for their nonconformity and their readiness to fight the bureaucrats, Russophile films emphasize the true intellectual's support for Russian values. Even if these intellectuals go awry, they are easily brought back to traditional tenets.

In several films, worthy intellectuals demonstrate their inclination to make sacrifices for the sake of the Russian people [i.e. Rodion Na-khapetov's *Do Not Shoot the White Swans* (1982), Kheifits's *Married for the First Time* (1980)]. In *Do Not Shoot the White Swans*, a young female teacher reveals her allegiance to Russian values in various ways, including prominently displaying a book on medieval Russian art with a picture of an icon. She also demonstrates her strong interest in Russian classical literature that has strong religious overtones. Most important, of course, is her self-effacing behavior and selfless service. In *Married for the First Time*, the main hero is a self-taught intellectual in the countryside who works to create a museum in the local church and enhance culture in the village.

An intellectual's repentance is shown in Vadim Abdrashitov's *The Turning Point* (1979), which is explicitly influenced by Dostoevsky's *Crime and Punishment* and is imbued with highly religious overtones. The hero of the film, a prosperous, middle-aged intellectual, neglects Russian Christian values. He becomes absorbed with vain and petty issues, such as his scientific career and prestigious vacations.

An accident in which an old woman is hit by the hero's car becomes the turning point in his life. At the beginning of the ordeal, he remains involved in his career and desperately tries to avoid imprisonment. As events unfold, however, he concludes that he is guilty not only of hitting the woman but in a broader sense as well. He begins to realize that his life has been emotionally cold and meaningless. Like Dostoevsky's Raskolnikov, he is ready to be imprisoned in the hope that suffering will purify him.

The hero is acquitted by the court, however, and seems to return to his old life-style. Still, the spiritual awakening triggered by his time of trial and uncertainty is not completely lost. Viewers are given the impression that he is on the path of moral rehabilitation. This theme—the moral recuperation of an intellectual gone astray in a life full of temptation—is seen in other films as well, such as Nikita Mikhalkov's *Kinfolk* (1982).

Russophile movies present the Western life-style as the major threat to the Russian intelligentsia, youth, and, of course, society at large. In *Kinfolk* Western values are blamed for destroying the life of a young girl who, like her mother, is completely under the influence of the West. The girl is too absorbed with the roaring sounds of a Western song and its constant refrain of "I love you" to take the time to answer her mother.

A female professional in Vladimir Men'shov's *Love and Pigeons* (1984), who is an admirer of Western culture, is depicted as deeply unhappy and lonely despite having a successful career. The same theme is presented in *Married for the First Time*, in which young people craving Western pleasures find themselves empty and frustrated.

In Russophile films, Western culture is primarily identified with consumerism and sexual promiscuity. These movies do not ignore the efficiency of the Western economy and science; they simply do not praise such achievements. Moreover, in portraying village life as more virtuous than urban life, Russophile films imply that technological progress is an enemy of high moral values. For this reason, it is ultimately not intellectuals, with their close links to science and to the West, who emerge as the true bastions of Russian values and the hope of the country: It is ordinary people.

Mikhalkov's *A Few Days from the Life of Oblomov* (1980) altered the classic interpretation of Goncharov's novel by portraying Oblomov, who avoids any professional activity or career, as a positive hero. Oblomov is contrasted with Shtolz, who is condemned as a hustler who is unable to appreciate lofty and sublime ideas like his friend can.

Andrei Tarkovskii's films have a special place among movies inspired by Russophile ideology. Representing the liberal wing in the Russophile movement, Tarkovskii was far from xenophobic and he did not explicitly portray Russians as the model for the world. He instead focused on specific features of Russian culture that he admired and that were close to him. In addition, he did this without demonstrating aggressiveness toward other people. His *Soliaris* (1972—based on the novel by the Polish writer Stanislav Lem), in which the director muses about mankind and its future, demonstrates how broad-minded he was. In this movie the heroes, a team of intellectuals, look at the Earth with awe, understanding how vulnerable the population is to any space enemy and how important is the unity of humankind to combat eventual threats.

However, his most important films of the 1970s, including *Andrei Rublev* (1971) and *Mirror* (1975), were about Russia and its destiny. In the first film he continued the line he started in *Ivan's Childhood* (1962), poeticizing spiritual nobility and humbleness. The hero is a Russian painter of the fourteenth century, the famous artist of revered icons. However, Tarkovskii depicts life in Russia at that time in a unflattering way. Such a depiction revolted the Soviet authorities, who were against aggressive Russophiles. In the film, Russian princes invite Mongols to participate in their struggle with each other and easily justify the slaughter of Russians by their allies. At the same time, the Russian people are presented as cruel and savage. This background was necessary for Tarkovskii. He wanted to show his hero as untouched by the reckless environment around him and totally devoted to the lofty ideas of Christianity. The presence of such people was a guarantee of God's support for Russia.

In his somewhat autobiographical film *Mirror*, Tarkovskii was again absorbed with the fate of Russia. He referred to the polemic between Alexander Chaadaiev, a Russian philosopher in the beginning of the nineteenth century, and his famous contemporary, the poet Alexander Pushkin. The director sided with the poet and argued against Chaadaiev's pessimistic vision of the future. The characters of the movie, refined Russian intellectuals, commend Russia for the salvation of Europe from both the Mongol invasion and the Nazis. Even Stalin's terror has some positive implications in that it would cleanse Russians through suffering, thereby raising their spirituality.

The Negative Portrayal of Intellectuals

Although many film directors tried to emphasize the noble features of the intellectuals, others were much more critical of the intellectual community (of which filmmakers are clearly members). In some cases, critical filmmakers presented intellectuals as no better than bureaucrats or the masses. Intellectuals are shown yearning for the same things as bureaucrats (i.e., material comfort and prestige), and as cynical, conformist, and engaged in the perennial quest for pleasures and Western goods.

In their depictions of modern Soviet intellectuals, neo-Leninist films, especially those made prior to 1986, strongly emphasized their sexual permissiveness. A major reason for this focus was that filmmakers, intending to portray the complete cynicism of modern educated individuals and their contempt for any principles and ideals, were unable to discuss the political attitudes of their characters. Due to censorship, filmmakers focused on their characters' total disregard for moral principles in sexual relations in order to make their point.

Love affairs are not always presented as symbols of cynicism, however. Involvement in romance can be the result of the boredom of provincial life, or a woman's compassion for a loser [as in Kheifits's *The Only*

One (1976)]. It is also the result of the younger generation's rebellion against parental domination [Lapshin's *Prolong the Enchantment* (1984)] and of real passion [(Aida Manasarova's *A Fantasy on Love Themes* (1981), Nikolai Lebedev's *Accuse Klava of My Death* (1980)]. In most cases, however, promiscuity or cheating is portrayed as a symbol of the cynicism of Soviet intellectuals and of society in general.

For the most part, libertinism is regarded by filmmakers as a product of Soviet society, not of cultural traditions. Thus, filmmakers always try to avoid national stereotypes. For example, they did not present Caucasians as philanderers although they had a reputation in the USSR for a proclivity toward a sexually loose life-style. In fact, Caucasian men are quite often presented as exemplary family men [*Vanity of Vanities* (1979), *Married Bachelor* (1983)].

Neo-Leninist filmmakers show their heroes cheating and lying not only in connection with their love affairs, but in other arenas as well. The heroes of Georgii Danelia's *Autumn Marathon* (1979) and Roman Balaian's *Flights in the Night and Daydreams* (1983), for example, lie to their wives, mistresses, friends, and colleagues. In fact, they are so enmeshed in lies that they cannot free themselves from the habit even when they want to do so.

The licentious heroes justify their carnal behavior with expressions of concern for the public good—a direct allusion to the hypocrisy of official Soviet ideology. A hero in Bazhanov's *Most Charming and Attractive* (1985), a design institute engineer, is eager to help his institution finish an important project in a province. Although the project requires travel to a distant town, he is ready to sacrifice his time. In truth, however, he really needs this time for another reason: He is a married man in search of a brief affair. The hero's willingness to use bombastic official slogans and cliches that he apparently does not support makes him typical of cynical Soviet intellectuals. The hero of the film *Flights in the Night and Daydreams* is presented in a similar manner. He asks his superior for a day off to meet his elderly mother, but actually wants the time to visit his mistress.

In these films, women are rarely presented as victims of lecherous men (*The Director of a Children's Home* is one exception). Cynical promiscuity is shown to involve females as well as males. The intellectuals and party officials in all of these films are generally rather tolerant of the love affairs of their colleagues, friends, and relatives. They apparently accept lying as well, except when done in excess or to friends. Moral degeneration and cynicism are viewed by intellectuals not as aberrations but rather as normal behavior and sometimes even as positive traits.

In *Most Charming and Attractive*, viewers see a husband and wife who are members of the intelligentsia. The husband openly cheats on his wife. The wife apparently knows about her husband's behavior but this knowledge does not spoil their relationship. In fact, the viewer can easily imagine that she is similarly involved. The film's other heroine, also an intellectual, married a man she did not love. She is enchanted by eighteenth-century French culture (known for its erotic tastes) and quotes La Rochefoucauld. The reference to eighteenth-century French culture by the heroine, who is apparently of dubious reputation, implies that she is not opposed to cheating on her husband. She apparently assumes that by doing so she would be imitating the great courtesans of the French court.

In *Vanity of Vanities*, the female friend of a lonely divorced woman finds her a lover for consolation, but the lover turns out to be married. *Valentin and Valentina* also depicts a liaison between a female intellectual and a married man.

Women do more than fail to regard their partner's cynicism as a negative quality; they openly appreciate it. Cynicism, especially when combined with intellectual sophistication, is considered attractive. It is deemed a characteristic of members of the elite, so people occasionally outwardly demonstrate their libertinism in order to be identified as part of the elite (see, for instance, *Fell in Love at My Own Request*).

Intellectuals are sometimes presented as lazy shirkers (*Autumn Marathon*, *My Dear Edison*). They visit their place of work only to chat and flirt. They sometimes even spend their workdays at home, where they engage in various private activities while still receiving their paychecks. They regard their jobs as a form of welfare (e.g., *My Dear Edison*).

Furthermore, intellectuals and their offspring boast about their privileges in comparison with ordinary people. Higher education (especially in such prestigious establishments as Moscow University), knowledge of foreign languages and cultures (as in *Valentin and Valentina*), and possession of highly sought-after foreign goods are symbols of their privileges. Their contempt for the masses is even greater than their distaste for the bureaucracy. They openly mock their intellectual forefathers, the Populists, who sacrificed their careers to serve the people (*The Top Guy*).

In fact, the majority of intellectuals are depicted as being as attached to their privileges as are the bureaucrats. A hero in *My Dear Edison* is informed that only the connections and high position of one's parents can open the doors of prestigious universities and colleges. Only a few representatives of the common people are fortunate enough to be accepted among the chosen intellectual elite. Edison, the bright fellow at the center of *My Dear Edison*, is among these. However, deprived of a strong and influential parental hand, he can only postpone and not prevent his eventual failure. Instead of graduate school or a good research institute, he is assigned to work in a provincial institution where he apparently is unable to manifest his talents.

Viewers of *Prolong the Enchantment* learn that the Union of Soviet Writers is a closed and privileged caste. Not only do its members enjoy various privileges, including better material conditions than the rest of the population, but they are also able to push aside any competitors. One of the main heroines of the film, a talented poet, was unable to publish her work for this reason.

Special shops are depicted as the exclusive domain of a select group of intellectuals and representatives of the bureaucracy. The film *Married Bachelor* presents a young man, apparently the son of a highly positioned bureaucrat or intellectual, who brags about "certificates" (special checks that allow their holders to purchase coveted goods in special shops) that allowed him to buy a car. In *Director of a Children's Home*, viewers see a youngster whose highly placed intellectual parents have traveled abroad and procured prestigious Western clothes for him. In order to obtain popular Western consumer goods, intellectuals are also depicted as eager to turn to the black market (*Fell in Love at My Own Request*, *Most Charming and Attractive*, *The Blonde around the Corner*).

In Raizanov's *Garage*, the members of a scientific institution engage in bribery in order to ensure the building of a garage. They also frantically struggle to limit the number of those allowed to participate in their garage cooperative. In *The Blonde around the Corner*, even one of the most respectable heroes is tempted to obtain food through illegal channels. Thus, intellectuals are portrayed as people of weak will, a trait that often leads to involvement in criminal or semicriminal activity.

Not only are intellectuals happy with their privileged positions in Soviet society but they are intent on passing them along to their children. In *Director of a Children's Home*, one of the heroes is convinced that higher education is reserved only for privileged groups and that orphans are destined only for factory benches. The movie's hero, though presented as a likable character, sees nothing wrong with this type of caste stratification.

Whereas neo-Leninist movies tend to denounce the intellectuals for their vices and try to appeal to their consciences, neo-Stalinist movies take an altogether different position.

To a certain extent, neo-Stalinists see intellectuals as children who, unable to manage even their own affairs, require a strong power placed above them. An example of this perceived relationship between the ruling elite and the intellectuals is seen in *A Train Station for Two*. The central hero is an intellectual who, having taken the blame for a crime committed by his wife, is placed in a camp. He eventually comes to resent his wife for visiting so infrequently. When he hears that she has arrived and awaits him in a nearby village, the hero refuses to visit her. The camp chief, a militia man, understands that the hero's decision could irreversibly damage his family life. He also understands that the hero, a musician and quite an emotional person, is incapable of reason, even in dealing with his own personal problems. The chief therefore orders the man to see his wife. Although the visitor is not actually his wife, but another woman who loves him, the film implies that this visit was a great consolation for the imprisoned musician. In addition, he had the strong but paternalistic militia man to thank for compelling him to do what was best for him.

The Masses in Liberal Movies

Soviet movies vary more in their portrayal of the masses than of any other group. Russophile movies present a picture of the masses that is very different from that presented in movies influenced by the other three ideologies.

With few exceptions, the Russophiles consider only true ethnic Russians eligible for membership in the masses and Russophile movies generally describe ethnic Russians very positively. By contrast, filmmakers with other ideological orientations do not distinguish between Russians and non-Russians. They tend to describe all of their compatriots rather disparagingly.

The Russophile's sympathetic approach to depicting the ordinary people is examined first.

Ethnic Russians as a Distinct Group

Russophiles strongly emphasizes the basic differences between Russia and the rest of the world, particularly the West. Russophiles view ethnic Russians as the only Christian people able to demonstrate the qualities of meekness, natural nobility, devotion to lofty spiritual principles, and self-sacrifice (see Nesterov 1984; Melentiev 1986). Endowed with such characteristics, Russians have no need of technological progress and economic growth in order to lead happy lives. This explains why Russophilism was so eagerly accepted by the Brezhnev regime in the 1970s. In fact, it was, to a certain extent, incorporated into official ideology as a rationale for stagnation.

Russians during Wartime

One of the most important subjects in Russophile films is war. War is seen as an almost religious experience, providing abundant opportunities to reveal such Christian qualities as meekness and willingness to sacrifice. Peacetime, by comparison, is seen as a time of earthly temptations (e.g., the pursuit of a career and material well-being) when Russians often deviate from the Christian model of behavior. During wartime, the Russian national character manifests itself fully and provides the major base for the nation's strength. Russia's victory in the Second World War is often portrayed as having been due primarily to the emergence of the Russian national character.

Russophile films about the Second World War generally present soldiers and civilians alike as martyrs who are repeating the ordeal of Christ. Film directors avoid showing Russians inflicting suffering on others or killing foreign soldiers on the battlefield [Alov and Naumov's *The Shore* (1984), Igor Talankin's *Shooting Stars* (1982), V. Mosenko's *Children's Home* (1982), Gavriil Egiazarov's *Back Home* (1983)].

The Russophile movies of the 1970s, which portrayed peaceful periods in Soviet history, nevertheless retained a focus on military and army issues. One of the heroes in *Kinfolk* is a war veteran. He is depicted as a vain drunkard abandoned by all, including his wife on whom he constantly cheated. His daughter is shallow and infatuated with the West, and his son is not much better. The single positive character is the veteran's wife, who lives in the countryside.

The conscription of the veteran's son becomes a turning point for all of the family members as they come to bid him farewell, an event that reveals the true essence of their souls. The film culminates with a scene at the railway station where the recruits assemble. The old drunkard-veteran is particularly affected by the event. Wearing all of his war medals, he is overcome with emotion and urges his son to serve the motherland well. The son and his sister, both of whom are strongly affected by the situation, forget their petty personal interests and demonstrate their deep affection for each other, their parents, and the people around them. The entire scene evolves into a sort of religious ceremony in which people repent and attempt to redeem their sins.

The purgatorial role of the army is also depicted in *Muzhiks* (1981), although not as strongly as it is in *Kinfolk*. In *Muzhiks*, a man refuses to marry his fiancée who has allegedly been unfaithful to him. He also rejects a daughter born to him by this woman. Although his elderly parents urge him to adopt the girl, the hero stubbornly refuses. He changes his mind, however, at a wedding party. Immediately following the party he will be entering the army, a fact central to those attending the gathering. At the end of the party, the man talks with the young girl. He decides not only to accept her as his daughter but also to adopt two male children of other fathers, including one who is mute.

The long quarrels between spouses in *Love and Pigeons* also come to an end when their son enters the army. Once again, this sacred institution inspires the most noble feelings in the film's characters.

Russians during Peacetime

War provides the most frequent opportunities for Russians to manifest their noble and spiritual values. However, Russophile movies portray most Russians as behaving in accordance with Christian morals during peacetime as well. There are, of course, numerous Russians who abandon their Christian standards and it is the task of society to help them regain their Russian values.

The true repository of the highest national virtues is the countryside. As a result, Russophile movies directly or, more often, indirectly praise the technological backwardness of the countryside.

The hero of *Do Not Shoot the White Swans* is a village resident with no formal education beyond elementary school. He is neither an achiever nor a hard worker. He does not read books, does not go to movies, and in general does not display any interest in the outside world. Although he is not without creative skills, he exercises them only when he is in a good mood or if he likes his job. If both of these conditions are not met, his professional performance is abysmal. Not only is he unable to adequately perform any official job, he is also unable to sustain his family, the poorest in the village.

Still, he is endowed with several very positive qualities. Like Karataev in Tolstoy's *War and Peace*, he is absolutely content with his daily life. He is absorbed with love, not only for human beings, but for all living creatures. He is extremely generous and absolutely free of vanity and ambition. He possesses artistic talents but does not exploit them. This is not because of his resistance to bureaucratic routine but his absolute carelessness and childlike irresponsibility.

The man, a noble fool, is portrayed as the sole defender of nature against the offenses of civilization. Having been appointed forester, he decides to repopulate a lake with swans, which left it many years earlier. Using money given to him to attend an ecological conference, he buys swans for his lake and dies defending them from poachers. His death, full of religious overtones, is not in vain. Civilization retreats and the lake, as in the remote past, is once again filled with life.

The hero of *Love and Pigeons*, a member of the masses so highly regarded by the Russophiles, also displays the Russians' characteristic low level of education, discomfort with modern life, and passionate love of nature and living things—in this case pigeons. Both the hero and his equally unsophisticated wife are depicted as happy, in contrast to those who try to live by Western standards.

Similar praise of the countryside and its denizens, the sole bearers of compassion and humanism, is seen in Kheifits's *To Whom Do You Belong, Old People?* (1989). Two elderly, homeless people, rejected by a city obsessed with the pursuit of material goals, finally find refuge in the home of a poor peasant woman who, many years ago, had been a neighbor to one of them.

Themes of sacrifice, prominent in war movies and present in the peacetime movies of the 1970s and early 1980s, are also found to a much lesser extent in the movies of the first years of the Gorbachev era. In V. Krishtovich's *Single Woman Wants to Date Someone* (1989), for example, an ordinary seamstress attempts to find a husband. Instead, she encounters a committed drunkard whom she selflessly helps. Similarly, in B. Konunov's *Small Favor* (1988), a single woman in her late thirties rejects her last chance for a normal family life by refusing to marry a famous singer whom she loves. Instead, she persuades him to return to his family even though his wife is an alcoholic. In V. Buturlin's *Gardener* (1989), Lekha, a true Russian, passionately continues to tend a collective farm's garden despite the total indifference and even hostility of others, including his superiors. Likewise, the hero of V. Zheleznikov and V. Lonskii's *Lethargy* (1983), passive and indifferent to both his work and his family, realizes the futility of his life. In a moment of revelation, he nobly sacrifices his life by saving a girl who is being attacked by hooligans.

Another important aspect of Russophile ideology is its antifeminist perspective. In fact, Russophiles regard the emancipation of women as one of Western civilization's greatest vices. *Love and Pigeons* provides a good example this view. This theme is also forcefully portrayed in a number of other films, such as Ilia Frez's *Quarantine* (1983) and Kheifits's *Married for the First Time*. In all of these films, poorly educated, unpretentious, kind, and loving women are contrasted with Westernized, liberated, modern women.

The Masses in Non-Russophile Movies

The neo-Leninist and neo-Stalinist ideologies are even more unanimous in their attitudes toward the masses than they are with respect to the intellectuals. The movies influenced by these two ideologies all reveal a high level of contempt for ordinary people. They portray them as lazy individuals deprived of elementary moral virtues.

Workers and peasants in these films display a weak work ethic (e.g., *Fell in Love at My Own Request*, *The Top Guy*) and are often involved in consumerism [e.g., Adzhar Ibragimov's *Business of the Heart* (1974)]. Members of the public are portrayed as being involved in fraudulent activity, securing positions for which they are not qualified (e.g., *A Train Station for Two*, *Kind People*), obtaining material and equipment for their

businesses through illegal channels, and hoarding scarce goods to obtain useful connections (e.g., *The Blonde around the Corner*).

The involvement of the masses in private activity is clearly shown to
interfere with their performance on the job. In *The Top Guy*, for example,
the peasantry is intensely involved in cultivating private plots while
collective farms are utterly neglected.

Similarly, private activity is regularly portrayed as being connected
with semilegal, if not openly illegal activity. The heroes of *The Kidnapping
of the Century*, for example, must occasionally resort to illegal means to
obtain the services required for them to operate their private business.
Those involved in private activity are also shown dabbling in speculation [Leonid Gaidai's *Sportloto-82*, (1982)] and gold and currency trading
(*Confrontation*), using state equipment to accomplish their speculative
ventures.

Like bureaucrats and intellectuals, the masses crave Western consum-
er goods and are often sexually promiscuous [e.g., *My Dear Edison*,
Mikhalkov-Konchalovskii's *Siberiade* (1979), *The Only One*, *Valentine and
Valentina*, *A Train Station for Two*, *The Life of Vacationers*]. In addition, the
masses are plagued by drunkenness [e.g., *Fell in Love at My Own Request*,
Autumn Marathon, and V. Dosortsev's *A Foreign Case* (1985)].

The public's quest for foreign goods and sexual adventure is shown to
provide further inducement to illegal activity. Desire for video cassettes
(*A Train Station for Two*), Western clothes (*A Train Station for Two*,
Sportloto-82), and other Western goods often leads ordinary people to
participate in the black market.

The masses are also depicted as having a weak sense of social solidarity (*The Only One*, *Fell in Love at My Own Request*) and little social
prestige (*Married Bachelor*, *Fell in Love at My Own Request*). They apparently loathe the bureaucracy and the intellectuals because of the privileges enjoyed by these two groups. These feelings are prompted not
by egalitarian ideals, however, but by envy. In addition, the common
people are portrayed as being equally susceptible to corruption (*My
Dear Edison*). The masses demonstrate little interest in democracy and
are quite content to have their superiors appointed from above (*The
Top Guy*).

Those employed in the service industry receive equally cold treatment
in Soviet movies. Films portraying kind and industrious service workers
usually also present their negative counterparts—workers who are
rude, lazy, or both (e.g., *Director of a Children's Home; The Blonde around
the Corner; And Life, and Tears, and Love; Married Bachelor*). The negative
portrayal of service workers in *We, the Undersigned* includes workers
displaying extreme rudeness in dealing with clients. In addition, it is
implied that these workers, particularly salespersons, are involved in

the theft and hoarding of scarce goods. Private activity in general, such as renting apartments in resort areas [*Please Be My Husband* (1981), scriptwriter E. Akropov)] and distributing hotel beds through bribery, is also depicted negatively. It is implied that the people's indulgence in private activity fills them with greed and alienates them from others.

CONCLUSION

It took almost two years following Stalin's death for Soviet filmmakers to emerge from their oppression. After 1956 many of them radically changed their attitudes toward their work. During Stalin's time, they were absorbed mostly with physical survival and fear, even if they attempted from time to time to use some new artistic means to convey propaganda. However, after Stalin's death they were finally able to convey their own views about life and reality.

The Khrushchev regime remained totalitarian, however, and filmmakers were still far from being able to do films as they wanted. Nevertheless, they did begin to experiment with official ideology and its guardians. For the first time, they were concerned about the gap between their movies and Soviet reality and tried to insert material reflecting the harsh reality of life in the Soviet Union. They also watched developments in the Kremlin closely, trying to exploit the conflicts inside the ruling elite in order to make more truthful films.

Cinematographers, as well as other intellectuals, were generally supported by the broader intelligentsia. Even ordinary people, deprived of access to uncensored information, avidly looked to movies, as well as novels and poetry, for the truth, however defined. Practically all of the films of this period, regardless of their ideological perspective, portray such moral decay among the Soviet people that a moral revival of society is a distant dream. Such moral decay also renders radical economic and social progress extremely unlikely.

These movies provide a rather profound portrait of the Soviet bureaucracy, for example, in a period in which they enjoyed unprecedented autonomy and privileges. The movies, taken together, trace the degeneration of Soviet bureaucrats from Stalin's time to the end of the Brezhnev era. Soviet films are particularly attentive to the use of sophistry, obfuscation, and propaganda by bureaucrats in defense of their position and privileges.

No Soviet sociological data exist that can provide as comprehensive a description of this stratum as movies can. As such, no serious student of Soviet society can afford to ignore Soviet movies as a source of information.

Soviet movies are second only to the mass media in detailing the special role played by the Soviet intellectuals in criticizing Brezhnev's regime. The movies help to illustrate the nature of the country's resistance to the dominant regime in the 1970s. Specifically, they depict a few courageous individuals, prepared to fight for the interests of society, facing off against hostile or, at best, passive bureaucrats, intellectuals, and ordinary people whose attitudes doom any heroic efforts.

Characters representing Russophile ideology emerge as opponents of modernization, of technological progress, and of active, energetic, and professionally competent individuals. They prefer that Russians be motivated by religious and other traditional values.

NOTES

1. Paradzhanov once tried to defend a new script to the authorities, arguing in a letter that the script satisfied all criteria of official ideology, including "Soviet patriotism," "proletarian internationalism," "the socialist motherland," and "trust in the party" (*Iskusstvo Kino* 12, 1990, pp. 32–34).

2. One of them—Ivan Lukinskii's *A Rural Detective* (1969)—describes Aniskin, a village policeman, as a fatherly local official who, with his tolerance for human weaknesses, tries to help everybody while actually abusing his power.

V

Soviet Cinematographers Reject Official Ideology:
Cinema during the Last Years of the Soviet Empire

The last seven years of the Soviet Union were extremely turbulent for the Soviet movie industry, and it went through rapid transformations. The movies made in 1989 were radically different (ideologically) in comparison with the movies of 1987, while movies made in 1991 and 1992 would not have see the light of day only two years earlier. But before moving to the ideological revolution in Soviet movies, let us examine briefly the major political developments in Russia since 1985, when Gorbachev came to power.

Gorbachev emerged, with the support of the political establishment, in March 1985. He vowed to prevent the decline of Soviet military power, to accelerate economic and technological progress, and to clean up a corrupt bureaucracy, which he felt was the major obstacle to progress in Russia.

This direction followed neo-Leninist ideology as it was shaped in the 1960s, during Khrushchev's thaw. In the economic sphere Gorbachev (following his mentor, Iurii Andropov) supported the decentralization of economic management through a series of measures that reflected this neo-Leninist ideology. Two examples are the election of managers by workers and state control over the quality of goods. His position toward private business was more ambivalent. He cautiously supported limited privatization in agriculture (family farms) but resorted to administrative measures to fight nonlabor income (i.e., profit from private enterprise).

In the political sphere Gorbachev initiated *glasnost* in order to encourage the public critique of bureaucracy and legitimize his regime. This step radically expanded (in comparison to the Brezhnev years) opportunities to express critical views about the present state of the society as well as its history. However, it included one condition: that socialism and the Communist party be accepted as necessary for Soviet society.

Recognizing the failure of his first economic reforms, Gorbachev began (in 1987) to consider radical transformation of the political system. He hoped to combine the dominance of the Communist party with a democratization of the political order that included relatively free elections. Between 1987 and 1989 Gorbachev pushed this agenda and was met with extensive resistance by the party apparatus. However, it was supported by intellectuals in Russia and nationalists in non-Russian republics. Developments in these years helped to transform the official ideology into the ideology of liberal socialism, which came to be known as "socialism with a human face."

The first partially free election for the Soviet parliament, in March 1989, demonstrated unequivocally that people hated the Communists. Communists suffered defeats in Moscow and the main industrial centers throughout the country. This election gave momentum to the opposition and reduced Gorbachev's control over the political, national, and economic processes in the country. Between 1989 and 1991 the people finally began enjoying real political freedoms. This helped push the Soviet empire to its collapse in August 1991. New independent states emerged from the collapse of the entire Communist structure.

Developments between 1989 and 1991 were accompanied by the emergence of liberal capitalism, which confronted the ideology of liberal socialism as well as two old but still living ideologies: Stalinism and Russophilism. Liberal capitalism promoted democracy over authoritarianism, private instead of public property, market economy over planned and centralized economy, the priority of the individual over the state, and human rights over patriotism and loyalty to the state.

Historically, this ideology began inundating the Russian political establishment when the economic and social situation in the country rapidly deteriorated. Economic reforms, initiated in 1987, led to hardship instead of improved living conditions. Liberal ideology was especially prominent after the August revolution in 1991 when the democrats, led by Boris Yeltsin, came to power after the failed coup of the conservatives. The months following August 1991 led, however, to growing discontent of the masses. Their lives were not improving and the new democratic regime turned out to be even more corrupt and inept than the previous Communist regime. Russians also witnessed many other negative developments in their country: the weakening of the state, increased separatism inside Russia, and increasing conflicts with former Soviet republics caused by discrimination against Russian minorities in their territories.

These processes led to two important developments. The first was a deep demoralization of the Russian population that led to the rejection (especially by the young) of social values and the popular espousal of an individualistic, hedonistic ideology. The second was the revitalization of old ideologies like Communism and Russian nationalism. These ideologies shared many common values, especially an emphasis on the priority of the state.

All of these developments led to an extremely complex economic, political, and ideological atmosphere in 1991 and 1992, a fact reflected in the movies produced during this period.

12

The First Years of Freedom: The Beginning
of the Offensive against Official Ideology

When Gorbachev started his program of reforms in 1985, no one, including Soviet cinematographers, could predict that the Soviet system, ideology, and empire would all be dead in five to six years. Therefore, in 1985–1988 Soviet film directors only gradually emancipated themselves from their fear of the state and from official ideology. Their movies of this period are still respectful of socialism and the Soviet political machine. Only after 1989 would their quest for total freedom from the totalitarian state end.

MOVIEMAKERS AND THE POLITICAL STRUGGLE
IN GORBACHEV'S TIME

From the beginning of *glasnost* moviemakers were active supporters of the new direction. Film directors and painters were second only to writers in their level of confrontation with the political elite and party apparatus. Like writers, theater and film directors are dependent on public reaction. Consequently, they are inclined to stage plays and make movies that reflect real human thoughts and feelings. They put a high premium on creative freedom and the opportunity to be in touch with the public. In addition, their role among critical intellectuals has always been extensive. This was especially so between 1985 and 1988.

The Fifth Congress of the Union of Moviemakers in 1987 was one of the most remarkable events of the first period of *perestroika*. It was the first case in which intellectuals openly attacked the leadership of their union (and implicitly the Central Committee that appointed it). They also hissed and booed at the official speakers, and elected their own leaders—Elem Klimov, Sergei Soloviev, and Andrei Smirnov, among others.

Alexander Gel'man was one filmmaker who, like some other liberals, was not afraid to join Gorbachev's *glasnost* in 1986. His articles in 1986–1987 stand as some of the bravest challenges to the *nomenklatura* (Gel'man 1986, 1988; see also *Moskovskie Novosti* 23 April 1989).[1]

The Movie Club became a center for gatherings that promoted democratic ideas and demonstrated support for various liberal newspapers (*Moscow News*, among others) and organizations.[2] During this time *Iskusstvo kino* (*Art of Cinema*) became the main forum for the liberal intelligentsia to publish sharply critical political materials.[3]

Between 1989 and 1992 the political activity of cinematographers continued, even though the role of moviemakers (as well as intellectuals in general) in the political struggle had somewhat decreased.[4] The Sixth Congress of the Union of Moviemakers was much less politically significant (*Sovietskaia Kul'tura* 9 June 1990).

Two of the most politically active liberal filmmakers in 1989–1992 were Stanislav Govorukhin and Oleg Basilashvili. The political activity of Basilashvili was mostly confined to the Russian parliament. Govorukhin appeared as a sort of tribune or biblical prophet, who denounced both Communist and "democratic" authorities.

Govorukhin found himself in the center of the political struggle with his movie *We Cannot Live This Way Anymore* (1990) as well as with *Russia, Which We Lost* (1992). The former film portrayed the Communists as members of a criminal party and Lenin as the leader of the gang that seized Russia in 1917, while the latter bemoaned Tsarist Russia.[5]

Also remarkable was the activity of filmmakers in individual republics. For example, Davlat Khudonazarov, a Tadzhik director, was elected (in June 1990) chairman of the Union of Cinematographers. In the following year he left his public role in Moscow and became a leading figure of the opposition to the Communist leadership, and even ran for president in his republic (*Souz* 24, 1990, p. 20; *Nezavisimaia Gazeta*, 9 November 1991).

Otar Ioseliani, Georgii Khaindrava, and Lana Gogberidze, all prominent Georgian cinematographers, were members of the opposition that toppled Zviad Gamsakhurdia. Gamsakhurdia, a former dissident and the first president of the Georgian Independent Republic, was viewed by many as a dictator and the fierce enemy of the Georgian intelligentsia, filmmakers included (*Izvestia*, 17 April 1992, 6 December 1991; *New York Times*, 10 January 1992).[6]

THE SELF-DEFENSE OF THE OLD CADRES

When Gorbachev's regime moved to its second stage, it became evident that the course toward democracy was stable. Many people, intellectuals in particular, began to explore their own (and other's) behavior in the past.

Attention was first paid to the group of filmmakers who became prominent during Stalin's time, particularly those who received medals and various other signs of the Kremlin's approval. As with other intellectuals, these filmmakers attempted to explain and justify their work and life in those terrible times. One argument was that they had been true believers at the time. In 1987, Iosif Kheifits contended that he was proud of the movies he had made during Stalin's time, such as *A Member of the Government* (1940) and *Baltic Deputy* (1937).

Alexander Shtein, a prominent playwright and scriptwriter, referred to "the music of the revolution" and "the revolutionary conviction" of his generation to avoid condemnation of his activities. He criticized one of his most Stalinist films, *The Court of Honor* (1945, director Abram Room). However, he suggested that he and his colleagues were able to justify the mass repressions of this time due to the imminent war (Shtein 1987). Shtein's sentiments were echoed by the actress Tamara Makarova, who said that, despite the repression of members of her family, "there was full trust . . . in the party and its tasks," and that she was proud of the "heroic movies" of the times (*Sovietskaia Kul'tura*, 23 May 1987).

Filmmakers also suggested that during this period they had attempted to remain above politics and simply to make movies about ordinary people. In this vain, Iulii Raizman (who was awarded six Stalin prizes) tried to vindicate his work by saying that "politics is not my business" (Raizman 1988).

Only a few filmmakers were bold enough to acknowledge that much of their work distorted the truth. Evgenii Gabrilovich, the scriptwriter of three movies about Lenin, recently described Lenin in an extremely unfavorable light. This was in stark contrast to the portrayal of Lenin in his movies (which he made with Sergei Iutkevich). He justified his earlier distorted portrayal by saying that "everything besides wisdom, nobility, and kindness was rejected by censorship" (*Zerkalo*, 28 May 1991).

Filmmakers justified their boundless conformism by pointing to their all-embracing fear of the state. This same argument was also used by filmmakers during the 1960s and 1970s, when the regime was not so repressive and when refusal to cooperate with the authorities did not imply the loss of one's life. Such refusals meant, however, the termination of professional work and the loss of various privileges like traveling abroad, good schooling for their children, and special hospitals and rest homes.[7] One extreme case involved Alexei German and Kira Muratova, who were forbidden to make films for many years. Another involved Alexander Askol'dov, who, after refusing to modify *Commissar* (1989), was barred from the movie industry.

Sergei Soloviev, who became one of the great activists of *perestroika*, tried to explain why he was "beloved by superiors" before 1985. He argued that it was, in part, because he was not a Jew, he never used corrupt means to influence decisions, and he never spoke with his superiors "seriously" and "always adapted my ideas to their intellectual level." He even praised the leaders of the Soviet movie industry (such as Sizov and Ermash), describing them as "simple good people" and "producers with remarkable talents" (*Ogoniok* 34, 1990, pp. 25–27). In reality, both of these officials were active in the persecution of Tarkovskii and other nonconformists.

THE IDOLS OF THE SOVIET MOVIE INDUSTRY

With the expansion of *glasnost*, by 1989 Soviet moviemakers began to elaborate their own mythology and create their own saints and villains. The first among the saints was, of course, Andrei Tarkovskii (1931–1986). Each of his movies was instantly declared a masterpiece and any critique of his work or personality was ignored. Furthermore, every event in his life and each meeting with him were described with the highest reverence (see Freindlikh, *Moskovskie Novosti*, 5 April 1992; Strugatskii, *Ogoniok*, 29 July 1987, pp. 7–8; *Komsomolskaia Pravda*, 4 April 1992; *Nezavisimaia Gazeta*, 8 April 1992; *Izvestia*, 3 April 1992, 4 April 1992; *Iskusstvo Kino* 2, 1989, pp. 94–150).

The second idol was Sergei Paradzhanov (1924–) [*The Shadows of Our Forgotten Ancestors* (1965), *The Color of Pomegranate* (1970), *The Legend of Suram Fortress* (1984)]. As with Andrei Tarkovskii, he was included in the assembly of movie martyrs because of the persecution he endured before the Gorbachev era (*Nezavisimaia Gazeta*, 16 November 1991; *Koza*, 12 October 1991; *Literaturnaia Gazeta*, 1 August 1990; *Iskusstvo Kino* 7, 1990, pp. 48–60; 12, 1990, pp. 32–71; 4, 1991, pp. 107–25).[8]

The third idol was Vasilii Shukshin (1929–1974), a filmmaker with Russophile tendencies whose best movies were from the 1970s [*Peculiar People* (1970), *Shop Crumbs* (1972), *Red Snowball Tree* (1974)]. Shukshin was especially glorified by Russian nationalists. As a film director, as well a talented scriptwriter and actor, he was closer to the soul of the Russian people than any other filmmaker (*Iskusstvo Kino* 7, 1989, pp. 92–98).

The New Figures

During the first stages of *perestroika* new filmmakers had little impact. However, many who had been on the fringe before became more promi-

nent in its later stages. These intellectuals, now in their fifties and sixties, were previously unable to surface in public life primarily because of
their liberal convictions. Among them were the film directors Andrei
Smirnov, Alexander Sokurov, Kira Muratova, and Alexei German.

THE POLITICAL STRUGGLE AROUND NEW MOVIES
BETWEEN 1986 AND 1989

In the Soviet past, the production of most films was controlled primarily by the central party apparatus. Regional party committees, with
the exception of republic capitals and some cities with movie studios
(Leningrad, Sverdlovsk, Odessa) had little influence on the making of
movies.

However, after 1987 the centralized power in the country was greatly
diminished. Under such circumstances, local party committees became
increasingly involved in the ideological struggle surrounding movies.
Local officials, being much more conservative than the center, tried to
stop the circulation of movies that they regarded as hostile to official
ideology.

By 1989, officials in several regions (for instance, Omsk, Krasnodar,
Tomsk, Kiev, and Stavropol) forbade the showing of such movies as S.
Snezhkin's *The Extraordinary Event of District Importance* (1988). This movie exposed the lack of morals of Komsomol leaders. V. Pichul's *Little Vera*
(1988) was also forbidden because it conveyed a gloomy picture of the
life of ordinary people (*Izvestia* 4 March 1989).[9] Furthermore, conservative newspapers and magazines (see *Pravda, Sovietskaia Rossiia, Literaturnaia Rossiia, Nash Sovremennik,* and *Molodaia Gvardia* during 1987–1991)
often denounced new movies.

THE FIRST MOVIES IN THE SPIRIT OF GLASNOST (1986–1988)

Due to the length of the production process, filmmakers could not
produce movies in the new spirit as fast as poets or journalists could
produce new literature. However, by 1986 several movies were made
that were much more critical of the system than the bravest movies
made a few years earlier. Such movies as Isaak Friedberg's *My Dear
Edison* (1986) or A. Sirenko's *The Top Guy* (1986) would have never found
their way to theaters in the 1970s and early 1980s.

However, only by 1988 could filmmakers offer films made completely
in the spirit of *glasnost.* But, due to the rapid changes that were occurring

in society, even these movies did not adequately reflect the current public mood as revealed in the mass media and in public opinion polls. Among the first true movies of *glasnost* were Mamin's *Fountain* (1988) and Riazanov's *Dear Elena Sergeevna* (1988).

Still, during this period filmmakers were not as free as in the last two years of *perestroika*, when many of them abandoned any (even symbolic) ties with socialism. At this point many started to make movies openly hostile to the official ideology. Among several topics that remained forbidden during the early years of *glasnost* were the direct comparison of Stalinism to Nazism and of socialism to fascism. In a 1988 article about Mikhail Romm's famous film *Ordinary Fascism* (1966)(which was severely edited in the 1960s), the author still could not discuss the main underlying theme of the movie—the similarity between Hitler's and Stalin's regimes (*Nedelia* 1 May 1988).

NOTES

1.   In the 1970s Alexander Gel'man, a scriptwriter, belonged to the group of liberal cinematographers who enthusiastically advocated the ideology of neo-Leninism with strong liberal overtones. One of his scripts, used in Mikaelian's *Bonus* (1975), was about a conscientious foreman who persuades his team to reject a bonus for their work, claiming it is unfair and simply a way for the bosses to conceal the problems in the firm. Though the premise of the script— the refusal to take money offered to them—was absurd, the author exploited this artificial conflict to demonstrate the corruption and incompetence of Soviet management. The same theme—the struggle of an honest individual against bureaucracy—was used by Gel'man for the same purposes in his own movie, *We, the Undersigned* (1981).

Gel'man continued to publish his political articles in various periodicals (see, for example, his articles in *Iskusstvo kino* during 1990–1991), but their political resonance was incomparably lower than in 1986–1987.

2.   In February 1989, filmmakers organized a meeting with the editors of *Moscow News*, the leading liberal weekly (*Moscow News*, 5 March 1989). Two years later (9 March 1991) at the Movie Club, Yeltsin made his most aggressive speech against Gorbachev, who by that time was siding with the conservatives.

3.   One of the most significant publications was Ilia Kabakov's novel *Defector* (*Nevozvashchenets*), which described life in the country after the success of a conservative coup. To some degree this novel foreshadowed the developments to come in 1991.

4.   As a journalist from *Komsomolskaia Pravda* mentioned in regard to his contacts with the famous movie couple director Gleb Panfilov and actress Inna Churikova, "our conversations about theater and movies always ended with politics" (*Komsomolskaia Pravda*, 4 April 1992).

5.   About the debates over Govorukhin's films, see *Nezavisimaia Gazeta*, 16 November 1991; see also Govorukhin, *Sovetskaia Kul'tura*, 2 June 1990; *Iskusstvo Kino* 12, 1990, pp. 3–7.

6. Revaz Chkheidze, Georgian film director and author of one of the most patriotic Soviet movies [*The Soldier's Father* (1965)], as well as a positive movie about the party secretary [*Your Son, Earth* (1981)], in 1990 renounced the Lenin prize awarded to him in 1982 for the latter movie.

7. The Union of Moviemakers, for instance, had a number of rest homes (those in Bolshevo, close to Moscow, were the most prestigious), which were open only to those favored by the authorities.

8. Paradzhanov was arrested several times, apparently because of his homosexuality, which was regarded as a serious crime.

9. Such could not have occurred during Stalin's time. Stalin would not have tolerated any decision by his local officials regarding the movies people should or should not see. However, in Brezhnev's era, with the gradual decline of the central power, some local bosses dared to prohibit the viewing of movies they did not like. Among them was Shukshin's *Red Snowball Tree* and Riazanov's *Garage*.

13

Movie Heroes 1986–1989

With the ideological shift toward neo-Leninism and liberal socialism, Soviet filmmakers strove to debunk the old official ideology. Instead, they presented a realistic picture of Soviet life. In the beginning they concentrated their attention on two groups: bureaucrats and youth.

BUREAUCRATS

As has been demonstrated, liberal moviemakers viewed Soviet bureaucrats as their enemies and used any opportunity to expose the masters of Soviet society. However, only with *glasnost*, and then only very slowly, did film directors begin to reveal their genuine feelings about apparatchiks. Filmmakers felt it their duty to demonstrate the indifference of bureaucrats to the interests of society. Their depravity and corruption were also brutally exposed. The filmmakers inveighed against bureaucrats passionately because they represented the hated ideology and regime. They were the oppressors of the people and art, as well as the source of the backwardness of Russia.

The Top Guy was one of the first movies in which apparatchiks were attacked to a degree unheard of before *glasnost*. In this film bureaucrats, the leaders of the rural districts, are depicted as individuals who are absorbed with their own power and totally disregard the welfare of their communities. The film's portrayal of the terrible plight of agriculture is accompanied by an extremely optimistic radio broadcast enumerating various achievements in the countryside.

Bureaucrats were also depicted as spreading anti-Semitic feelings. One of the heroes of *My Dear Edison*, an able scholar, is a Jew. It is obvious to moviegoers that his ethnic origin is behind his troubles (in particular, finding a different job). His ethnicity is also exploited by the institute's director, who pressures the hero into preparing a dissertation for him.

Anti-Western propaganda is also portrayed as being central to the ideological arsenal of the bureaucrats. Blending Russophilism with Marxism, bureaucrats present the West as inhumane and depraved. The corrupt West is juxtaposed with the benign and moral Soviet Russia in order to dupe the masses and hide the bureaucrats' incompetence and corruption. *My Dear Edison* openly mocks officials who rail against the corruption of the West, but are, in fact, its admirers. A despicable bureaucrat, quite proud to have visited various Western countries, brandishes his Japanese pen as a symbol of his high social position and success.

With the progress of *glasnost*, film directors were able to create even more poignant and negative images of bureaucrats. Riazanov's *Forgotten Melody for Flute and Orchestra* (1987) suggests that bureaucrats are so corrupt that they are simply unable to change their iniquitous life-style. This life-style includes total indifference to their jobs and a permanent interest in promotion. The hero is an able flutist who marries the daughter of a high official and becomes an apparatchik involved in the meaningless activities of the Directorate of Leisure Time.

The bureaucracy was also under fire in Nikolai Gubenko's *The Danger Zone* (1988). This movie examines the aftereffects of a tornado that destroyed a rural village and left dozens of families homeless. The political and cultural elite live close to the area of disaster but are not affected by the tornado. Most of these bureaucrats turn out to be callous and egotistical people. They are totally indifferent to the fate of a populace they regard as untouchables. Without any concern for the tribulations of ordinary people, the bureaucrats discuss what threat the homeless people present to them. Their discussion takes place while some of them play tennis and their children dance. Furthermore, while discussing *perestroika* most of them, even the most "progressive" officials, express their doubt that the Russian people will ever be productive workers.

Vadim Abdrashitov's *Servant* (1988) shows that Soviet bureaucrats created a class of subordinates—servants—who are morally no better than their cynical and cruel masters. In the movie "the old man," Andrei Gudionov, is a big shot who encounters Pavel Kliuev, a successful choral conductor who had been his personal driver in earlier days. He reminds Kliuev that his career would have gone nowhere without his help. In fact, Kliuev had been so controlled that Gudionov even hand-picked his wife. In the film, Kliuev continues to accept the role of servant to Gudionov because he is involved in criminal activity with him. Thus, the power imbalance continues.

This was one of the first films to create a comprehensive image of the Soviet bureaucrat. Bryzgin, a retiree and old critic of Gudionov, addresses him (as a representative of the whole Soviet bureaucracy) as follows:

You are the genius of evil: You destroy nature, push the rivers backwards; you enslave nations, obliterate their memory and tradition; you destroy in order to build and build in order to destroy; you encourage corruption, pervert people and then put them in prison; you present virtue as vice and vice as virtue.

In essence this movie portrays a pessimistic climate in the country. The ruling elite and the masses deserve each other and there is no real hope for the resuscitation of the country. However, the movie does not address many fundamental realities of Soviet society (for instance, patriotism, internationalism, or the army). Furthermore, some characters do display moral virtues and continue to struggle with the bureaucracy even while risking their lives. And finally, although the portrayal of life is quite bleak in this movie, the social fabric, its main institutions, and its main social ties, remain uncriticized.

BUREAUCRATS AS THE ENEMIES OF PERESTROIKA

The advent of *glasnost* allowed for the emergence of many movies that depicted bureaucrats as committed enemies of *perestroika*, liberalization, and economic reform. In these democratically oriented movies, party and state officials appear to hate the new regime. They exploit its difficulties and anxiously await its failure and the subsequent restoration of the old regime.

An official in L. Kvirinadze's *The Actress from Gribov* (1988) promises that "our time will come, and it will be thrust under the noses of all reluctant people." A similar hope is held by Kropotov, the director of a large Leningrad enterprise in I. Khamraiev's *Red Arrow* (1986). Rude, power hungry, and practiced in the art of demagoguery, Kropotov hates *perestroika* with all his heart and longs for its demise. The party officials in the TV movie *Nadia Rodionova* (1989) obstruct democratization in their city by using their influence to corrupt the election of a deputy of the Soviet parliament. All the while, they ignore the real mood of the masses.

The hostility of apparatchiks to *perestroika* is the major theme in Riazanov's *Forgotten Melody for Flute and Orchestra*. In this film, most of the bureaucrats pretend that they work in the spirit of reform—they even use the new terminology of *perestroika*. However, in their hearts they actually long for its end. Furthermore, they understand (and their prognosis was quite correct) that the logic of liberalization—which started in their Directorate of Leisure Time when a chorus dared to sing a song with some frivolous (by Soviet standards of the time) words—

will lead to the election of managers, the liquidation of their offices, and other unspeakable developments. In their dreams they see themselves asking for alms like beggars in the subway.

"DEMOCRATIC BUREAUCRATS" IN GORBACHEV'S TIME

The first years of *perestroika* seemed very promising for filmmakers. Aside from denouncing the old party apparatus, they tried to portray honest officials who would implement the reforms proclaimed by Gorbachev. However, these personages soon totally disappeared from Soviet movies.

In Gubenko's *The Danger Zone*, an apparatchik suggests that one should "look at the issue of property with open eyes." He further suggests that propertyless individuals cannot respect themselves. However, even more important than some skepticism about the Stalinist ideology is the figure of Vera Tretiakova, chairman of a local government. She is a devoted woman who works to aid those in need. Her example leaves hope that with *perestroika* people like her will infuse new blood into the Russian bureaucracy.

In the following year this same issue was addressed by pro-Gorbachev apparatchiks in Brovkin and Solntsev's *Three People on the Red Rug* (1989). Mikhail Soshkin, the new chairman of a collective farm, fervently argues with his opponent, an old party apparatchik, in defense of privatization in the countryside. Soshkin denounces existing economic relations as being responsible for the deterioration of agriculture. He refers to the ancient Roman Empire, which "perished because of the wrong attitudes toward work."

In *Forgotten Melody for Flute and Orchestra*, Leonid Filimonov, a high official, comes under the influence of the new direction and falls in love with an honest nurse. At the end of the film he proposes that the Soviet people should be freed from rigid bureaucratic control. He suggests that, like a bird released from the hand, they will not fly away. This is an allusion to the naive belief of liberals that if the Soviet people are freed, they will remain faithful to the system.

Despite these examples, in the years that followed, positive apparatchiks, along with happy endings, disappeared completely from Russian movies.

SOVIET YOUTH IN THE FIRST YEARS OF PERESTROIKA

Soviet youth were the second target of Soviet movies in the first years of *glasnost*. In order to understand why liberal cinematographers felt this audience to be so important, it is necessary to recall how youth were treated in Stalin's time (and until the 1990s).

Ideological control over youth was always a high priority for the Soviet leadership. This fact was well known by filmmakers who until Stalin's death did their best to aid in this indoctrination. The most popular Soviet movies made during Stalin's era were about young people who were genuine bearers of socialist ideology. They were in opposition to the more conservative and reactionary, even counterrevolutionary, old people.

Grigorii Kozintsev created a three-part series about a young Bolshevik involved in the revolution and fighting its enemies [*Maxim's Youth* (1935), *Maxim's Return* (1937), and *The Vyborg Side* (1939)]. These films exemplify the portrait of youth that the establishment hoped to put forth. Other famous movies during this period also glorified young people's devotion to socialism and the motherland. Examples include Ivan Pyriev's *The Rich Bride* (1938) and *Tractor Drivers* (1939), Leo Arnshtam's *The Girlfriends* (1936), and Sergei Gerasimov's *The Bold Seven* (1936), *Komsomolsk* (1938), and *The Young Guard* (1948).

With Stalin's death, the portrayal of youth in Soviet movies changed only slightly. Liberal cinematographers began to expose the false image in the 1960s (during Khrushchev's thaw) but were often reprimanded by the authorities for even mild attempts to expose the truth [two of the most noteworthy examples are the story of Marlen Khutsiev's movie *I Am Twenty* (1965) and *Rain in July* (1967)]. For the most part, filmmakers continued to follow the official line and portray young people as members of the Komsomol and faithful soldiers of the party.

However, some nonconformist films did portray youth in radically different ways. They often depicted them as being even worse than the older generations. In fact, young characters often seemed indifferent to social values (especially those related to socialism) and cruel to old people and to each other. They were totally absorbed by consumerism and entertainment (primarily rock music). They were portrayed as hypocrites and liars. They were also seen as extremely vain and craving any form of prestige. Of course, youth were also characterized as being extremely libertine in their sexual behavior.

This type of portrayal was usually made with many reservations and in no way implied that most young people behaved in this way. Moreover, such negative portrayals were tempered by the presence of some positive young characters. Furthermore, sometimes young people appeared evil at the beginning of a movie, only to be transformed by the end [see, for example, Sergei Mikaelian's *Fell in Love at My Own Request* (1982) or Menshov's *Prank* (1977), where one of the main characters, a cynical schoolboy obsessed with the desire to make a career for himself, is contrasted with a number of good children].

In fact, only a few movies painted a pessimistic picture of the Soviet youth. In *Who's Knocking at My Door?* (1983, scriptwriter T. Kholopliankina) and R. Muradian's *A Photograph for Remembrance* (1985), the offspring of well-to-do families are seen robbing people in the streets. In Kheifits's *The Only One* (1976), the hero starts out as a young worker full of idealistic visions of life, including a happy family and carrying out exciting work for the public good. Under the pressure of circumstances, however, his dreams collapse. By the end of the film, he is an absolutely broken man.

With the progress of *glasnost*, liberal filmmakers began to portray the young generation much more realistically. By 1989–1991, they could openly address the realities of young people's lives. Four main topics, all of which were only cautiously mentioned in the past, became important themes in movies during this period: youth's alienation from society and socialist ideology, their cynicism, the social differentiation among young people, and their rampant criminal activity.

Alienation

For the most part, Soviet young people were portrayed as surly and bitterly disappointed with their lives, their parents, and society in general. Iuris Podniesk's *It's Not Easy to Be Young* (1987) was especially indicative of this new portrayal of Soviet youth. This film was a revelation for the Soviet audience because it portrayed adolescents as unsure about what to do with their lives, as being prone to violent acts and vandalism, as passionately loving rock music (disparaged by the authorities), as loving money, as being able in desperation to commit suicide, and as doubting the honesty of adults. However, this movie was optimistic and expressed hope for a dialogue between generations and for the ultimate adaptation of Soviet young people to their changing society. Only a few years later a movie with such ultimately optimistic views would be unheard of.

Leina Laus's *Games for Teenagers* (1986) is about the total alienation of Marie, a teenager, from her father and from the teacher in the foster home where she was placed after her mother's death. Her world is cruel and lifeless. The children's parents are mostly drunkards, prostitutes, and child abusers.[1] However, like in previous movies, this film leaves hope for Marie through love and friendship.

Soloviev's *Assa* (1988) also exemplifies the new portrayal of Soviet young people. Banan, the hero, typifies the new Russian youth through his defiance of the authorities. He would rather be arrested than acquiesce and stop wearing a ring in one of his ears. This is a direct allusion to the period when young people were arrested for the length of their pants or hair.

Youth's total alienation from the state, its authorities, and its ideology was further demonstrated in V. Rybarev's *My Name Is Arlekino* (1988). This film mocks an official lecturer who denounces the younger generation's dress, the emblems they wear, and their interest in modern pop music. It is evident from the movie that all this ideological humbug only irritates teenagers and pushes them into even greater nonconformist behavior.

There are dozens of other movies that portray the alienation of youth from Soviet society. Mikhail Tumanshvili's *Avaria—A Cop's Daughter* (1989), Vadim Zlobin's *Sunday at Six-Thirty* (1988), and S. Proskurin's *Children's Playground* (1987) are a few examples.[2]

Rock music plays a special role in these movies. The music is itself a sort of ideology because it was harshly persecuted by the Soviet authorities. For the film *Assa*, the director enlisted the best rock groups in the country, all of which had been illegal in the past. The glorification of rock music and the anti-Soviet songs performed by young rock singers, as well as the ecstasy that this music aroused in young people, continued to challenge Soviet ideology in 1988.[3] In fact, rock music was an indispensable part of almost all Soviet movies about youth. Victor Volkov's *Publication* (1988) ends with a powerful rock concert filled with brave songs. It is a direct and evident challenge to the hypocrisy and dishonesty of society as depicted in the movie.

Along with rock music, Soloviev and other film directors depicted other attributes of the youth subculture that had been denounced by Soviet authorities since the late 1950s—clothing, makeup, manners, and so on. Soviet movies also became filled with all types of youth populations—hippies, "metal-heads," etc.

Cynicism and Cruelty

Most movies made between 1987 and 1992 depict Russian teenagers as devoid of social values, indifferent to the interests of society, and absorbed only with their material well-being and pleasures. Such a portrait of Soviet young people was regarded by filmmakers in the second half of the 1980s as their contribution to the struggle against the false description of Soviet life by state propaganda.

In Viacheslav Sorokin's *Seduction* (1987) and Riazanov's *Dear Elena Sergeevna* (as well as other movies in which high school students discuss their future), none of the students mention any social cause that they might champion. Life abroad and work that permits long trips to foreign countries are the typical dreams of the young heroes.

Russian youth are also presented as very cruel and merciless to their parents, teachers, and peers. Such harsh descriptions can be seen in Zlobin's *Sunday at Six-Thirty* (1988). Here the young characters, completely devoid of compassion, desert a dying girl at a picnic in order to avoid contact with the police. In the film, a son visits his lonely father and forces him to go out to a movie theater, where he has a heart attack and dies. The audience then learns that the son needed his father's room so he could meet his mistress.

Another example is Abdrashitov's *Pliumbum* (1986). In this movie, a teenager is shown reveling in his power as a voluntary assistant to the police. He even gleefully arrests his father for an insignificant violation. Later in the film he fails to prevent the death of a girl who loves him.

In Evgenii Gerasimov's *Amusements of Youth* (1987) college students are depicted as totally immoral. They send Svetlana, a nineteen-year-old girl, to seduce an old man (the gymnastics instructor) in order to black-mail him and get high grades. As with other movies of the first years of *perestroika*, this movie is not devoid of references to the old values of honesty, nobility, and love. However, these values are expressed not by the teenagers, but by the old teacher. He experiences a sudden burst of affection for the girl and leaves his job and the city in order to avoid harming Svetlana, who has fallen in love with him.

In *Dear Elena Sergeevna*, the children of wealthy and educated parents attempt to persuade their high school teacher to raise their marks on the final exam. They begin with expressions of appreciation and gratitude but soon move to blackmail and death threats. The children are depicted as cruel liars, cynics, and hypocrites.

The teenagers in Friedberg's *Little Doll* (1989) are equally vicious. In the film a malicious girl is easily able to talk her classmates into betraying their teacher (whom they seemingly respected and loved) by not going to her birthday party. They instead watch a Western horror movie on the VCR. The majority of the high school and college students in *Publication* and *Blackmailer* (1986, director unknown) are also extremely cynical.

Social Differentiation

One of the most pervasive myths about socialist society is that there is no social differentiation. Soviet filmmakers often used gatherings of young people to demonstrate the existence of extensive social differen-tiation among teenagers belonging to different social classes. In Ryba-rev's *My Name Is Arlekino*, the gang consists of teenagers from working families who feel they have no future in this world (many of them live in hostels and can only dream about their own apartment and going to college). These young men continually lose their girlfriends, who aban-don them for wealthier suitors who are often from the "adult" criminal world.

By torturing their well-to-do peers, these teenagers get sadistic satisfaction and recompense for their low social status. The heroes of *My Name Is Arlekino*, as well as the heroes in the American film *Colors* (by Dennis Hopper, 1988), look for confrontations with other gangs. The gang in *Arlekino* also rely on official propaganda to choose their scapegoats, as when they attack people dressed as hippies.

In *My Name Is Arlekino*, the destitute teenagers regard their solidarity (based mostly on criminal deeds) as the single antidote against the hostile world. As the gang leader Arlekino suggests to his comrades, "We can only grab what belongs to them" (the wealthy youngsters). His speech is full of class anger, evidently mirroring the director's feelings. Finally, the portrayal of these adolescents is not all bad. Arlekino and other gang members demonstrate many positive traits like devotion to their mothers, friends, girlfriends, and even poetry.

Sorokin's *Seduction* (1987) continues this theme. In this film Zhenia Rodimtseva, who is of the lower class, falls in love with Boris Ogorodov, who belongs to "the cream of his class." These are students whose parents travel abroad, bring them foreign clothes and electronics, drive them to school in limousines, and live in luxurious apartments. Because she has moved to a new school, Zhenia is able to keep her real social position a secret for a while. However, when she is finally discovered she is deeply humiliated. Even Boris abandons her when he finds out that the shoddy room in which they had sex is not her aunt's, as she pretended, but her own.

In most films, the upper-class young have no compassion for those on the lower social rung. In *Seduction*, upper-class children often demonstrate their contempt for others; they humiliate them by flaunting their jewels, modern dress, fancy restaurants, and access to special sport facilities, and by refusing to invite them to their birthday parties (complete with bartenders!) and other gatherings.

The theme of *Seduction* is mirrored by Volkov's *Publication*, where we find the same social division in the graduating class, the same confrontation between rich and poor and the same contempt for the latter by the former. However, this movie also demonstrates that the administration of the school and the mass media support the rich children in their conflicts with lower-class children. But it is the poor teenagers who are noble in the defense of justice. In this case, they stand by the honest and uncorrupted old teacher who was ousted due to a slanderous article in the local newspaper.

Criminal Activities

During this period several movies revealed that youngsters were involved in extensive criminal activities. Probably the first scene to depict this occurred in *It's Not Easy to Be Young*. Here, a gang destroys the cars, seats, and windows of a commuter train. The gang in *My Name Is Arlekino* also makes regular incursions onto trains, scaring the passengers.

THE MASSES

In Soviet ideology, terms such as "the ordinary people," "the proletarian" or "socialist" masses, "the average Soviet citizen," "the working class," and "the collective farmers" were considered sacred for the most part. Of course, the image of the average Soviet individual was not static. In Stalin's time the gap between heroes and the masses was relatively small and anyone could be a hero. A series of films about ordinary people who became famous in the motherland, such as Zarkhi and Kheifits's *A Member of the Government* (1940) or Pyriev's *Swineherd and Shepherd* (1941), demonstrated that the official propaganda supported this idea.

In Brezhnev's time, official ideology was less demanding and filmmakers were allowed to depict some weaknesses of the average individual as long as their alliance with Russophile ideology remained intact. They shared the postulate that the people are inherently good and the real bearers of morals.

With the new political climate surrounding *glasnost*, filmmakers were finally allowed to freely express their views about the Soviet people. Many movies of the *glasnost* era portray the Soviet people as hostile to conscientious and hard work. They are also shown as prone to alcoholism and violence. Gradually, this critique addressed not only the Soviet people demoralized by the Soviet system but also the masses, or proletarians—those sacred people who made the revolution.

We see this contempt for ordinary people in Vladimir Bortko's *Dog's Heart* (1988), the movie version of the 1925 Bulgakov novel of the same name. The masses are depicted as cruel, lazy, and immoral. This film also depicts the intelligentsia as self-deluded and irresponsible. The masses are also condemned in Lev Kulidzhanov's *To Die Is Not Frightening* (1991), in which citizens during the revolution are presented as uncontrollably destructive.

The masses in Mikhail Ptashuk's *Our Armored Train* (1989) are portrayed with great contempt. They are presented as a herd of cattle who deliriously cheer each leader during parades in Red Square, regardless of what he did to the Soviet people and what he said of his predecessor.

This negative depiction of the masses is even harsher when directors portray their contemporaries. For example, in A. Itychikov's *Humble Cemetery* (1989) funeral workers are depicted as devoid of any moral values, including respect for the dead. Piotr, the hero of V. Popkov's *Sinner* (1988), is seen by others as a violator of moral norms. He is persecuted and even beaten by his supervisors and colleagues because he refuses to work slowly (he easily completes a full day's quota of work in one hour). V. Pichul's *Little Vera* (1988) portrays the people as aggressive brutes with few positive or redeeming qualities.

Only a few films in this period (which developed the Russophile traditions of the 1970s) supported the view that ordinary people are better than the bureaucracy and official intellectuals. Gubenko's *The Danger Zone* is one such movie—it demonstrated how bravely most ordinary people faced a disaster that deprived them of their homes.

DISBELIEF IN THE SUCCESS OF PERESTROIKA

Joining Gorbachev's drive for the modernization of Soviet society, several directors from the very beginning were quite skeptical about the success of this new attempt of Russia to join the family of democratic nations.

One such skeptic was Riazanov. In *Forgotten Melody*, a nurse, representing the liberal and humanistic part of society, urges the major protagonist (who symbolizes Brezhnevian bureaucracy) to change his life. His heart attacks symbolize the dire consequences of this life-style (read: the policy of Brezhnevian bureaucracy) for him and his family (the country). Yet despite her warnings, he continues his life-style and dies, even though ultimately understanding the necessity of change.

Genuine pessimism about reforms was clearly manifested in the isolation of positive bureaucrats, the spearheads of revolutionary change. They represented Gorbachev, and their isolation and violent demise demonstrated that a sense of impending doom had started to infiltrate Soviet movies during the early stages of *perestroika*. In S. Linkov's *Because of a Change of Job* (1986), a local party boss is transformed into a sort of quasi-Christ with a party card. At an informal meeting that resembles the Last Supper, he admonishes his subordinates to change their authoritarian approach to the masses and retain the humanistic and democratic essence of socialist teaching. He is extremely kind and forgiving to everyone, including his avowed enemy—he states that the villain is also a victim of the system, and thus should be liberated from oppression and have the right to speak his mind. Despite his effort to rally support for his changes, however, the hero finds himself isolated and he is finally killed by the Stalinist villain. This Christian martyrdom is similar to Russophile movies, with one important difference: In Russophile movies the death leads to significant changes; in *Because of a Change of Job* the death of the hero symbolizes the futility of his efforts to change society.

In G. Pavlov's *Objective Circumstance* (1987), a female major (representing Gorbachev), calls on the city (representing the USSR) to help her save the country from economic and ecological disaster. Unfortunately, the residents are apathetically indifferent to her call.

NOTES

1. In the past, child abuse by parents was never mentioned in Soviet movies.
2. In this last movie a girl who was raised in a children's home and is now a worker is heard exclaiming, "I hate all people."
3. See the angry review of *Assa* in the conservative paper *Molodaia Gvardia* (3, 1990, pp. 284–86).

14

Total Freedom from Totalitarianism and Its Ideology

Even in his wildest imagination, an Eisenstein or Dovzhenko, harassed by a merciless state demanding him to be a trivial propagandist of official ideology, would not have been able to predict what would happen to the Soviet movie industry in 1989–1991. Some of their colleagues and friends were fortunate enough to live long enough to see how the cruel tormentors and ideological watchdogs of Soviet cinema were ousted from their positions while monuments to Lenin and his comrades-in-arms were destroyed across the country. However, they too could hardly have expected all the controversial developments that freedom brought to Russian cinema.

THE RADICAL IDEOLOGICAL SHIFT (1989–1992)

Until 1989–1990, most Soviet movies were vehicles for the propagation of neo-Leninism and liberal socialism. Despite all their criticisms of Soviet society, filmmakers still felt themselves linked to the ideas of socialism. This was either by conviction or because of continuing ideological control by authorities. In fact, the ideological space of movies has remained basically unchanged since Stalin's death, even if the proportion occupied by various ideologies in 1986–1988 was very different in comparison with previous periods. As was mentioned earlier, since 1989 the ideological space has changed radically because new ideologies entered it—especially the ideology of liberal capitalism with its anticommunist overtones.[1]

THE EMERGENCE OF A NEW IDEOLOGY IN MOVIES

The dominant ideology of the Soviet movie industry in the last year of *perestroika* stressed individualism, political freedom, democracy (and a

Western style of life), capitalist economy, and universalism in world history (i.e., that all countries follow the same developmental path). In fact, it was quite similar to Western conservative ideology. As a Soviet film critic put it, "it is the philosophy of affluence, success, profit, freedom, and individualism" (Gladil'shchikov 1992).

Although praising the ideology of liberal capitalism, a number of movies between 1988 and 1990 were mildly critical of *perestroika*. The program was felt to be inconsistent, timid in reforms, and mild toward apparatchiks [see, for instance, Soloviev's *Black Rose Stands for Sadness, Red Rose Stands for Joy* (1989) and Riazanov's *Forgotten Melody* and *Chosen Heaven* (1991)].

However, between 1986 and 1991 almost no one directly attacked Gorbachev's leadership for mistakes in the restructuring of Russian society. Filmmakers, regarding themselves as the activists of *perestroika*, did not want to help conservatives with their critique of the Kremlin. Therefore, they could afford only minor criticism of *perestroika*. Such criticism was often attributed to secondary personalities as, for instance, in Soloviev's *Black Rose*.

However, most Russian movies in 1989-1991 were influenced not so much by the new ideology of liberal capitalism as by a negative anticommunist ideology. This ideology did not offer any new ideals and seemed content to simply debunk and ridicule the official Soviet ideology. In fact, this negative ideology reflected the moral vacuum that was already being felt in 1990.

This negative ideology, as manifested in movies and painting, was dubbed *Sozart* by Moscow intellectuals. It is a clear allusion to official Soviet ideology in the literature and arts of socialist realism. This ideology also shares characteristics of postmodernism with its predilection for absurdities in human life.

The major heroes of Sozart movies, portrayed with great sympathy and compassion, were diametrically different than the heroes in the classic movies made on the basis of socialist realism. Conscientious workers were replaced by drunkards and loafers, faithful women by prostitutes, brave soldiers by cowards, and so on.[2]

Aside from creating new heroes, Sozart movies ridiculed the classic heroes of socialist realism (Stakhnovites, pioneers, Red Army generals, heroes of the civil war, party leaders, and African Americans such as Paul Robeson or Angela Davis, who were presented as supporters of Communism[3]) by depicting them as idiots or simpletons. In M. Pezhemskii's *The Trek of Comrade Chkalov through the North Pole* (1990) the famous Soviet pilot Valerii Chkalov and his colleagues, honored by the whole world after completing the first nonstop flight from Moscow to the United States in 1936, are presented as a group of fanatics. In the film,

Chkalov and his comrades overcome the resistance of various counter-revolutionary bandits. Upon reaching the North Pole, they change the slope of the Earth's axis and force the globe to rotate "in our [Soviet] direction."

Friedberg, in his *Little Doll*, addressed Soviet sport, so touted for its international successes. The film demonstrated that state-controlled sports organizations acted like an inhuman factory. It produced young champions who ultimately turned out to be, like the heroine Tatiana (a former world champion in gymnastics), morally and physically handicapped.

Other targets of Sozart films were any symbols of the previous era. These include revolutionary songs, the ship *Aurora*—the emblem of the October Revolution (according to legend its salvos broke the resistance of the provisional government), medals, military parades in Red Square, various solemn ceremonies devoted to "the struggle for peace," and the activity of pioneers. In *Black Rose* many of these sacred symbols are ridiculed. In one scene, set in a psychiatric hospital, patients (presented as various types of degenerates) watch Brezhnev's funeral with joy. In another scene, Stalin's meetings with the pioneers, as well as other sacred symbols, are satirized.

In Soloviev's *The House under the Starry Sky* (1991) and Riasanov's *Chosen Heaven* (1991), the target was the solemnity of the party congresses and conferences. The mockery of socialism was often delivered by rock singers. This device was used especially by Soloviev in corroboration with Boris Grebennikov—the most famous Russian rock musician.

The Derogation of Official History

Special targets of cinematographers were the official version of history and Russian national myths incorporated in official ideology. Alla Surikova, in the quasi-historical comedy *Cranky People* (1990), describes the adventure of Otto von Goerstner. He was an Austrian inventor who came to Russia during the reign of Nicholas I in order to build the first railroad in Russia. The film obviously speaks to the present and is full of allusions about events that happened long after the time of Nicholas I.

The film depicts Otto as a naive inventor who, with the help of his altruistic Russian friends, is able to overcome obstacles to his project. However, most Russians, and especially the elite, are depicted as being extremely conservative, egotistical, xenophobic drunkards and loafers. The movie also demonstrates the stupidity, dishonesty, and corruption of the Russian bureaucracy as it advances idiotic arguments against the railroad project. Finally, the omnipotence of the political police and the omnipresence of its spies and informers underscore the salutary role of foreigners as the single bearers of progress in Russia.

THE ABSURDITY OF SOVIET REALITY

In attacking Soviet society, filmmakers began to include various absurdities in their films. The evolution of Sergei Soloviev's films is typical. His first great movie during *perestroika*, *Assa*, was quite realistic. But in *Black Rose*, he introduced a number of bizarre personalities and situations. Among them was Stalin. Despite his famous manners, gestures, and words, he is concerned only with his constipation. Absurdities were also pervasive in his third movie, *The House under the Starry Sky*. It suggests that Russian life is full of absurdities to which people have simply become accustomed. In the film, the KGB enlists the devil as an agent. In one scene, he cuts a woman in half as a trick at her father's birthday party. Unfortunately, he forgets how to put her back together again although the members of her family seem to accept this as normal. Many other strange events occur in the movie, and the director appeals to his viewers to be shocked only to the extent that they are shocked by their own experience in Soviet life.

The popularity of absurdity explains why the status of crazy people and former psychiatric patients has changed radically in Russian movies. Like Tolik, a psychotic from *Black Rose*, people with mental disorders seem to fit in quite well in such an abnormal society. They are often depicted as being even smarter than their "normal" neighbors.

Absurd plots, unthinkable only five years ago, proliferated in the movies of 1989–1992. In N. Khutov's *Body* (1990), which purported to be a realistic film, we see a plethora of implausible situations revolving around the accusation of a groom by his bride of rape, even though they had been lovers (and in love) for some time.

RUSSIAN CRITICS DISCOVER SOCIALIST REALISM
IN AMERICAN MOVIES

It is remarkable that with the rejection of socialist realism in the Russian movie industry, and with their new understanding of the arts in other countries, Russian movie critics discovered the extensive role of socialist realism in American movies. They found that many American movies are based on extremely rigid ideological, or "politically correct," precepts. This is so prevalent that it is often possible to predict the behavior of many characters. For instance, various minorities including blacks, women, homosexuals, and handicapped people often have pat reactions to events. It is also possible to predict various political developments and the attitudes of positive heroes toward issues such as colonialism or the causes of poverty (Genis 1992).

Lawrence Kasdan's *Grand Canyon* (1991) is one such movie. The proportion of good and bad black characters is such that it avoids any hint at prejudice against African Americans. There is a scene in which a gang in Los Angeles almost kills the hero, who prophesies that "the whole country is going to hell" (unknowingly foreshadowing the Los Angeles riots in April 1992). However, toward the end of the movie these events are downplayed. The movie closes with a melodramatic and happy ending.

Waterdance (1992), which Russian critics would also label socialist realism, demonstrates how people of different races and occupations, stricken with paralysis, are able to achieve solidarity after their initial clashes.

Happy endings in American movies, in which ideologically positive heroes are triumphant, are similar to those of socialist realism. Ivan Reitman's *Kindergarten Cop* (1990) is, in the opinion of Sasha Kisilev, an example of this sort of movie (*Literaturnaia Gazeta* 18 September 1991). In this film a policeman, using a day care center to catch a criminal, earns the love of children, their parents, the principal and, of course, a divorced woman. He also saves her former husband.

THE TRIUMPH OF EXISTENTIAL NIHILISM

Loyalty to the ideology of liberal capitalism was very limited even in 1991. No filmmaker was able to make a businessman a positive hero. Filmmakers like Muratova, Riazanov, Soloviev, and Sergei Livnev began to shift from the negation of the Communist utopia to an even more negative and pessimistic ideology. This ideology stressed the vulgarity, absence of moral laws, apathy, and atrophy in the world today. The leading filmmakers of the 1990s believe in the dominance of evil and mutual hatred in human society. They have discovered for themselves some sort of enmity to humanity as a species. In fact, the opposition of animals to human beings, with clear sympathy for the animals, was typical for many movies of 1989–1991 [in particular Muratova's movies—see, for instance, *Asthenic Syndrome* (1990) and *The Sensitive Militiaman* (1990)].

The bleak and dreary mood in Russian movies increased dramatically between 1989 and 1992. By the end of the period, Russian movies tended to portray society as totally sick, close to disintegration and collapse, and lacking any positive heroes or hope for the future.

THE EXTENT OF PESSIMISM IN RUSSIAN MOVIES

According to the data of *Iskusstvo Kino*, in 35 percent of Soviet movies made in 1989–1990 heroes either die, commit suicide, or degenerate completely as personalities. Furthermore, "82 percent of Soviet movies demonstrate negative attitudes toward life, reality, and human relations, as well as feelings of fear, desperation, and violence. Only 18 percent of the movies even hint at kindness, morality, nobility, and love" (*Iskusstvo Kino* 3, 1991, p. 11; about the gloominess of Russian movies see Sirivlia 1991; Lukshin 1991).

The social nihilism in Russian movies during the last years of *perestroika* fell into two levels. Although there was a general tendency toward increasing social pessimism, in several cases very gloomy movies were followed by movies with a lower degree of pessimism.

The First Level (Mostly 1989–1990)

Films of the first pessimistic level present the world as sinister and are more philosophical than critical films of the previous era. The first movie of this type was Mamin's *Fountain*. A large crumbling multiunit apartment building is used to symbolize the country and the tragedy of a decaying socialist society. The residents of the building are obedient beings willing to tolerate and rationalize any and all suffering imposed on them by their superiors. When the heating system fails they submissively accept the cold. They react similarly when they lose their electricity. The building's residents are portrayed as sheep, patiently awaiting their building's (i.e., their country's) collapse.

The heroes of Riazanov's *Chosen Heaven* reject almost all social values. This is in contrast to his warm movies of the past in which good people and noble values ultimately win out. This movie derogates the party, the army, the police, the Soviet intelligentsia, and war heroes. It suggests instead that the residents of a Moscow slum are actually the noblest people in the country. The movie also implies that there is no hope for the salvation of Russia. The heroes (forty-three residents from the slum) wait for an extraterrestrial spaceship to take them to another world where there is "human life." Although this film advances few positive values, it does point to friendship as a virtue that can help people to cope with their terrible lives. Furthermore, some characters, like the painter Fima or the colonel, could be considered positive since they try to help other people.

The heroes of *The House under the Starry Sky* also do not find solutions to their problems in Russia. Some of them leave for America. Others, like the protagonists in *Chosen Heaven*, prefer to start a journey, this time in a balloon, without knowing where it will land.[4]

The Second Level (Mostly 1990–1992)

Movies of the second level of pessimism basically describe the country as a totally absurd and disorganized mess. Muratova's *Asthenic Syndrome* is, of course, the peak of this nihilism. In this movie, as one critic noted, "the two main personalities decompose into molecules of disconnected acts and impulses" (*Nedelia*, 21 January 1990). The title refers to the medical condition in which people become extremely sensitive. Their mood can be changed instantly by the pettiest circumstances. They constantly vacillate between desperation and excessive hilarity. This condition metaphorically conveys the absolute instability of society.

Ultimately, this syndrome causes one to lose stable contact with others, and again parallels Russian society. What is more, those with asthenic syndrome are often cruel, or at best indifferent to each other, and lose control of themselves. The film's famous scene depicting people waiting in line for fish is a symbol of people's hatred of each other while struggling for survival.

The film opens with Nikolai Alexeievich, an English teacher and the main character, watching a movie about a doctor whose husband has just died. The heroine, in her despair, violates all norms of decent behavior. She has sex with a vagabond one day after the funeral and swears repeatedly on a crowded subway. However, this sad film has no effect on Nikolai. He has his own tribulations to worry about. These include his wish to become a writer and leave the abject school, his insensitive wife, and his stupid colleagues and students. The single sane reaction to this crazy world is to fall sleep at any moment, and Nikolai does this often—in the subway or during a school meeting (about this movie see Freilikh 1990; Bogomolov 1991; Plakhov 1992; see also *Komsomolskaia Pravda*, 2 June 1990; *Nedelia*, 21 January 1990; *Sovietskii Ekran* 4, 1990, pp. 18–19).

Dozens of similar movies were made in Russia at this time, but none matched the quality of *Asthenic Syndrome*. One example is Victor Aristov's *Satan* (1991), which depicts an equally gloomy portrait of society. All the characters are extremely hostile and unfriendly to each other. The heroes are involved in criminal activities and their victims are morally no better than the gangsters. Even children are presented as nasty and unpleasant beings. In fact, there is no single protagonist capable of spurring any positive feelings in the viewer.[5]

FROM THE CONQUEST OF THE COSMOS
TO THE FLIGHT TO THE COSMOS

The first three decades after the Bolshevik Revolution, and in particular the first ten years, were permeated with messianic ideas about the transformation of nature and even the conquest of the cosmos. The official ideology stressed the centrality of humanity in the biological pecking order, but also the almost divine role of technology. In fact it was technology that would assert humanity's final domination over nature and the cosmos. Consequently the earth became, de facto, the logical center of the universe, which was to some degree the restoration of Christian views of the cosmos. This Promethean humanism, or Promethean anthrocentrism, was one of the most important elements of Soviet ideology in its early stages. Marxism and Russian cultural traditions fed these millenarian sentiments. It is not surprising, then, that some of the early Soviet movies (e.g., Eisenstein's *The Old and the New*), as well as several intellectuals like Konstantin Tsiolkovskii (1857–1935)—the universally recognized founder of space science—were under the direct influence of Nikolai Fedorov, a Russian self-made philosopher who preached the resurrection of the dead and recommended relocating them in space.

Official ideology suggested that the October Revolution was of Promethean significance and marked the turning point in humankind's (and the universe's) history. The Soviet people were viewed as the chosen nation, while humankind on the whole was regarded as a chosen species, whose destiny in the universe was radically different from all other life on Earth and in space.

Aelita, mentioned before, is only one of the films with a strong belief in the happy future of human beings as the victors of space. Vasilii Zhuravlev's *Cosmic Voyage* (1936)—which used Tsiolkovskii as a consultant—told about a flight to the moon and even about a trip to its mysterious unknown side. Dovzhenko's *Michurin* (1949) was one of many movies that glorified human control over nature.

Notions about the conquest of nature and the cosmos continued to circulate in the post-Stalin era, but with less scope. The launching of the Soviet *Sputnik* in 1957 and Gagarin's space flight in 1961 revived the cosmic theme in Soviet public life and the leading role of Russians in the conquest of space. Vladimir Voinovich, the future Soviet dissident and author of numerous scripts very critical of Soviet reality, wrote the lyrics for a very popular song promising that cosmonauts "will leave their traces on remote planets." Daniil Khrabrovitskii's *The Taming of Fire* (1972) was about the Soviet space program and its successes.

Perestroika, with its freedom of expression, radically changed the public's attitude toward the space theme as well as the idea of the transformation of nature in Soviet life. The official infatuation with the cosmos and the hubris about mastering nature was attacked for various reasons. First, the liberals accused the state of spending gigantic resources on space programs while the standard of living in the country was very low. Second, all experiments with space and changing the Earth's nature were seen as dangerous for the future of humankind. Third, dreams about conquering the cosmos, as well as transforming the climate and changing the course of rivers, were castigated as a part of the utopian approach to reality so typical of Marxism.

Bortko's *Dog's Heart* (1988) based on Mikhail Bulgakov's novel was typical in this respect. The movie ridiculed the obsession with space, science, and the belief in transforming nature in the early years of Soviet society. Another movie, Pezhemskii's *The Trek of Comrade Chkalov through the North Pole*, ridiculed the heroes who wanted, as was mentioned earlier, to change the rotation of the Earth. In Naumov's *Law* (1991) Lavrentii Beria, the chief of Stalin's secret police and the man responsible for the development of Soviet rockets and atomic weapons, was compared with the devil. The rejection of cosmic claims was combined with the abandonment of the idea about the role of Russia as the vanguard of the transformation of humankind in the world as a result of the victory of the Bolsheviks. This, of course, had been an essential part of official ideology up to the late sixties.

The slow retreat from this idea started in the seventies with the growing role of Russophilism in official ideology. Facing the growing Soviet economic retardation and relinquishing the idea of catching up with the United States in technology, Russophiles proclaimed themselves conservationists. They accused the West of plundering nature with its technological progress and advanced Russian claims of moral superiority. We noted this development in the Russophile movies of the seventies and early eighties. Several movies, also influenced by Russophilism, proclaimed the defense of nature at the expense of technological progress as one of the Russophiles' most important tasks. This is a leading theme in Gerasimov's *By the Lake* (1970) and *Do Not Shoot the White Swans* (1982). Attitudes toward space were also changing. Tarkovskii's *Soliaris* (1972) treated an alien civilization not as an object of conquest but with respect and awe. Moreover, civilization revealed itself mostly through the psychological drama of one of the protagonists. The heroes emerged not as the representatives of the socialist motherland who were eager to explain the benefits of communism to aliens, but as the representatives of a planet that looked small and vulnerable from space.

Movies of 1990–1991 had already dismissed the Russian claim to superiority in any area. Furthermore, many directors went so far as to present the Russian drama as the tragedy of human beings in general. They began to describe humankind as a sort of biological outcast among other earthly creatures. Human beings were depicted in the films of Muratova, Soloviev, and several others as ugly and vicious to their own kin, and ready to destroy themselves and the planet. Human ascendance (read: Soviet Russia or Russian history) was depicted not as a triumph of evolution, but actually a terrible aberration for which nature would pay dearly. In this context, one could understand why recent Soviet movies were filled with extremely ugly personalities, both in behavior and external appearance, and why animals and not people began to be the positive heroes. Although not antihumanistic (i.e., attacking such values as love, compassion, and respect for life and dignity), Russian movies became antihuman. Humanity (Russia) was transformed into some sort of negative messiah—the only species able and willing to destroy the Earth. In such movies as *Chosen Heaven* and *The House under the Starry Sky* —both with titles related to space—heroes left the Earth as did the heroes in the old movies. However, they did not conquer other planets but looked for refuge from the ordeals of terrestrial life.

THE LACK OF HOPE IN MOVIES

Only a handful of films during this time offer the viewer any hope for the future. Muratova's *The Sensitive Militiaman* is one example. Although centered around the sentimental story of a policeman who adopts a child, the director depicts many idiocies of Soviet life. The regular lack of water in the city, caused by absurd problems, sets the tone for the movie. However, by focusing on the new baby and the warm relationship between the young couple, this movie is not nearly as tragic as *Asthenic Syndrome*.

The plot of Abrashitov'a *Armavir* (1991) revolves around a cruise ship that, due to a catastrophe, leaves its passengers with amnesia about their parents, relatives, and the other participants of the voyage. The hero is a passenger named Marina whose father and husband search frantically for her. When they are united, they begin to gradually reestablish their relationship with her to give some hope for the future. The analogy with the collapse of Soviet society is evident, and was later confirmed by the director (*Komsomolskaia Pravda*, 14 November 1992; *Iskusstvo Kino* 12, 1991, pp. 86–90).

Nikolai Dostal's movie *The Cloud Paradise* (1991) can also be considered a relatively optimistic film. It depicts the extremely boring life in a provincial city. However, the residents are very nice people. They help the hero, Kol'ka, when he jokingly says he wants to go live in the Far East.

His friends practically force him to pack a suitcase brought by one of them and to get on the bus. However, the movie is hopeful only on the surface, because the hero and his friends are unable to change their boring and evidently meaningless lives.

Not surprisingly, due to this trend toward apocalyptic and pessimistic films, the number of comedies declined greatly between 1989 and 1992. Some directors continued to claim that their movies were comedies, such as Riazanov's *Chosen Heaven*. To most viewers, however, they obviously were not.

PESSIMIST IDEOLOGY AS A REFLECTION OF RUSSIAN REALITY

Unconstrained by state censorship, Soviet filmmakers in 1989–1992 were finally able to follow the moviemaking guidelines used by their Western colleagues. That is, they could make movies guided (and thus self-censored) only by their desire to please their audience and their wish for commercial success. These two factors greatly influenced the Russian film industry during this period.

Most films made between 1989 and 1992 reflect the enormous struggles of a society moving from Communism toward a new social system. This new system, a sort of capitalism, seemed only moderately attractive to many Russian filmmakers. The Russian movies produced during this time help document a remarkable period in Russian history. They provide a unique source of information for sociologists studying contemporary Russian society. In addition, these movies will prove extremely useful to future historians focusing on this period.

The gloomy mood of the movies of 1989–1992 reflects the popular mood in Russia during this period. This mood is confirmed by the sociological data of the time. According to surveys conducted in 1989–1992, 80 percent of the population offered gloomy assessments of their lives and pessimistic predictions for the future. They foresaw hunger, civil war, technological disasters, economic collapse, and numerous other dire developments. The only disaster not consistently predicted was nuclear war. In fact, this was regularly omitted from the Soviet people's roster of imminent evils. In the same polls, the majority of the Russian people also criticized Soviet society's moral level and decried the disintegration of the social fabric and the degradation of basic human virtues (see Levada 1990; Grushin 1991–1992).

Still, even though the gloom common to the movies of 1989–1992 reflected the mood of the people, it is unclear whether the movies (or the popular mood, for that matter) were "fair" to reality and free from exaggeration. That is, it is unclear to what extent the movies and public opinion abandoned the distorting lenses used prior to 1985.

Of course, the question of whether the movies of 1989–1992 accurately reflected reality is quite complex. It was debated intensely by Russian intellectuals during 1991–1992. Among the issues discussed were whether the movies and public opinion adequately reflected reality and to what extent they were both part of that reality. Predictably, little consensus was reached regarding these questions.

ANOTHER SOURCE OF IDEOLOGICAL INSPIRATION: POPULAR HEDONISM

Between 1986 and 1989, filmmakers continued, in one way or another, to be embroiled in the ideological struggle. Therefore, they usually had some ideological target (the old Marxist ideology, the liberal ideology, the Russophile ideology, etc.). However, after 1989 this changed somewhat. Moviemakers began to reflect the unconstrained hedonism of the masses. They were in fact reflecting a new individualistic and hedonistic ideology that began to be espoused by millions of Russians. Everyone found themselves in an ideological and moral vacuum after the collapse of communism.

At this point, movies began to reflect a mixture of many ideologies, including liberal capitalism and the negative and hedonistic ideologies. We will discuss the impact of this mixed ideology later.

THE RUSSIAN QUESTION IN THE MOVIE INDUSTRY

Between 1989 and 1991, Russophile ideology became increasingly prominent. This was in particular contrast to the early years of *perestroika*, when its advocates were in disarray. For the Russophiles, the processes occurring since 1985 directly threatened the Russian people, culture, traditions, and even their state.

In the movie industry, however, Russophile ideology lost influence, unlike in the 1970s and early 1980s when Russophiles dominated the industry. By 1989, the Russophiles were reduced to publishing articles in the Russophile press decrying the Westernization of the movie industry. They also raged about filmmakers' responsibility for Russia's demoralization and the weakening of Russian traditions and morals. In the early 1990s, the single prominent Russophile director has been Sergei Bondarchuk, who has continued to make movies in the old Russophile tradition.

A less renowned director whose movies were influenced by Russo-phile ideology was Nikolai Burliaev. In 1987 he made *Lermontov*, about the great nineteenth-century Russian poet. Among other things, the movie suggests (against all available evidence) that the poet's death in a duel was arranged by Masons and that his killer, Martynov, was a Jew.[6]

In 1990, Burliaev made *All Ahead* (1990), which was based on an earlier movie by Vasilii Belov. It revolves around the struggle between Nikolai Medvedev, a true Orthodox Russian, and Mikhail Brish. The latter is a Jew who conspires against Russia, participates in Zionist propaganda, and gets good Russian fellows drunk in order to ravish their wives.[7]

In 1992, Burliaev established a production company called Russian Film (see *Russkii Vestnik*, 3 January, 21 January 1992; *Sovietskaia Rossiia*, 19 May 1992). He was aggressively supported by several other Russo-philes who demanded the resurgence of "the ethnic Russian movie industry" and the transformation of the Moscow Institute of Cinemato-graphy into a "real Russian institution." Their demands were accom-panied by charges that the institute gives Jews preferential treatment as both students and faculty (Bokoch 1992).

Furthermore, Bondarchuk, Burliaev, and their Russophile admirers accused the liberal mass media and liberal critics of carrying out a well-orchestrated campaign against their works. They charged that the cam-paign was based not on artistic merit but on the fact that the Russophiles were defending the Russian people's national interests (*Nash Sovremen-nik* 8, 1987, pp. 164–74).

Only a few other filmmakers of the period could be considered sup-portive of the Russophiles' views, among them Nikita Mikhalkov. He is well-known for his 1970s era Russophile movies (see the interview with him in *Argumenty i Fakty* 36, 1991).[8]

Govorukhin also moved toward a moderate Russophile ideology by releasing *Russia, Which We Lost* (1992)—an apologia for the Russian mon-archy (*Nezavisimaia Gazeta*, 14 April 1992; *Izvestia* 18 May 1992; Annenskii 1992). Nikolai Gubenko, the filmmaker and actor who, in 1990–1991 was the minister of culture, also belonged to this group of Russophile sympathizers.

Russophile filmmakers and their supporters were especially infuriated by the spread of Western movies in Russian theaters. Their anger was particularly sharp toward American and French filmmakers, whom they accused of aggressively defending their own movie industry against foreign imports (*Russkii Vestnik*, 24 July 1992).

Because Russophilism was promulgated in few movies, Russophile ideology drew little attention from filmmakers espousing other ideolo-gies. Among the few movies directed against Russian chauvinism was Mamin's *Whiskers* (1990). It is a satire of Russian Nazis who idolized

Pushkin (since Pushkin had whiskers, this became part of the uniform for these Nazis), the great Russian poet who used violence to try to create a new totalitarian society.

PRIVATIZATION, MARKETIZATION, AND IDEOLOGY

The privatization and marketization of the Soviet economy greatly influenced the Soviet movie industry, including its ideologies. The disappearance of state movie organizations (Goskino disbanded in January 1992) and the emergence of approximately five hundred private firms (compared to only a few dozen state firms operating earlier) completely liberated filmmakers from state organizations.[9] The competition that emerged in the movie industry was perhaps more intense than in any other sector of the Soviet economy (although it was restrained somewhat by the creation of ASKIN, the large monopoly that controlled the country's movie theaters).[10]

At the same time, however, the withdrawal of state support from the movie industry forced several good movie firms to close, especially in the provinces and the former Soviet republics (such as Kirgizia and Lithuania). Loss of state support also contributed to the lamentable state of the single educational institute for moviemakers. Without state funding, it became much more difficult to make "highbrow" films, which was a constant, ambitious goal for many Russian cinematographers (*Kommersant*, 13 January 1992). Filmmakers quickly realized the difficulty of making art films on a market basis and agreed that such art requires state support.[11]

Economic relations in the post-Communist world created an atmosphere in which many filmmakers, including those often victimized by the Brezhnev regime, felt a sort of nostalgia for the past, when they were freer to create "serious" movies. With the advent of the market, the ideology of success and pandering to the masses replaced the once-sophisticated ideologies of many film directors.

The hunt for "green" (American dollars) became an overwhelming passion for most people engaged in moviemaking. Demanding film directors such as Alexei German were unable to find actors and producers to make movies due to the unavailability of hard currency for films about lofty issues (see the interview with German in *Komsomolskaia Pravda*, 29 February 1992; *Nezavisimaia Gazeta*, 3 June 1992).

Privatization introduced filmmakers (as well as much of the rest of the country) to the cult of the high life—conspicuous consumption and defiance of social equality, which were at least hidden in the past. The Moscow Movie Club began organizing highly publicized receptions for various occasions, with lavish feasts for members of the new political and cultural elite. These fetes contrasted sharply with the poverty experienced by the majority of Muscovites and the rest of the country in 1992.[12]

It is remarkable that, with privatization and marketization in full swing between 1989 and 1992, even liberal filmmakers could not produce movies with business people as positive characters—engines of economic progress and the country's capitalist transformation.[13]

THE EMERGENCE OF NEW BOSSES

The end of the Soviet empire led almost instantly to the dismantling of the Union of Soviet Cinematographers, which was transformed into the Confederation of Filmmakers. It recognized film unions in new states, which angered the Russophiles and Stalinists, who bemoaned any reminder of the death of the Soviet empire (*Literaturnaia Rossiia*, 12 November 1991). Still, even the new, loose confederation had little chance of survival. By 1992 there were almost no organizational ties between moviemakers in the former Soviet republics.

As a result of privatization and marketization, party apparatchiks were gradually replaced by new bosses such as money magnate Ismail Tagi-Zade, who made his fortune selling flowers in Moscow. Unfortunately, however, the new bosses were no more concerned about the quality of movies than the old bosses. Tagi-Zade, who became head of ASKIN,[14] was joined by financiers such as Mark Rudinstein and Babek Serush, who gained notoriety through financing the movie industry and movie festivals.[15]

The influence of these new Russian money moguls on the movie industry was, in Dondurei's opinion, quite negative. They inundated the Russian market with low-quality foreign movies, fostered violence and hopelessness in the movies, and remained totally indifferent to the mood and the morale of the nation (Dondurei 1992; see also German 1991; Dondurei 1991).[16]

Dondurei argues that this process has gone so far that illegal and semilegal economies form the economic basis of the Russian movie industry. As such, Dondurei predicts that should this economic base disappear, the Russian movie industry would collapse (Dondurei 1992).

THE WEST AND IDEOLOGY IN RUSSIAN MOVIES

With the advent of *glasnost*, Soviet filmmakers could enter the world film market on their own, without an intermediary and without permission from the state. Moreover, they entered into joint filmmaking ventures with foreign firms. Among the most successful movies made through such joint agreements was Pavel Lungin's famous *Taxi-Blues* (1990), made with French economic support (*Nezavisimaia Gazeta*, 29 January 1992).[17]

The West, with its highly coveted hard currency, began influencing the ideology presented in Soviet movies. This influence stemmed from Soviet filmmakers' attempts to please Western audiences. The filmmakers wanted especially to attract Western liberal intellectuals because they believed that they set the tone of Western public opinion.

At first, Soviet filmmakers created movies that corresponded to the West's image of Russian society (as the filmmakers understood it) and movies that they believed corresponded to the Western postmodern esthetic. Alexei Balabanov's *Happy Days* (1990), based on Samuel Beckett's play, is typical of such movies. So is Alexander Mitta's *Lost in Siberia* (1991).

Often, though, Russian moviemakers and critics failed to predict Western reaction to their movies. Occasionally a movie that Moscow critics dubbed primitive and outmoded—by Western standards, of course—was quite successful in the West. Lidia Bobrova's *Oh, You Geese* (1990) is a good example. Although Moscow connoisseurs declared it "deeply provincial, naive, poor, exotic, and black-and-white," and rejected it as a bad imitation of 1960s era Soviet movies, it was received quite well in the West (Timofeievskii 1992a, 1992b; see also Gladil'-shchikov 1992).

In 1991–1992, after the first wave of Russian films hit the West, Russian filmmakers began gradually changing their perceptions of Western tastes. Specifically, they began reassessing their initial judgment of postmodernism as the surest road to success in the West.[18]

RUSSIAN DIRECTORS IN THE WEST

In the early 1970s, a few Russian filmmakers, mostly of Jewish origin appeared in the West as a result of the so-called third wave of emigration. Having emigrated, they lost all contact with the Soviet movie industry and were totally isolated from Brezhnev's Russia. As such, they tried to identify themselves with the moviemakers of their new countries (primarily in America and Israel). As a rule, however, they did so rather unsuccessfully.

Tarkovskii, the most prominent of these filmmakers, stayed in the West for six years and refused to return to the USSR in 1982 when he officially proclaimed his defection. (He remained in the West until his death in 1986.) Unlike other Russian directors who had emigrated to the West, he always considered himself a Russian filmmaker. During his stay in the West he made a few excellent movies. They were all about Russia and included *Stalker* (1979), *Nostalgia* (1983), and *Sacrifice* (1986).

When the Russian political order relaxed in 1987–1989, a throng of Russian filmmakers rushed to the West. They were looking not only for favorable conditions for their work but for more comfortable lives. They either remained in the West or returned to the motherland with hard currency in hand.

Andrei Mikhalkov-Konchalovskii (sometimes referred to simply as Konchalovskii), who left Russia before 1985, was clearly the most successful of these filmmakers. He made movies totally devoid of Russian elements [such as *Maria's Lovers* (1984), *Runaway Train* (1985), *Duet for One* (1986), and *Tango and Cash* (1989)], as well as movies inspired by Russia (such as *Black Eyes* and *The Inner Circle*; about his life in the West see Konchalovskii 1988, 1989; see also Plakhov 1989; Dementieva 1990).[19]

Other former Soviet directors and script writers who worked in the West included Otar Ioseliani and Iraklii Kvirikadze.

NEW HEROES OF RUSSIAN MOVIES (1989–1992)

The prominent characters in the movies of 1991–1992 are radically different from the those in movies released in the early years of *perestroika*, not to mention those in movies from earlier stages of Soviet history. Most of the characters are in conflict with laws, ideology, and even with the Ten Commandments. In general, Russian movies are ambivalent toward these characters. They sometimes romanticize them as enemies of a despicable social order, hypocrisy, and bigotry. Sometimes they condemned them and the society that produced them.

FORMER NEGATIVE HEROES

Criminals

Of course, criminals appeared in hundreds of earlier Soviet movies. However, they were always presented as evil people. The official Soviet ideology was strongly hostile to any violence or other illegal act performed without the permission and blessing of the party. And the party was hesitant to encourage violence against the anyone no matter how indirect the encouragement or noble the motive.

Moreover, given the official dogma that there was no social basis for crime in a socialist society, official ideology prohibited even remotely justifying criminal behavior by reference to social causes. Even mild romanticization of offenders was impossible in Soviet movies. A related official dogma held that crime, especially organized crime, was rare in socialist society. And, of course, the official ideology prohibited mention of any connection between criminals and the party and state apparatuses.

Thus, prior to 1985, criminals were depicted in Russian movies as ugly people, social outcasts, partners of external or internal enemies of the Soviet system, and totally responsible for their actions. This representation can be seen, for example, in Semenov and Lianozova's *Confrontation* (1985).

Criminals received sympathetic treatment only if they demonstrated some sign of social recovery. Such recoveries were usually attributable to the positive impact of socialist society. One of the first Soviet talkies, Ekk's *Pass for Life* (1931), depicted the joyous return of lawbreakers to good Soviet life.

Given this history, the release of Shukshin's *Red Snowball Tree* (1974), which was strongly opposed by officials, was a major event. In the movie, a former criminal, Egor Proskudin, is presented as morally superior to many "honest" Soviet people. Even Riazanov's comedy *Beware the Car!* (1966) was accepted with great reservations by officials. In *Beware the Car!*, Detochkin, an altruistic fellow, steals cars from people who have enriched themselves through illegal means. Although he uses the money from the stolen cars to help kindergartens, he does so by taking justice into his own hands. The Soviet regime could not support such action. When presenting criminal behavior, Soviet filmmakers initially felt bound by *glasnost* to reveal the major official myths regarding this social issue. Later, however, as they did with other topics, they began catering more to public tastes and expectations.

The Scope of Criminality

With *glasnost*, movies with criminals as central characters changed radically. First, directors could finally portray crime as a mass phenomenon in Soviet society. One of the first movies after 1985 to show the extent of crime in the country was Iurii Kara's *Thieves in Law* (1988). Khabibulat Faiziev's *Jackals* (1991) suggested that criminals totally controlled the whole city, (apparently Kazan').

The Origins of Crime

After 1985, Soviet film directors, like many of their American counterparts, began examining the social origins of crime. They gradually shifted responsibility for crime from the individual to society. *My Name Is Arlekino* was among the first movies to look for the social roots of youth crime. *My Name Is Arlekino* explains crime in terms of social class. It points out that gangs consist primarily of boys from working-class neighborhoods who loathe the rich kids from downtown.

Romanticization of Criminals

Understanding the social causes of malfeasance and forgiving the criminal is one thing. However, romanticizing the culprit is another altogether, and this second step was totally prohibited before 1985. It became quite popular in the era of *glasnost*, however, even if some directors like A. Proshkin in *The Cold Summer of 1953* (1987), in which criminals were described as beasts, did not follow the new fashion.

Although most film directors did not go so far as to present criminals as positive heroes, many directors did endow criminals with some positive features (such as generosity and courage). The criminal in *Assa*, for example, is a murderer and a swindler. Still, the character, as played by Stanislav Govorukhin, arouses some sympathy compared to the other petty individuals of the Brezhnev era. In Friedberg's *Little Doll*, the single positive teenager in the ninth-grade class is Panov, who is under police supervision for being a hooligan.

Of course, Kara's *Thieves in Law* (an antediluvian *Godfather*, according to its detractors in Moscow) went much farther than did *Assa*. Artur, the main character in *Thieves in Law*, is a noble mobster. He is an admirer of poetry who robs only the rich. However, he resorts to the cruelest tactics to get his way (torturing his victims with a hot iron, for example). Law enforcement officials are portrayed as corrupt and arouse no sympathy. One Moscow critic noted that, "the script appears rather trivial in the world of cinematography with its numerous Robin Hood characters, but in the Soviet past such a script would have been unbelievable" (*Iskusstvo Kino* 6, 1990, pp. 15–16).

In *Satan*, Vitalii, a devilish character (among other things he kills the ten-year-old daughter of his lover Elena and rapes the bride of his friend at their wedding), refuses to take his part of the ransom for a kidnapped girl. He declares to Elena, in quite a quite plausible way, that he killed her daughter only because Elena rejected him as a lover.

In several movies, filmmakers actually endorsed their heroes taking justice into their own hands and killing the bad guys. In *Assa*, the bandit's mistress murders him after he kills a boy, Banan, with whom she had secretly fallen in love. In A. Muratov's *Beast* (1990) and Viacheslav Sorokin's *Marked* (1991) we see noble people as avengers who punish criminals and mafiosi without the participation of the police.

With the romanticization of crime, and the criminalization of the Soviet population, the jargon of criminals and profanity made its way into Russian movies beginning in the late 1980s. At first, as with other topics, this happened primarily as a challenge to the puritanical official ideology and the hypocrisy of Soviet life. Later, however, it became postmodernist chic. Along with naked bodies and sexual acts it became a fixture of many, if not most movies. The peak of this use of language comes in *Asthenic Syndrome*. The main female character, a doctor, has a monologue in a subway consisting entirely of four-letter words. Moreover, some filmmakers went so far as to use expletives in the titles of their movies. Efim Gal'perin, for example, named a film *Blia* (1990), which is inadequately translated as "whore."

Organized Crime: Mafias

Contemporary organized crime figures finally appeared in Soviet movies in 1989. Earlier *glasnost* era movies, such as German's *My Friend Lapshin* (1984), had depicted criminal gangs as operating in the distant past. *Thieves in Law* was among the first films to show well-organized gangs operating in contemporary Soviet society.

In the final scene of G. Ivanov's *Shtemp* (1991), two gangs meet by a restaurant in a Moscow suburb. Although the audience expects a bloody confrontation, the leaders of both mafias agree to divide the capital into zones that each of them will control. The mafias are presented as being more powerful than the state. One mafia boss, furious that his bodyguard has had a love affair with his mistress, tries to exact revenge even though the bodyguard is in prison.

Connections with the Bureaucracy

Between 1989 and 1992, filmmakers also portrayed the Soviet mafias as closely intertwined with the state and party apparatuses. In *Jackals*, for example, a local gang known for its cruelty is directly linked to the regional first party secretary. The first secretary, in turn, is connected to the Moscow leadership. The gang is not only involved in drugs and racketeering; it also participates in political struggles and is prepared to help local Nazis seize power. A similar merging of crime and politics in seen in *Satan*. Here, the head of the local government asks mafia leaders to help her find a kidnapped girl. The government leader is convinced that the mafia will be far more efficient than the police.

In Poliakov's *Corruption* (1990), the KGB plays a leading role in the functioning of a large mafia. This mafia, which concentrates on fraud in the building industry, is headed by Elena, a young and attractive woman.

Prostitutes

The characterization of prostitutes in Soviet movies closely followed that of criminals. It went from total rejection to an understanding that their behavior, although deplorable, is socially determined. In fact, many prostitutes, with their frankness and cynicism, appear more principled than either the hypocritical representatives of the dominant class or their honest but ignorant parents.

Piotr Todorovskii's *Intergirl* (1988) revolutionized the presentation of Russian prostitutes. *Intergirl* was not only the first movie about Soviet prostitutes, it was also the first movie about the Soviet prostitutes (referred to in Russian slang as *putana*) who work only for hard currency. The movie describes the nature of the occupation, including both its advantages (such as living the good life) and its disadvantages (such as regular conflicts with the police). Tatiana Zaitseva, the movie's heroine, is presented with compassion and sympathy.

The film also recognizes that her behavior is, at least in part, driven by her environment. Tatiana has a monologue about her miserable life and lack of basic goods: She cites the ever-present lies and hypocrisy in Soviet society, and describes her kindness toward her mother (a naive Soviet teacher), patients (Tatiana is also a nurse), and friends. The monologue creates sympathy for her predicament. It also clarifies that her illegal occupation is the only way out of the life imposed on her by socialism.

Mikhail Mel'nichenko's *Top Class* (1991) develops a theme that is only briefly touched on in *Intergirl*: the KGB's use of prostitutes in its work with foreigners. *Top Class* reveals nothing of how its heroine, Vera, became a prostitute. Viewers are led to believe that the KGB pressured her to collaborate and also plans to do the same with her daughter. The film provides another example of prostitutes as victims of society. In *Top Class*, however, we see that not only has the KGB exploited Vera as a spy, it has also blackmailed her to prevent her from marrying a foreigner and relocating to Germany, which is her only hope of escaping her terrible life in Russia.[20]

Drunkards, Drug Addicts, Beggars, and Loafers

Like criminals and prostitutes, characters engaging in other forms of socially deviant behavior were also presented differently in movies of the *glasnost* era compared to earlier films.

For decades, socialist realism and official ideology looked down on those not properly contributing to the state's prosperity and might. This stance was absolute during the Stalin era. Beginning in the 1960s, however, moviemakers began adopting a milder stance toward those who violated socialist morals, particularly if they showed signs of improvement.

Attitudes toward deviants relaxed significantly during the 1970s under the influence of Russophile ideology. Directors espousing Russophile ideology wanted to prove that Russians were better than others because of their deep devotion to spiritual values and their contempt for material success. Thus, Russophile directors were quite tolerant toward drunkards and loafers as long as they were good and noble people. This can be seen in Menshov's *Love and Pigeons* (1984) and Mikhalkov's *A Few Days from the Life of Oblomov* (1980).

Glasnost took the process of rehabilitating immoral persons even further. However, this was not because *glasnost* era filmmakers followed Russophile precepts. It was because they regarded positive treatment of immoral persons as another blow to the official ideology. The moviemakers' behavior resembled the idolatry of tramps seen in Gorky's famous stories from the late nineteenth century.

Drunkards and loafers were seen in numerous Russian movies between 1989 and 1991. In *Chosen Heaven*, for example, a painter named Fima chooses to become a beggar in order to be free of society's demands. Lia Akhedzhakova, who played Fima, describes her character as "a genuine aristocrat of spirit, a person who can do without all material goods" (*Komsomolskaia Pravda*, 4 January 1992). Heavy drinking is similarly romanticized in *Humble Cemetery*, *Little Vera*, and other movies made between 1989 and 1991.

In Livnev's *Kicks* (1991), the female lead is a drug-addicted singer. Entertainment industry bosses replace her with a clone and then throw her out a twenty-seventh-floor window.

Sexual Enthusiasts

As mentioned earlier, sex was taboo in pre-*glasnost* Soviet movies. Although Soviet movies praised romantic love, this love was always based on noble motives ranging from respect for heroic labor (as seen in the movies of the 1930s) to spiritual affinity for one another (as seen in the movies of the 1970s). It was never based on sexual desire.[21]

Soviet moviemakers regarded Smirnov's *Autumn* (1975) as a milestone and great victory in their struggle against hypocritical puritanism. *Autumn* contained an unbelievable scene: two lovers (completely covered, of course) in bed together.[22]

In the early years of *glasnost*, cinematographers considered the expansion of sexual matters in movies to be another important aspect of the struggle against official ideology. This sexual offensive was carried out on several fronts:

1. Sexual relations were presented as facts of life that should not be hypocritically ignored.

2. Sex was presented as pleasurable in and of itself, as opposed to the previous focus on romantic and even platonic elements of relationships.

3. Partners in sexual relations were presented as much more diverse than previous movies and propaganda had suggested.

4. The prevalence of prostitution in socialist society was revealed. Prostitution was presented as being forced on Soviet women by their circumstances.

5. Party apparatchiks were shown exploiting their positions to get sexual favors from their subordinates.

6. Teenagers were seen beginning their sexual lives much earlier than had been admitted in official propaganda.

Thus, the movies of 1986–1988 presented a strong challenge to official ideology. In addition, film directors immediately understood that the people's hunger for eroticism could greatly boost the popularity of their films. Predictably, the conservatives declared this sexual offensive to be a threat to the entire political and ideological order. Needless to say, they tried exhaustively to stop it.

These sexual topics were presented quite graphically (at least by contemporary Soviet standards) in *Little Vera*, *The Extraordinary Event of District Importance*, and *Intergirl*. These movies not only showed naked people but scenes of lovemaking (albeit without visible details).

Little Vera, for example, with its relatively explicit depiction of two young people making love, presents carnal passion as a normal part of human relations. It thereby defies the dominant ideology.[23] *The Extraordinary Event of District Importance* shows Komsomol leaders, absorbed by their sexual desires, using their status to get sexual pleasures. These are often presented as violent. *Intergirl* reveals the pervasiveness of sex and the frequency with which women (including those with jobs in the official world) earn needed additional income by selling their bodies. Similar themes dominate S. Ashkenazi's *Criminal Talent* (1988).

In Andrei Razumovskii's *Nice Little Mug* (1990), Iulia, the daughter of strict, highbrow intellectuals, discovers that sex is an extremely pleasurable part of life. Her sexual desires lead her to marry the scoundrel Gena. She tolerates his licentious behavior, and even forgives him for giving her a venereal disease. This is another hard fact of life that was ignored in earlier Soviet movies.

Several Soviet movies depict unusual sexual partners. Examples include an old teacher and a girl in *Amusements of Youth*, a female teacher and her secondary school student in *Little Doll*, and, in a highly explicit love scene, a woman in her forties and a teenager in *My Name Is Arlekino*. Several movies, including *My Name Is Arlekino*, depict teenagers as quite sexually active, something else that Soviet society had previously denied.

Over time, sexual themes lost their ideological overtones and became simply a popular subject for viewers. The amount of graphic sex in movies increased substantially in 1989. This was the beginning of competition between Soviet movies and foreign films for the number of naked women and sexual scenes depicted. In fact, it seemed to many journalists and critics that the Soviet movie industry had become obsessed with graphic sex.

In Elena Nikolaieva's *Sex Fairy Tale* (1991), the main character changes lovers in rapid succession but fails to seduce a woman played by the famous actress Liudmila Gurchenko. The main characters in Ol'ga Zhukova's *Merry Christmas in Paris* (1991) are young lesbians who lure partygoers to their apartment to beat, rob, and even kill them in a graphic way [see also V. Tregubov's *Tower* (1989) and V. Shevelev's *They Could Not Get Along* (1989); about sexual themes in Soviet movies in 1987–1989, see *Pravda*, 21 November 1989; *Literaturnaia Gazeta*, 29 September 1989; *Komsomolskaia Pravda*, 5 October 1991].[24]

Directors dealing with issues unrelated to sex seized any opportunity to at least show a naked breast or buttock. Thus they both defied the old ideological prudery and attracted viewers [see, for instance, Georgii Danelia's *Passport* (1990), about the life of Georgian emigrants in Israel; Karen Shakhnazarov's *Tsar's Murder* (1991); M. Kats's *Desert* (1991), about the life of Christ, which depicts the debauchery in King Herod's court; and Snezhkin's *Failure to Return* (1991), into which the filmmaker, apparently without reason, inserted a scene with three naked women]. Of course, the depiction of naked actors is sometimes vindicated by esthetic considerations, as in Muratova's *The Sensitive Militiaman*. This film opens with young spouses awakened by an alarm clock.

Even historical figures drew special attention because of their sex life. See, for example, Victor Merezhko's *The Kremlin Secrets of the Seventeenth Century* (1991), with Ivan the Terrible—complete with sexual vices—as the main hero.[25]

The depiction of sex in Soviet movies became so widespread that, in December 1991, a festival was held entitled "Sex Exists."[26] Of the forty-nine movies presented at the festival, forty were heavily loaded with sex scenes (*Kommersant*, 16 December 1991).

Suicide

Before 1985, suicide by Soviet people was taboo in both movies and books. Only enemies of the state were permitted to kill themselves. After 1985, however, suicide became the subject of several films.

In most cases, filmmakers presented suicide as a tragic but somewhat unavoidable escape from the anguish of life. In Leon Menaker's *Dog's Feast* (1990), for example, a nice, single woman in her forties living in a small city picks up Arkadii, an ex-convict, in a railway station. Although she hopes to start a family with him, he has an affair with a neighbor. This betrayal, combined with the misery of her life, the alcoholism all around her, and the total indifference of socialist society, is too much for her. She leaves the gas on in the kitchen.

In *Intergirl*, Tatiana Zaitseva intentionally collides with a truck because she cannot see a way out of her problems. In *Games for Teenagers*, Mary, isolated from everyone around her, tries to kill herself.

Emigrants

The treatment of emigration in Soviet movies has changed considerably over the years. During the first fifteen years of legal emigration (from 1971 to 1986), emigration was simply ignored by filmmakers. Because official ideology held that nobody would want to leave the socialist paradise, emigration could be addressed only indirectly. A movie could, for example, depict the tribulations of postrevolutionary Russian emigres suffering far from their motherland. This theme is explored in S. Vronskii's *White Snow of Russia* (1980). It follows the life of Alexander Alekhine, the Russian world chess champion who left the country after the revolution. His life is, of course, wretched.

During this initial period, Georgii Danelia and R. Gabriadze's *Mimino* (1978), which was considered quite brave, was probably the single exception to the rule of ignoring or denigrating emigrés. In *Mimino*, the hero tries to call his friend living in the Azerbaidzhani city of Telavi. Because of an operator's mistake he reaches Tel Aviv instead and, by chance, a Georgian Jew. Crying, they sing a Georgian song together. In this scene, the filmmaker kills two birds with one stone: He follows the ideological line that all emigrés should agonize for the motherland, and also suggests that at least some emigrés are not monsters.

The next major step in the depiction of emigration came after 1985, with Alexander Tovstonogov's *Sholom Aleichem 40* (1987). This movie suggests that many emigres leave the motherland unwillingly and under pressure from unscrupulous relatives. In the movie, a Jewish couple loyal to Russia are forced to emigrate by their two greedy sons. Along with presenting a more sympathetic view of emigration, *Sholom Aleichem 40* broke other ground as well. One of the characters is a Russian man who disapproves of emigration. He also happens to be romantically involved with the daughter of the emigrating Jewish couple. Despite his disapproval, he maintains his relationship with her. He is even prepared to escort her to the airport.[27]

As *glasnost* progressed and "the Jewish question" became less taboo, potential emigrants were portrayed with increasing respect. Panfilov's *Theme*, which was made in the late seventies but was shown only in 1986, was the first movie to present emigration as defensible, although not totally justifiable. *Theme*'s hero, a failed bearded scholar who could not fulfill himself in Soviet society, finds himself working as a grave digger. He eventually decides to leave the country, even though his lover Sasha refuses to follow him.

In *Passport*, Danelia continues this trend toward acceptance of emigration. *Passport* presents two brothers—Iakob, whose mother is Jewish, and Merab, whose mother is Georgian. Iakob wants to emigrate to Israel but Merab cannot even consider leaving Georgia. Iakob, however, is being pressured to emigrate by Inga, his Russian wife. She believes that Israel will be a land of milk and honey. Through a case of mistaken identity (the brothers are twins), Merab finds himself in Israel. He then discovers that all of his old compatriots either dream of returning to the homeland or try to preserve their Georgian traditions. After several misadventures, Merab returns to Georgia and finds Iakov, who has abandoned any thought of emigrating.

The power of patriotism is seen in *Intergirl*. Here, a prostitute married to a foreigner cannot bear her boring life away from the motherland and commits suicide. The filmmaker seems to side with the ordinary people who denounce Tania for marrying a foreigner and leaving the motherland. In I. Maslennikov's *Winter Cherry-2* (1990), the heroine abandons her lover, who in the first part of the movie will not marry her despite all his promises. She goes to America, but despite her outward happiness is disillusioned and unhappy. This is a tribute to the old dogmas about life in the West.

Eventually, emigrants came to be characterized as decent and even noble people. The heroine in Valerii Todorovskii's *Love* (1991) decides to go to Israel—a decision presented sympathetically, given her suffering in Russia.

Moreover, in the movies of 1991–1992, the decision to emigrate is presented as the single respectable way out of the morass in which the Soviet people find themselves. In Soloviev's *The House under the Starry Sky*, one of the characters is the son of the director of the Russian space program. He exhorts his relatives to leave the country immediately, "for the sake of the children" and to kiss the "concrete-surfaced soil of Kennedy airport." This is one of the most glaring challenges to the fundamentals of Russian patriotism ever presented in a Russian movie. Similarly, emigration is praised in *Failure to Return* as an alternative to potential pogroms.

Jews as Heroes

Jews, their religion, and their culture were nonexistent in Soviet movies (as well as in the theater and literature) in the four decades prior to *perestroika*.[28] If these subjects were mentioned at all, it was in a negative context.[29] It is impossible to name a single positive character in pre-*glasnost* Soviet movies who can be identified as a Jew. Likewise, anti-Semitism, which was rampant following the war, was totally ignored in Soviet movies.[30]

This situation changed little during the first years of *glasnost*. In 1986, Friedberg made an initial, rather timid attempt to discuss the Jewish question in *My Dear Edison*.

One of the main heroes of *My Dear Edison*, as already mentioned, seems to be a Jew, although this is never confirmed explicitly. He is a prominent scholar with an ambiguous last name, who was expelled from Moscow to a provincial research center in the early 1950s during the acerbic anticosmopolitan campaign, in which many Jewish intellectuals were fired or arrested. Viewers are led to believe that his ethnic origin causes many of the troubles in his life.

Askol'dov's *Commissar* was the first movie in five decades to use Jews as the central positive heroes. It was officially banned until 1988—twenty years after it was made. The main character in *Commissar* is Klavdia Vavilova, a Russian female commissar. In her fight for the revolutionary cause she is merciless to everyone she regards as impeding victory. Without remorse, she shoots Emelin, a deserter who is the father of her unborn child.

She is contrasted with Efim Magazanik, a poor Jewish tailor whose humanism recognizes neither ethnicity nor class. At great risk to his and his family's life, he cares for the newborn child while the revolutionary mother joins the Red Army in its retreat from Berdichev. This city, prior to World War II, symbolized Jewish settlements.[31] *Commissar's* appearance in movie theaters meant that, after fifty years, it was possible to make new movies examining Jewish issues.[32]

Efrem Sevela's *The Parrot That Speaks Yiddish* (1990) followed *Commissar's* humanistic example. It tells, with great compassion, the story of a Jewish boy born in Vil'nius before the Second World War. The film does not hesitate to focus on the close relationship between the boy and his Jewish mother—a relationship that is the butt of numerous anti-Semitic jokes.

In Todorovskii's *Love*, the central love affair revolves around the fact that the woman is a Jew from the capital and the man is a Russian from a province. The drama stems from the woman's determination to go to Israel (she has been raped by a gang, and the district attorney—an anti-Semite—refuses to prosecute the men involved) and the man's decision to stay home. The director's sympathy is clearly on the side of the heroine.[33]

Jews are mentioned warmly in Kulidzhanov's *To Die Is Not Frightening* (1991). This movie reflects the liberal Russophile ideology combining praise of the prerevolutionary past and Orthodoxy with benign attitudes toward Jews. In the movie, a peasant who falls victim to collectivization warmly remembers Semen Abramovich, an old Jewish doctor. He says that it would be "nice to have more such Jews." It is a comment that meets with only lukewarm approval from his old landlord. In each of these movies, the message is the same as that delivered by Shylock in his famous soliloquy from *Merchant of Venice*: "We Jews are also human beings."[34]

Still, despite progress between 1990 and 1992 in accurately describing the life of the Jews, few directors dared challenge the widespread anti-Semitism. Mamin did so indirectly in *Whiskers* by depicting an increase in Russian Nazism. Aristov did so much more explicitly in *Satan*. Here, a villainous wedding guest makes an insidious toast against Jews and other non-Russians who, in his opinion, downgrade and plot against the Russians.

During this same period, several films approached the Jewish theme from another angle and played to the anti-Semites (although probably unintentionally). Shakhnazarov's *The Tsar's Murder* (1991) examines the killing of the last Russian tsar and his family in 1918. The movie's main character is Iakov Iurovskii, a Jew assigned by Lenin to kill Nicholas II and his family. Thus, the last Russian tsar and his beloved are presented as being victims of the Jews and other non-Russians. The role of Russians in this heinous act is reduced almost to nothing (see Annenskii 1991; see also *Nedelia*, 11 November 1990).

The Tsar, the Landlords, the Bourgeoisie, and the Counterrevolutionary Intellectuals

Between 1989 and 1992, a favorite twist of moviemakers was to present former exploiters and their intellectual servants as better than the revolutionary masses. These are the same masses that robbed, tortured, and killed such exploiters at the request of Bolsheviks. One of the best of these movies was, of course, Bortko's *Dog's Heart*, based on Mikhail Bulgakov's novel. In *Dog's Heart*, a wealthy doctor who despises the revolution, Marxism, and the proletariat is presented quite sympathetically. His opponent, however, is a typical representative of the working class and is seen as totally immoral and stupid. The doctor created him by putting a dog's heart into a dead drunkard.

Kulidzhanov's *To Die Is Not Frightening* is far more critical of the revolution. It praises the old landlords as hard workers and builders, and only briefly notes the gap between their material lives and those of their peasants. Among the movie's heroes are the old landlord Nikolai Mikhailovich and his daughter Ksenia Nikolaievna. They demonstrate complete moral superiority over their persecutors during the terror of the 1930s.

Defying the theory of class struggle, the director presents the landlord and Ivan, his peasant, as united in their suffering under the cruel new order. Still, the primary hero is Ksenia Nikolaievna. A thin, frail woman, she prefers to go to prison and leave her two little daughters alone in the world than to serve as an informer for the secret police. Her resolve influences Fedorenko, her prosecutor, to commit suicide rather than continue "to steep my hands in blood." In Sergei Sel'ianov and Nikolai Makarov's *The Day of the Ghost* the single positive character is the grandfather of the main protagonist. An open monarchist, he refuses to yield to any Soviet regime and spends many years in the *Gulag* rather than change his views.

The most remarkable change, of course, was the sudden appearance of Tsar Nicholas II in numerous movies. He first appears in Klimov's *Agony* (1981), where he is depicted rather negatively but not as in Soviet textbooks. He is shown simply as a human being unable to govern his country. Within a few years, however, the Russian tsar was being presented far more sympathetically. In the movies of *perestroika*, such as *The Tsar's Murder*, the tsar and his wife become positive and decent people. Nicholas II is presented here as a noble and courageous individual who accepts his death and the death of his family with great dignity. Panfilov, in discussing his new film about the tsar, described Nicholas as a "tragic figure, . . . an intellectual, [a] deeply religious person, [and as a] valiant individual [who] found the pluck to voluntarily abdicate from the throne" because he realized his inadequacy for the position (*Nezavisimaia Gazeta*, 13 March 1992).

Religious Figures and Martyrs

By 1990, religion had begun its triumphal comeback in Russia. In the past, the direct praise of religion, even in Russophile movies, was almost impossible. At best, Soviet directors could afford to make some indirect allusions to the usefulness of religion for weak people, as was done in Georgii Natanson's *All Is Left to the People* (1963) or in Stanislav Rostotskii's *From the Four Winds* (1962).

During *glasnost*, the movie industry began to produce, for the first time since 1917, movies depicting biblical figures. Kats's *Desert* is a narration about the life of Christ told against the backdrop of the metaphorical moral desert. Several other movies about biblical events were made between 1989 and 1992.

Religion and the church played increasingly significant roles in the lives of Soviet movie characters. The protagonists of *To Die Is Not Frightening* are deeply religious. The director devoted a great deal of time to scenes showing his main characters at church and participating in religious rituals.

Dead Bodies

In order to destroy Soviet ideology and its esthetic norms, Leningrad moviemakers created a new trend during the last years of the Gorbachev era. Necrorealism, which used corpses as its main characters, was, of course, another antithesis to socialist realism. Evgenii Iufit, the master of this genre, made *Papa, Santa Claus Is Dead* (1991). It is filled with degenerates, vampires, and corpses who make love to each other.

FORMER POSITIVE HEROES

Stalin

Filmmakers, like other intellectuals, considered Stalin to be the ultimate symbol of the system under which they lived. Until his death, most filmmakers followed the Orwellian precept that loving Big Brother was the best policy for survival. As described earlier, nearly all filmmakers presented themselves as Stalin's loyal devotees and glorified him in their movies. Prominent film directors who paid homage to Stalin included such well-known and respected directors as Mikhail Romm (*Lenin in October* and *Lenin in 1918*), Sergei Iutkevich (*The Man with a Gun* and *Stories about Lenin*), and the Vasiliev brothers (*The Defense of Tsaritsin*). Other directors who glorified "the greatest leader of all epochs" included Kalatozov, Kuleshov, Kozintsev, and Trauberg. Of course, Stalin's most enthusiastic minstrel was Chiaureli, who made offensive, fawning films about his patron.[35] Stalin, in turn, rewarded filmmakers' efforts with innumerable prizes, medals, and material privileges.

Filmmakers remained deferential toward Stalin until the late 1980s (their stance was inspired, in part, by Stalin's undeniably influential role in history, as heinous as it may have been). As late as 1989, Shuster's *Lost Time* (1989), based on Alexander Bek's *Appointment*, presented a rather positive image of the former Soviet leader.

Despite this public adoration, however, liberal intellectuals began in the 1960s to dream of unmasking Stalin. Due to official censorship they could not do so publicly until the late 1980s. Thus, beginning in 1989–1990, Stalin's presence could be felt in countless movies. He was either a main character, a secondary figure, or a symbol.

Two trends emerged in 1989–1990 regarding Stalin's characterization in Soviet movies. The first trend was to present Stalin as a monster. The second, less prevalent trend was to satirize Stalin's image. Occasionally, both of these trends could be seen in the same film.

Soloviev's *Black Rose* is one example of this type of film. In the beginning of the movie, the protagonist, a former *Gulag* resident, listens each morning to a recording of the official announcement of Stalin's death. He savors each word, knowing that the announcement means salvation for him and millions of his compatriots. Later in the movie, Stalin is satirized when he battles constipation.

Yevtushenko's *Stalin's Funeral* (1990) describes the terror on March 8, 1953, when hundreds of Muscovites died in a stampede during Stalin's funeral. The movie examines the cruelty of the Stalin era and is extremely hostile to "the great leader."

Other movies featuring Stalin as a main or supportive character include Kvirikadze's *Stalin's Trip to Africa* (1990), Kara's *Valtasar's Feast or the Night with Stalin* (1989), and Alexander Pavlovskii's *And to Hell with Us* (1991).[36] All of these movies present Stalin either directly or indirectly as a monster, a criminal, and a liar.

Stalin's Hangmen and Their Victims

For decades, the mass terror, the *Gulag* and the KGB's role as repressor were among the most strongly prohibited subjects for Soviet moviemakers. During the first thaw these issues were raised only indirectly. Kheifits's *Rumyantsev's Case* (1956) caused a sensation because, for the first time, a prosecutor (although only from the police and not from the KGB) was presented as a negative character. Vladimir Basov's *Silence* (1964), which is based on Iurii Bondarev's novel, took another step into the forbidden zone by discussing people who were unjustly accused and arrested in the past.

During the Brezhnev era, the *Gulag* and its victims appeared in several Soviet movies. Through various allusions, movies such as Todorovskii's

Wartime Romance (1984) introduced viewers to the period of repression. Still, it was not until late in *perestroika* that the *Gulag* became a leading theme in Soviet movies. It provided a sort of spiritual catharsis for filmmakers.

Abuladze's *Repentance* (1984) was among the first contemporary films about the *Gulag*. It was completed two years after Brezhnev's death, when feelings of imminent change were sweeping across the country. However, the movie reached a large audience only during *glasnost* (*Sovietskaia Kul'tura*, 16 January 1988; *Literaturnaia Gazeta*, 24 February 1988).

The movie was a frontal attack against Stalin's regime and its terrorist character. Parting with the ambiguous presentation of previous filmmakers, Abuladze flatly placed the origin of mass repressions in the inhuman character of the regime, which is portrayed as ready to sacrifice almost the whole nation to perpetuate its reign. The hero, Varlam Aravidze, combines the features of such persons as Beria, Mussolini, and Hitler. He is a shrewd and merciless leader who sends his best friends and colleagues to the gallows simply because he feels some remote danger to his personal power.

Of course, this film, made in 1983–1984, had to be quite allegorical. The director could claim that he was in fact depicting totalitarian society in general and not specifically Soviet society. As Iurii Karabchievskii, one of the few detractors of this movie pointed out, none of Stalin's characteristic trait's could be found in the movie's image of the dictator (*Iskusstvo Kino* 4, 1989, pp. 34–44). However, this movie was a historical milestone in the denunciation of Stalinism.[37]

One of the first films to make heroes of *Gulag* prisoners was Alexander Proshkin's *The Cold Summer of 1953* (1987). This film focuses on two wretched people who are unable to recover their zest for life after spending many years in a concentration camp. After Stalin's death, they live in a remote northern village without any hope for the future since they are not allowed back to "the continent"—European Russia. The sudden arrival of criminals, many of whom were also released in April 1953, makes these two former prisoners the defenders of the villagers.

A. Sirenko's *Sophia Petrovna* (1989), based on Lidia Chukovskaia's (1989) novel, is about the tragic days of 1937 when there were mass arrests all across the country. Sophia Petrovna, a typist, believes in the official explanation for these arrests until her own son is jailed. She is then confronted with the hostility of everyone around her. Due to her fear she burns her son's letter imploring her to convince the authorities that he is innocent.

Ptashuk's *Our Armored Train* (1989) was a huge step forward in the analysis of Stalinism and the psychology of its hangmen. The main character, Nikolai Kuznetsov, is a brave officer during the war with

Germany. After the war, he becomes the chief guard in a concentration camp. In the middle of the 1960s, the Brezhnev leadership decides to cover up the atrocities of Stalin's times. Nikolai, a true believer, tries to defend his past and Stalin's policy. He even defends his orders to shoot at prisoners who staged a demonstration proclaiming their innocence after Stalin's death. He appears as an unrepentant hangman, even though some of his former KGB colleagues are even worse, wishing for the restoration of mass terror.

In the next few years the aggressiveness of film directors toward Stalin's era increased tremendously. For example, in Vladimir Vasil'kov's *Damned Days Again in Russia* (1990), a camp worker and daughter of a KGB man falls in love with a prisoner. He is a student arrested for his love of Bunin, the Russian emigrant writer who wrote one of the first books on the Russian revolution, *Damned Days*. She is quite brave but dies while giving birth to their child. Her father, in order to avenge himself before his colleagues, participates in the cruel killing of the student. In the last scene of the movie the child, now grown, meets the old "Chekist" (KGB man) in order to find out the truth about his father's death. Instead, he finds the old man to be an unrepentant monster, representing the thousands of Stalinist hangmen who continue to dream of restoring the old order.

Rustam Khamdamov's *Anna Karamazoff* (1990) is about a woman who returns from the *Gulag* to her native city without any means of subsistence or hope. Evgenii Zymbal's *The Story of the Nonexistent Moon* (1991), fashioned after Boris Pil'niak's famous novel, tells the story of Stalin giving short shrift to Frunze, the head of the Red Army and Stalin's potential enemy. Frunze, also guilty of cruelty during the civil war, dies during surgery. The surgery is an event set up by Stalin. Several other movies glorified famous Stalin victims, such as Nikolai Bukharin, a leading Soviet commander who was murdered by Stalin in 1937 [L. Mariagin's *The Enemy of the People—Bukharin* (1989) and V. Eisner's *Marshal Bliukher* (1989)].

Intellectuals: Heroes or Bankrupt Individuals?

Developments during 1989–1992 had a tremendous impact on the place of intellectuals in Russian movies. As was discussed earlier, liberal intellectuals were the dominant positive heroes in countless movies of the 1960s and 1970s. In fact, there were probably more positive intellectuals than any other social group represented during these years. This stemmed from the conviction of filmmakers, as well as other intellectuals, that only they were consistent adversaries of Stalinism and the Soviet regime.

However, radical changes in the political sphere after 1989 allowed other political forces to come to the surface. This caused the role of intellectuals as the agents of change to diminish tremendously. At the same time, many intellectuals who came to power in the new administration revealed their unlimited yearning for prestige and material comforts. Furthermore, as knowledge about the behavior of liberal intellectuals in the past came to light, further damage was done to their image. Finally, there was also a growing disappointment with democracy among some intellectuals.

With their increasingly morose vision of the world, filmmakers did not even spare intellectuals, who had been their main positive heroes since the 1960s. This shift in the portrayal of intellectuals occurred gradually and was, of course, not linear. Gubenko's *The Danger Zone* (1988) was one of the last movies in which an intellectual-idealist (a musician) is ready to make sacrifices. In this movie, the hero helps the residents of a village destroyed by a tornado.

In *Little Doll*, Elena Mikhailovna, a school teacher, resembles the kind idealists of the previous era. She fights evil and tries to convey lofty and noble virtues to her pupils. She supports *perestroika* and is in conflict with the school principal (read: bureaucrat) because she attempts to introduce some elements of democracy into her classroom. She invites her class to vote whether they want her as a teacher or not. This was viewed as a bold act in the first years of Gorbachev's regime.

Leonid Filatov's *Bitch's Children* (1990) also hailed intellectuals. This time they are actors of a liberal vanguard theater in Moscow (evidently Iurii Liubimov's theater on Taganka). They bravely resist (by the threat of self-immolation and hunger strikes) authorities who, after Liubimov's defection to the West, want to force the actors to publicly condemn their master. However, these heroes are already far from being as morally impeccable as their colleagues in previous movies. Many of them are lascivious individuals for whom extramarital affairs are a normal way of life. They are also very vain and envious. They engage in physical fights and try to create as big a nuisance as they can.

However, these flaws are overshadowed by their determination to stand up to the totalitarian state. At the end of the film, Lev, the organizer of resistance, restores his relationship with Igor, the seducer of his wife, because he joins in the struggle.

In Lungin's *Taxi-Blues*, the portrayal of intellectuals is even more ambivalent, although still positive. In the film, Lesha Seliverstov, a brilliant saxophonist of Jewish origin, is opposed to Ivan Shlykov, a representative of the Russian masses. Lungin forces viewers to reconsider their stereotypes about both ethnic and social groups. Lesha, an intellectual, combines features that are attributed to Russians and the masses—

disorderly manners, devotion to creativity, drunkenness, poverty, lies, and an absorption with metaphysical issues. His antipode, Ivan, possesses those traits correlated in the public mind with Jews and intellectuals. He is a disciplined machinator and a calculating businessman. He is also a rather sober individual who is very concerned about his health.

The heroes' relationship could best be described as a love-hate situation. The plot revolves around Lesha's attempt not to pay Ivan, a taxi driver, his cab fare. This makes him dependent on Ivan and permits the taxi driver to torture the great musician. However, by the end of the film they ultimately understand that they need each other. This is an allusion to the closeness of Russians and Jews and the worker and the intellectual, even if their mutual attitudes are far from idyllic. Furthermore, the conflict between Lesha, a Russophile Jew, and Ivan, a Russian with fascist inclinations totally alienated from high culture, is a conflict between intellectuals and the masses—a conflict seemingly unsolvable in the near future (see the brilliant analysis of this movie in Vail and Genis 1990).

Aside from the films just discussed, most films made between 1989 and 1992 were openly hostile toward liberal intellectuals. This is in stark contrast to the movies of the previous epoch. The main hero of *The House under the Starry Sky* is Bashkirtsev, a member of the Academy of Science and the head of the Soviet space program. In order to ridicule earlier movies, Soloviev named the hero after the main character in a very "Brezhnevian" film, Khrabrovistkii's *The Taming of Fire* (1972).

In the new movie, Bashkirtsev is a blunt parody of the personage in the old one. However, the 1991 Bashkirtsev is not absorbed with state interests and is not nearly as creative as the 1972 Bashkirtsev. After demonstrating his inability to run the space program, the new Bashkirtsev is concerned only with trivial material issues.[38]

Contemptible and miserable intellectuals are also found in *Satan*. Andrei, an actor in the local theater (he performs a leading role in Chekhov's subtle *Uncle Vanya*) is the single intellectual in an almost totally criminalized provincial city. He tries to pretend that he is not infected by this world and he does not know that his wife is a gang leader. However, during a family crisis his wife angrily reminds him that without her friends he would not have a career.

In *Failure to Return*, based on Ilia Kabakov's novel, the main hero is a television journalist and an activist of *perestroika*. However, it turns out that he has been a KGB agent for many years. He has even reported on his close friends while receiving KGB support for his career.

The idea of cooperation of liberal intellectuals with the KGB is also a major theme in Mikhail Shveitser and Sofia Mil'kina's *How Do You Do, Carps?* (1992). The hero is a former KGB colonel named Innokentii Kartoshkin. He has a collection of 135,000 informers which includes people from all walks of life. Among these informers, the directors especially emphasize humanitarian intellectuals and future democrats. Thus, they promote the idea that the informers are in no way better than the KGB colonel. Furthermore, the colonel, unlike his intellectual squealers, finally repents and even denounces the intellectuals for their moral depravity. With this elegant twist, the directors equate the hangman and his victims. This is a characteristic example of the moral relativism prevalent in Russian films during the early 1990s.

In 1991, filmmakers began to move from the merciless portrayals of their contemporaries to angry analyses of intellectuals of the past. In the process they attempted to debunk the myths about them.

Cynics (1992), a film by Meskhiev based on Mariengof's novel, is about victims of the revolution and the civil war. The victims are people whose lives were destroyed by the Bolsheviks. However, unlike Kulidzhanov's film *To Die Is Not Frightening*, this movie has no positive heroes. The victims, Russian intellectuals, are just as cynical and corrupt as the commissars and new NEP businessmen. One of the main characters, a prerevolutionary historian, goes to a flea market and sells books from the library collection that his family had accumulated over many generations. He also shows his lack of scruples by becoming a pimp while living with his cheating wife.

Dubious Revolutionaries

Revolutionaries fighting for a new society did not disappear totally from movies. Compared to their predecessors, however, they were portrayed in a new light. As heroic but tragic figures who sacrifice their lives for the cause, they could not know the ultimate consequences of their bold activities. While continuing to praise these revolutionaries, filmmakers protested against the primitive revision of history and the new distortion of the past made by the heralds of *glasnost*.

Panfilov's *Mother* (1990), the fourth movie based on Maxim Gorky's novel, tried to revitalize this premier proletarian author and the founder of socialist realism who was an intrepid dissident in the prerevolutionary past, regardless of his evolution and behavior in the 1930s. Panfilov also wanted to show that the revolutionary Pavel Vlasov, from the city of Sormov, the protagonist of the novel and the movie, was really a noble person who took up the revolutionary cause due to his compassion for suffering people. At the same time, from a new perspective absolutely unknown to Gorky, Panfilov demonstrates how blood generates blood and how slavery and poverty are always combined with immorality.[39]

NOTES

1. It is interesting that some people described the fall of official Communist ideology as the "de-ideologization" of society. At their last meeting in November 1991, members of the State Committee on the State Prizes of the USSR agreed "to move away from ideological criteria in the assessment of films" (*Argumenty i Fakty* 47, November 1991).

2. Russian filmmakers also used other methods to offset socialist realism. In the early 1990s they began to remake old movies (these remakes were called parallel films). For example, Igor and Gleb Oleinikov used a famous movie from the 1930s—Pyriev's *Tractor Drivers* (1939) and satirized the original movie's portrait of happiness on Soviet collective farms.

3. One of the most famous Soviet movies of Stalin's time—Alexandrov's *Circus* (1936)—focused on the discrimination against African Americans in the United States, and their support by the Soviet people.

4. The film critic Miron Chernenko concluded his article about Soloviev's third movie *The House under the Starry Sky* by saying: "Please shoot another movie, Sergei Alexandrovich, but one that everybody will be able to understand—how and for what purpose we should live, and also tell us where we have to live" (*Iskusstvo Kino* 12, 1991, p. 93).

5. The main message of Avtandil Kvirikashvili's *Crazy Love* (1992), as formulated by a Moscow movie expert, is that "you all are in shit, and your rulers too" (*Nezavisimaia Gazeta* 8 April 1992). Pathological people, psychics, KGB agents, fools, presidents, journalists, Communists yearning for revenge, pangolins—all were crammed into this movie. Kvirikashvili's *Kharms's Old Woman* (1990) was filled with as many abominable gestures, actions, fluids, and creatures as possible. A critic melancholically noted that "fortunately the director could not use smells because otherwise it would be impossible to stay in the theater" (*Nezavisimaia Gazeta*, 28 November 1991).

6. The movie, which was artistically inept, was criticized by the public. Their reaction enraged Russophiles and Russophile filmmakers, all of whom accused "the Jews" of engineering a conspiracy (*Nedelia* 25, 1987).

7. The Moscow premier of Burliaev's *All Ahead* (1990) was followed by speeches denouncing Yeltsin, Jews, and Zionists (*Moskovskie Novosti*, 17 March 1991). A similar movie—V. Liubomudrov's *Hotel Eden* (1991)—also denounces the West as the kingdom of the devil, which tries to destroy Russia, using as its base a hotel on the Black Sea that serves only those with hard currency.

8. The Russophile press accused "Westernizers" of seizing control of Russian cinema and of the movie institute. These accusations regularly carried obvious anti-Semitic overtones (*Russkii Vestnik*, 3 January 1992).

9. Although several of the new private firms were headed by prominent filmmakers such as German, others were headed by previously unknown individuals (*Izvestia*, 8 February 1992).

10. Competition and a lack of state control over the industry led to fierce struggles among various groups of moviemakers and an unprecedented level of judicial wrangling, primarily regarding the division of state property and control over various movie houses and clubs.

One of the biggest conflicts occurred between the Confederation of the Alliances of Cinematographers (which included moviemakers from former Soviet republics) and the Union of Russian Filmmakers. Both organizations struggled fiercely to control the Moscow Movie Club. Confrontations between supporters of the two groups—which included the most prestigious figures in the film industry—were regularly accompanied by rude insults that would have been unthinkable in the past. Equally dramatic bickering occurred between the regional unions (especially Moscow, St. Petersburg, and the Russian Union). Again, prominent figures such as Soloviev and Bortko participated in the intrigues and squabbling (*Nezavisimaia Gazeta*, 9 January, 18 January, 28 January 1992; *Kommersant*, 13 January 1992; 13 April 1992; *Pravda*, 3 December 1991).

11.   Vadim Abdrashitov recently commented, "The previous censorship, despite being controlled by one party, had multiple points of entry [an allusion to the various factions operating in the building of the Central Committee] and one could dodge various hurdles. Therefore, I am not ashamed of any of my movies. Censorship by the ruble is, of course, a normal phenomenon. But in our country it is destructive, because it is implemented at the troglodyte level" (*Komsomolskaia Pravda*, 14 November 1991). See also the complaints about the grim consequences of privatization on the movie industry by such figures as Basilashvili and Nikita Mikhalkov (*Literaturnaia Gazeta*, 8 January 1992; *Argumenty i Fakty* 36, 1991).

12.   See the description of one of these regales in *Kommersant* (30 December 1991) and *Komsomolskaia Pravda* (7 June 1991).

13.   When asked whether he planned to make a movie about the new Russian businessperson, Riazanov said that, given his contacts with them, he would have to say no, because they are too primitive to be protagonists in his movies (see *Moskovskie Novosti*, 12 April 1992).

14.   Tagi-Zade maintained close relations with the Communist party prior to August 1991. He later invited former movie officials (such as Ermash, Sizov, and Pavlenok) and the general procurator (Sukharev) to participate in his firm. He was no doubt interested in the state money that they could bring to his organization (*Megapolis*, 8 April 1992; *Komsomolskaia Pravda*, 28 September 1991).

15.   New businesses, particularly those connected with mafias and criminal activities, found the movie industry to be an effective sector in which to launder money. As Dondurei described it, business people doing this would finance the production of a movie and then forge papers regarding the film's revenues, even if it was shown in only a few movie clubs (Dondurei 1992).

16.   Tagi-Zade, for example, closely controlled the production of a remake of Eisenstein's *Ivan the Terrible*, based on Tolstoy's *The Silver Prince*, making decisions about the script as well as the cast (*Komsomolskaia Pravda*, 28 September 1991).

17.   Hard currency lured even the KGB into working with Western filmmakers. In early 1992, the KGB contracted with several filmmakers to create a twenty-six-part movie about the KGB (*Komsomolskaia Pravda*, 18 January 1992).

18.   Iurii Gladil'shchikov, a prominent movie critic, cites Grigorii Pomerants, a popular liberal intellectual, who discussed misconceptions in Moscow about current Western cultural trends. He writes, "the West wants to stop and look around—to use the respite that economic development has created for it—to search for the spiritual values that bourgeois development has been taking away." This, argues Gladil'shchikov, is why Bobrova's *Oh, You Geese*, with its naive simplicity, was so enthusiastically accepted in the West (*Nezavisimaia Gazeta*, 2 April 1992).

19.   Konchalovskii and Tarkovskii, two of the best known Russian directors working in the West, had been friends in the past. Eventually, however, they

became hostile toward one another's work. Tarkovskii rebuked his former friend for the conformism evident in *Siberiade* (1979), and even suspected him of being a KGB agent (Konchalovskii lived in the West with the permission of the Soviet authorities—an extraordinary situation at the time). For his part, Konchalovskii declared almost all of Tarkovskii's movies to be "mannerish" (*Nezavisimaia Gazeta*, 12 December 1991; about Konchalovskii, see also the article by Mikhail Kosakov, an actor and a past friend of Konchalovskii's—*Nezavisimaia Gazeta*, 1 June 1991).

20. Similar compassion for prostitutes is seen in *Seduction*, in which a senior in high school earns her first income from sex. This act makes sense to her, because she was previously humiliated by rich classmates who despise their poor peers.

21. In this respect, Soviet movies of the 1960s and 1970s were radically different from American movies of this and later times, especially in presenting the nascent relations between men and women. Whereas intellectual discourse, spiritual rapprochement, and common views and tastes in literature, music, and politics were depicted in Soviet movies as integral ingredients of love, few American directors (an exception being Woody Allen) focused on the intellect as an aphrodisiac. Compare, for instance, Kheifits's *Lady with the Little Dog* (1960) and the American movie by Ulu Grosbard, *Falling in Love* (1984).

22. I (V. S.) happened to be in the Movie Club at the premiere of this film. At the banquet following the premiere, the film's creators praised one another not only for battling censors who wanted to cut "the bed scene," but for presenting the protagonists as lovers only, without reference to their occupational and social activity.

A humorous episode occurred in the late 1970s, when Leonid Gaidai, working with several Finnish producers, made *For Matches* (1980). In the script, a couple, having ended a long quarrel, reconciles in a bath. The Finnish partners demanded that both male and female performers (the husband was played by Evgenii Leonov, a famous actor) be naked. Soviet officials reluctantly agreed, but only for the Finnish version of the movie (see *Komsomolskaia Pravda*, 21 March 1992).

23. The success of *Little Vera* is incomparable with other movies that became prominent in the first years of *perestroika*. In various surveys this film was ahead of all others (Zhabskii 1989, pp. 23, 25).

24. Nashima's *In the Realm of the Senses* (1976), with its many scenes of graphic sex, was tremendously successful in Russia (see *Nezavisimaia Gazeta*, 3 April 1992).

25. Immediately after the release of *Intergirl*, several directors made semi-documentary films about prostitutes. The best known include Anchugov's *Grandmother's Flat* (1991) and Tofik Shakhverdiev's *To Die from Love* (1990). In both cases, the protagonists—real prostitutes themselves—tried to sue the film directors for showing these movies in public, contending that they had not been told about them and had not given their consent. These conflicts were followed closely by the most respected Moscow newspapers (*Literaturnaia Gazeta*, 22 January 1992; *Nezavisimaia Gazeta*, 31 March 1992; *Kommersant*, 21 October 21, 1992).

26. The name of the festival mocks the famous response of one of the Soviet participants in a Soviet-American "TV bridge," who, rebuffing an American question about sexual life in the USSR, said that "there is no sex in our country."

27. Given the fast pace of *glasnost*, this movie looked hypocritical and ridicu-

lous within a year of its release. In 1989, a satirical program on Soviet TV presented a hilarious parody of the movie.

28. In the 1920s and 1930s, several movies were made about the lives of the Jews. These included Vladimir Sablin's famous *The Seekers of Happiness* (1936), about American Jews who settled in Birobidzhan, an official Jewish administrative unit in the Far East. Other films include Herbert Rapport's *Professor Mamlok* (1938), about the persecution of Jews in Nazi Germany, and Tatiana Lukashevich's *Foundling* (1940), about a Jewish couple that tries to adopt a young boy who has lost his parents. *Foundling* was the last movie with a Jewish theme to be made for over four decades.

29. A funny thing happened to Alexandrov's *Circus*. In the original version of the film, several people of different ethnic origins express their desire to take care of a black infant who was rejected by his American parents. Each character, in turn, sings a lullaby in his or her native tongue. Among them is a Jew, played by the famous actor Mikhoels. However, in the later version of this film, the Jewish lullaby was edited out.

30. This fact is especially remarkable given that, despite the so-called anti-Cosmopolitan campaign of the late 1940s (which was directed against Jewish intellectuals), Jewish film directors continued from the 1960s to the 1980s to make up a significant part of the filmmaking community. Even more remarkable is that several directors of Jewish origin produced movies with strong Russophile tendencies, and thus anti-Semitic overtones [see, for example, Alov and Naumov's *Shore* (1984)].

31. Although *Commissar* was received favorably by liberals when it was finally shown to a limited audience in 1988, almost no reviews recounted the film's real history. Only a few liberals, such as Yevtushenko, enthusiastically praised the movie (*Sovietskaia Kul'tura*, 13 February 1988).

Between 1988 and 1990 the situation changed to such an extent that the movie was shown on prime-time TV. In an incredible challenge to Soviet anti-Semitism, the film aired on November 7, 1989—the anniversary of the October Revolution and the USSR's main official holiday.

The widespread release of *Commissar*, as well as the publicity it received, enraged the Russophiles, who considered the movie a tool of Zionist propaganda. In the movie, a Jewish tailor saves the children of a female Russian commissar during the civil war. According to an article in *Molodaia Gvardia*, the movie demonstrates "the moral superiority of Jews over Russians," an idea that supposedly inspired Askol'dov and the Zionists who supported him (*Molodaia Gvardia* 7, 1990, pp. 244–46; about Askol'dov and his movie, see Andrei Mal'gin's *"Put' k Komissaru," Nedelia*, 10 December 1988; *Pravda*, 8 November 1989).

32. Given Gorbachev's ambivalence regarding the Jewish question (he did not publicly condemn anti-Semitism until 1990), it was difficult even under *glasnost* to get permission to show movies with Jewish themes (*Nedelia*, February 1992, p. 3).

33. Other movies dealing with Jewish themes include L. Gorovets's *Lady Tailor* (1990), which appeared at various festivals (*Kommersant*, 10 February 1992); Vsevolod Shilovskii's *The Wandering Stars* (1991), based on Sholom Aleichem's novel; the movies based on Issak Babel's *Stories* [Vladimir Aleinikov's *Bindiuzhnik and the King* (1990), Alexander Zel'dovich's *Sunset* (1990)]; Georgii Iungwal'd-Khil'kevich's *The Art of Living in Odessa* (1990); and Dmitrii Meskhiev's *Gambrinus* (1991), based on A. Kuprin's story.

34. Ukrainian intellectuals, regretting the strong influence of anti-Semitism

in their now independent country, organized the special exhibition "Jewish Cinematography in Ukraine, 1910–1945," which was visited by prominent cultural figures as well as by delegations from America and Israel. Dovzhenko's movie firm acquired copies of "Jewish movies," which were partially represented at the exhibition (*Evreiskie Vesti*, 1 December 1991).

35. Chiaureli also maintained close relations with Lavrentii Beria, the head of the political police (*Iskusstvo Kino* 8, 1989, pp. 80–94).

36. Unlike most movies about Stalin, which focus on mocking the former leader, *And to Hell with Us* also reflects the yearning felt by millions of Russians for the great man whom they still identify with the glory of the country. In one scene, Stalin suddenly appears in a park and hundreds of ordinary people fall under the spell of his presence.

37. A leading film about the *Gulag* was Marina Goldovskaia's documentary *Solovetskaia Power* (1988), about the first concentration camp in the Soviet Union, which was created in an old monastery in the north of Russia.

38. Bashkirtsev's role in the new movie is played by Mikhail Ulianov, who in Brezhnev's time always performed the role of the most positive character. He was one of the most touted official actors and received many decorations. Later he permitted Khrabrovistkii to include excepts from the documentary movies in which he attended various official ceremonies and even gave speeches in the Kremlin. He allowed this as part of the satirical onslaught on the past, demonstrating that he had also abdicated his position in the old Soviet society.

39. This movie aroused hot debates in Russia, and several critics denounced Panfilov for his return to socialist realism (about this movie see Alla Gerber "*Etot nesovremennyi Panfilov*," *Nezavisimaia Gazeta*, 13 March 1992).

15

Russian Movies after the Fall of the Empire

The sudden fall of the Soviet empire and the old order in August 1991 made a great impression on filmmakers. Most of them had wished for the death of "the evil empire" but were shocked because it changed their lives so dramatically.

The disintegration of society in the first half of 1992 led to the pauperization of the population, the decay of culture and science, wild privatization, increasing violence, and the corruption of the new democratic authorities. Filmmakers were also flabbergasted by the outburst of nationalism in all parts of the former Soviet Union and the breach of their old connections with colleagues in other national republics.[1] Their disappointment that the August victory did not bring positive results but led to deteriorating conditions in the country was enormous. However, as we are writing this they have not had the time to produce movies reflecting their disappointment.

NOSTALGIC VIEWS OF FILMMAKERS IN 1992

The radical deterioration of life in Russia in 1992 pushed some film directors, mainly those who had prospered as liberals in the past, to express their disappointment with the new freedoms and the ascendance of democrats to power.

Riazanov, perhaps one of the most sophisticated personalities in the country, commented that although he had once been convinced that "freedom was most important and dear," current events in the country, including the terrible regression in culture and science, had led him "for the first time in my life . . . to wonder whether freedom is worth all these sacrifices." Moreover, after alluding to the lack of any real difference between the new, presumably democratic authorities and their opponents, Riazanov went so far as to say that "when you were squeezed in the past by the army, the KGB, and the iron curtain it was easier to live—not so much because there was relative abundance in stores, but because there was clarity, and I knew against whom I had to fight" (*Moskovskie Novosti*, 12 April 1992).

Among the intellectuals who criticize Russia's current democratic order, the most active and unforgiving is Govorukhin. A highly respected film director and publicist, he is one of the few liberal intellectuals who does not mince words when assessing developments since August 1991. Govorukhin likens Russia's newborn democracy to an ugly, crippled infant child who has no chance of becoming a normal person. In his opinion, Russia's so-called democratic leaders are prepared to sacrifice the people to achieve their goals. This makes them no different than Stalin and his successors. Govorukhin argues that the new freedoms have paved the way for massive corruption greater than in the 1970s, for crime rates higher than those in the postwar period, for the "clearance sale of the country" and its natural resources, and for interpersonal cruelty unprecedented in Russian history (*Komsomolskaia Pravda*, 4 September 1991; *Novoye Russkoye Slovo*, 28 April 1992).

Not surprisingly, the political activity of movie people began to ebb in 1992. Being absorbed with adapting to the market economy, filmmakers retreated from the front lines of the political struggle. Their union also changed radically and ceased to be the headquarters of the democrats as it had been previously (*Izvestia*, 4 April 1992).

Increasing disappointment with post-Communist Russia forced some filmmakers to wonder who the positive heroes of the country might be: new businessmen, rock stars, new politicians, farmers? Gabrilovich, the elder statesman of the guild of moviemakers, suggested that the best candidate for this role is the average Russian. Poorly dressed, ready to drink, and often loitering and stealing from the state plant or office, the average Russian has managed to survive under various regimes and ideologies (Gabrilovich 1992).

Of course, Russophiles were more furious about events in the country and the movie industry than any other social group. They pointed to the rejection in most movies of all social values, including love, family, patriotism, high culture, and traditions (*Nash Sovremennik* 3, 1992, pp. 3–18; 5, 1992, pp. 110–41; *Molodaia Gvardia* 5–6, 1992, pp. 144–92).

RUSSIAN VIEWERS REFUSE TO SEE SOZART MOVIES AND PREFER AMERICAN MOVIES

The popularity of critical movies in 1987–1989 apparently gave filmmakers expectations that, with yet more critical attitudes toward reality and Communist ideology, the public would be even more eager to see their movies. However, during the next period, 1989–1992, most Russians preferred Western movies that, while full of sex and violence, offered happy endings to the drama of social conflicts.[2] To some degree, it was a repetition of the NEP period, when foreign movies, and again principally American, left almost no room for domestic films. Now these films were helping Russians to escape their current reality, much as Hollywood comedies had helped Americans during the Great Depression. Of 313 films shown in Moscow in the beginning of 1991, only 22 were of Soviet origin (*Izvestia* 14 February 1991). According to the Russian TV program "News," (22 October 1992) no more than 10 percent of films in Moscow theaters were Russian.[3] Referring to the foreign movies shown on public and cable TV, in theaters, and on video cassettes, Dondurei stated that "the national filmmaker is disappearing from the mind of the population" (*Literaturnaia Gazeta*, 20 May 1992).[4]

The sudden expansion of Western (mostly American) movies—a direct result of *glasnost* and privatization—and the growing number of private VCRs and private video salons were important factors in this process. Of no less significance was the yearning of the public, kept for decades on a puritanical diet, for exciting movies with violence and explicit sex. This is a phenomenon that Russophile and Communist critics tend to attribute to mischievous cosmopolitan politicians who want to destroy Russian culture and statehood (*Pravda*, 15 August 1992).

These developments radically changed the Soviet movie market in favor of foreign films and delivered a powerful blow to Russian cinema. Leading movie figures, who only a few years ago had demanded the total marketization of cinema, were forced to ask the government to protect them against foreign movies. One way suggested was to create a network of state movie theaters.

This trend was exacerbated by the general decline of public interest in movies between 1989 and 1992. Attendance at movie theaters dropped almost threefold. According to a survey by Grushin in January 1992, 41 percent of Muscovites had seen no movies during the previous six months (Grushin 1992).

THE SUDDEN EFFECT OF THE OLD STALINIST MOVIES

Amidst the downfall of Communist ideology and the emergence of a sort of moral vacuum in the country, the initiative of Russian TV to show old Stalinist movies drew, quite unexpectedly, a great deal of attention from the public. One such film, Pyriev's *Party Card* (1936), is about the struggle against dissidents. It nurtured the hatred of Soviets against the omnipresent enemies of the people and legitimized Soviet power and Stalin's cult.

Calls and letters from viewers revealed that while many treated the movie as a monument to Stalinist oppression, many people accepted the movie at face value. It was seen as a document of the happy past and as evidence of Stalin's political genius. This genius predicted that enemies, like Gorbachev and Yeltsin, would undermine the party from within (*Nezavisimaia Gazeta* 14 December 1991). A few other movies shown in 1991–1992 produced the same positive reaction, in particular *Kuban Cossacks* (1950) and *Joyful Fellows* (1934)(see *Nezavisimaia Gazeta*, 1 September 1992).[5]

CONCLUSION

With the end of the Soviet system, Russian cinema completely rejected the official ideology. All its elements, even those that were in essence humanistic, such as social equality or collectivism, were discarded as false dogmas. The last Soviet movies presented Soviet life, and even life in general, in extremely pessimistic ways. There are probably only a few societies and only a few periods of their history (for example, the Roman empire before its collapse) in which such a melancholy and bleak view dominated the arts as it did in Russia during the last two years of the Soviet empire.

During the last years of the Soviet system, cinematographers were, for the first time since 1917, totally free. They were anxious to reveal the truth about elements of Soviet life and Soviet history. People were inundated with portrayals of many historical figures and Soviet social groups in a completely new light. However, due to their hatred of the past and Soviet ideology, cinematographers appeared to go too far. Their anti-Communist ideology was guilty of some distortion of the present and past, although less so than earlier ideologies.

The Soviet experience shows that movies in general are doomed to distort reality in one way or another, even if many filmmakers try to be as objective as possible. Such was the case with Soviet cinematographers during the 1960s and 1970s.

FINAL NOTES

The history of Soviet cinema is both a fascinating and tragic story. In many ways it is also quite unique. The battles fought around movies have no parallel in other countries or other historical periods.

The main struggle for Soviet cinematographers has always been with the official ideology. Regardless of whether one was a true believer or an enemy of the state, this ideology was always central to movies. However, filmmakers differed as to whether they took the road of blind acceptance of, or brave challenges to, the dictates of the party.

The history of Soviet cinema is also the history of systematic confrontations between the real Soviet world and the fictional reality created by directors attempting to obey the injunctions of the ideological apparatus. The scope of the confrontation between these two realities has no precedent in the history of cinema anywhere in the world.

Another unique feature of Soviet cinema involves the attempts by directors to hint at, usually surreptitiously through the use of Aesopean allusions, some reality in their films. In effect, each movie became a game of cat and mouse with the officials. Directors tried to outsmart the censors and sneak some reality into their films.

In fact, the relationship between Soviet authorities and cinematographers has always been extremely complicated and dramatic. On one hand, most directors tried to gain the benevolence of party bosses and adjust to their demands, no matter how absurd and humiliating. In Stalin's time, this conformism was due to ever-present fear. Later, their submissiveness was due to their desire, as with other intellectuals, to keep the jobs that most of them genuinely loved. They also hoped for the good life, privileges, and official prestige.

On the other hand, as soon as any direct threat to their life was removed, many cinematographers entered into (in some cases quite heroic) conflicts with the authorities. Of course, many of their colleagues preferred to maintain their cordial relationship with the party apparatus. They aimed to serve the current leader or at least some factions in the political establishment.

Relationships between colleagues were also quite interesting. Soviet history abounds with examples of undying friendship and loyalty. It also contains examples of betrayal and perfidy.

In the end, no matter how well filmmakers were able to conform to and justify what was expected of them, there was one enemy they could not escape: themselves. For many filmmakers, the internal battle with their own conscience was far worse than any struggle with authorities. Even the best cinematographers had to regularly choose between truth, as they understood it, and the requirements of ideological bosses. They also had to choose between supporting the brilliant work of their colleagues and the desire to demonstrate their fealty to the authorities by joining them in condemning these films. Very few, if any, film directors escaped the Soviet oppression without scars on their conscience. Most have harrowing memories of times in which they acted as cowards and traitors.

Although often volatile, the history of Soviet cinema includes many artistic innovations, especially in the revolutionary period when cinematographers were true believers. However, it is also a history of conservatism imposed on filmmakers by the party, which since the early 1930s viewed artistic novelties as ideological subversion.

Due to the rapid and unpredictable changes occurring as we write, it appears that Russian cinema will continue to prove interesting for historians and other social scientists. With the formal dismantling of the Soviet Union in December 1991, a new society continues to emerge in Russia: It is impossible now to figure out what type of society that will become. However, in all likelihood, these changes will continue in the next few years. It will indeed be intriguing for future historians to compare films and filmmakers from the Soviet and the post-Soviet epochs.

NOTES

1.   Some filmmakers (Riazanov, among others) could not reconcile themselves with the secession of Ukraine (*Iskusstvo Kino* 11, 1990, pp. 44–50; *Moskovskie Novosti*, 12 April 1992).

2.   For example *Servant* (1988), a strongly critical movie, has for the most part ignored by the public. In the movie theater Vitiaz' (Viking) located in the district with the highest proportion of the intelligentsia, hardly half the available seats were filled on the four days of its screening (see Zhabskii 1989, p. 13).

3.   Soviet viewers chose, as the best movie of 1990, the sentimental Brazilian film *The Female Slave Izaura*, while the immensely popular (in 1989) movies *Intergirl* and *Little Vera* were at the bottom of the list (*Izvestia*, 22 February 1991).

In 1992, the success of the Mexican serial *Rich People Also Cry*, an extremely sentimental story, was even greater. Almost the whole year, no less than half of the Russian population watched how Marianne, a rebellious girl, was becoming a decent woman. When Veronique Castro, the actress portraying Marianne, came to Moscow in September 1992, it became a great public event, eclipsing among other things the arrival of the general secretary of the UN and of Jean-Luc Godard, the French film director. In the opinion of Moscow critics, the phenomenal success of the serial could be attributed to the deep malaise in a Russian society torn up by the conflicts in the transition from socialism to another form of society. *Rich People Also Cry* appeared as a sort of medicine, promising a happy ending for Russians coping with their troubles (*Izvestia*, 11 September 1992).

4.   In Moscow in September 1992, I (V. S.) found out for myself that Russian movies, old and new, were practically unavailable in the capital. One of the few Russian movies—a new Govorukhin film, *Russia, Which We Lost* (1992)—was shown only once a day. To my great surprise, when I got to the theater I discovered that it was half empty (see also the article about the movies in Moscow theaters in the second half of September 1992, in *Vse dlia Vsekh* 35, 1992).

5.   What is more, a survey carried out by the Institute of Sociology in 1992 found that several Stalinist movies are deeply rooted in the public mind as the best ever seen by them. So, despite the fact that a high proportion of young people had never seen these movies, they were most frequently given in answer to the question, " What were the two most beloved movies of your youth?" *Volga-Volga* (1938) took first place with 5.8 percent, *Chapaiev* (1934) took second place with 4.8 percent, and *Joyful Fellows* (1934) took third place with 3.8 percent.

References

Althusser, L. (1984). *Essays on Ideology*. London: Verso.

Anderson, W. (1990). *Reality Isn't What It Used to Be*. New York: Harper.

Andrews, D. (1984). *Concepts in Film Theory*. Oxford: Oxford University Press.

Annenskii, L. (1991). *Lokti i kryl'ia: literatura 80-kh, nadezhdy, real'nost, paradoksy*. Moscow: Sov. pisatel'.

Aronson, E., and Lindzey, G. (eds.) (1985). *Social Psychology*, 3rd ed. New York: Knopf.

Banks, A. (1992). "Politics and Aesthetics in the Cinema of Postrevolutionary Societies." Pp. 194–205 in *Communication Yearbook/15*, edited by Stanley Deetz. Newbury Park, CA: Sage.

Barthes, R. (1972). *Le Degre Zero de l'Ecriture*. Paris: Editions du Seuil.

Bazin, A. (1985). "The Stalin Myth in Soviet Cinema." Pp. 29–40 in *Movies and Methods*, Vol. 2, edited by B. Nichols. Berkeley: University of California Press.

Berger, J. (1972). *Ways of Seeing*. London: BBC and Penguin.

Berger, P., and Luckmann, T. (1966). *The Social Construction of Reality*. Garden City, NY: Doubleday.

Bloom, A. (1987). *The Closing of the American Mind*. New York: Simon and Schuster.

Bogomolov, Iu. (1989). "Po motivam istorii sovetskogo kino." *Iskusstvo Kino* 8:67.

Bokoch, S. (1991). "Shkola grazhdanskogo Sluszhenia." *Russkii Vestnik* (3 January):13.

Braudy, L. (1976). *The World in a Frame*. Garden City, NY: Anchor.

Campbell, D., and Fiske, D. (1959). "Convergent and Discriminant Validation by Multitrait-Multimethod Matrix." *Psychological Bulletin* 56:27–39.

Chukhrai, G. (1991a). "Lichnost." *Iskusstvo Kino* 11:126–34.

——— (1991b). "Personality." *Iskusstvo Kino* 11:134.

Chukovskaia, L. (1981). *Opustelyi Dom*. Paris: Alagante.

Cohen, L. (1973). *The Cultural-Political Traditions and Developments of the Soviet Cinema, 1917–1972*. New York: Arno Press.

Coleman, J. (1990). *Foundations of Social Theory*. Cambridge, MA: Belknap Press of Harvard University.

Cook, D. (1990). *A History of Narrative Film*, 2nd ed. New York: Norton.

Cormack, M. (1992). *Ideology*. Ann Arbor, MI: University of Michigan Press.

Curran, J., and Porter, P. (eds.) (1983). *British Cinema History*. London: Weidenfeld and Nicolson.

Denzin, N. (1991). *Hollywood Shot by Shot: Alcoholism in American Cinema*. Hawthorne, NY: Aldine de Gruyter.

Derrida, J. (1981). *Dissemination*. Chicago: University of Chicago Press.

Dondurei, D. (1991). "Umeret' v nishchite ili vyzhit v obiatiakh spruta." *Nezavisimaia Gazeta* (23 February).

—— (1992). "Kino: Zhizn' posle smerti." *Nezavisimaia Gazeta* (6 February).

Dudintsev, V. (1987). *Belye odezhdy*. Moscow: Izd-vo Knizhnaia palata.

Dumnov, D., Ruthaiser, V., and Shmarov, A. (1984). *Budzhet Vremeni Naseleniia*. Moscow: Finansy i Statistika.

Dyer, R. (1985). "Entertainment and Utopia." Pg. 220–32 in *Movies and Methods*, Vol. 2, edited by B. Nichols. Berkeley: University of California Press.

Eagleton, T. (1991). *Ideology: An Introduction*. London: Verso.

Eisenstein, S. (1956). *Izbrannyie Stat'i*. Moscow: Iskusstvo.

Ellis, J. (1989). *Against Deconstruction*. Princeton, NJ: Princeton University Press.

—— (1976). *Cinema et Histoire*. Paris: Denoel/Gonthier.

Fiske, J. (1982). *Introduction to Communication Studies*. New York: Methuen.

Fitzpatrick, S. (1970). *The Commissariat of Enlightenment; Soviet Organization of Education and the Arts under Lunacharsky, October 1917–1921*. Cambridge: Cambridge University Press.

Foucault, M. (1977). *Power/Knowledge: Selected Interviews and Other Writings*. New York: Random House.

Freilikh, S. (1990). "Sindrom Odinochestva." *Izvestia* (3 March).

Freindlikh, A. (1992). "Zhena Stalkera." *Moskovskie Novosti* (5 April).

Gabrilovich, E. (1992). "Opyt vnevedomstvennoi biografii." *Literaturnaia Gazeta* (12 December).

—— (1991). "Iz knigi Podzemnyie perekhody'." *Iskusstvo Kino* 4:87–98.

Galichenko, N. (1991). *Glasnost—Soviet Cinema Responds*. Austin: University of Texas Press.

Geertz, C. (1973). *The Interpretation of Cultures*. New York: Basic Books.

Genis, A. (1992). "Kannibal i Zagovorshchiki. Posle 'Oskara.'" *Nezavisimaia Gazeta* (23 April):3.

German, A. (1991). "Maska, ia tebia znaiu." *Moskovskie Novosti* (12 May).

Giannetti, L. D. (1990). *Understanding Movies*. Englewood Cliffs, NJ: Prentice Hall.

Gladil'shchikov, I. (1992). "Provintsial'noe Kino." *Nezavisimaia Gazeta* (2 April).

Goffman, E. (1959). *The Presentation of Self in Everyday Life*. Garden City, NY: Doubleday.

Golovskoy, V. (1986). *Behind the Soviet Screen: The Motion-Picture Industry in the USSR, 1972–1982*. Ann Arbor, MI: Ardis.

Goodman, N. (1978). *Ways of Worldmaking*. Indianapolis, IN: Hacket.

Goulding, (1989). *Post New Wave Cinema in the Soviet Union and Eastern Europe*. Bloomington: Indiana University Press.

Granin, D. (1987). "Ekho dal'neie i blizkoie." *Literaturnaia Gazeta* (27 May).

—— (1988). *Miloserdie*. Moskva: Sov. Rossiia.

Grenville, J. (1971). *Film as History: The Nature of Film Evidence, an Inaugural Lecture Delivered in the University of Birmingham on 5th March, 1970*. Birmingham: University of Birmingham.

Groshev, A., Ginzberg, S., Dolinskii, I., Lebedev, N., Smirnova, E., and Tumanova, N. (eds.) (1969). *Kratkaia istoriia sovetskogo kino (1917–1967 Uchebnik)*. Moscow: Iskusstvo.

Grossberg, S. (1988). *Marxism and the Interpretation of Culture*. Urbana: University of Illinois Press.

Grushin, B. (ed.) (1991–1992). "Mir mnenii i Mnenia o mire." Pamphlet, nos. 1–12, 1991; nos. 1–12, 1992.

Hall, S. (1980). "Encoding/Decoding." Pp. 129–49 in *Culture, Media, Language*, edited S. Hall et al. London: Hutchinson.

Habermas, J. (1975). *Legitimation Crisis*. Boston: Beacon Press.

——— (1984). *The Theory of Communicative Action*. Boston: Beacon Press.

Hughes, W. (1976). "The Evaluation of Film as Evidence." Pg. 49– 80 in *The Historian and Film*, edited by P. Smith. Cambridge: Cambridge University Press.

Iampol'skii, M. (1990). "Zensura kak torzhestvo zhizni." *Iskusstvo Kino* 7:97–104.

Iutkevich, S. (ed.) (1986). *Kino Entziklopedicheskii Slovar*. Moscow: Sovietskaia Entziklopediia.

Izod, J. (1988). *Hollywood and the Box Office, 1895–1986*. New York: Columbia University Press.

Jarvie, I. C. (1978). *Movies as Social Criticism: Aspects of Their Social Psychology*. Metuchen, NJ: Scarecrow Press.

Kelly, M. P. (1991). *Martin Scorsese: A Journey*. New York: Thunder's Mouth Press.

Kheifits, I. (1987). "O druziakh-tovarishchakh." *Sovietskaia Kul'tura* (20 October).

——— (1989). "Vzlet i padeinie 'Moiei Rodiny.'" *Iskusstvo Kino* 12:99–103.

Klimov, E. (1989). "Vlast'—vot v chem vopros!" *Moskovskie Novosti* (19 June).

Kornilov, V. (1988). "Pol'za vpechatlenii." *Literaturnaia Gazeta* (13 July).

Kovaleva, M. (1989). "Mefisto na sklone let." *Iskusstvo Kino* 8: 80–90.

Kozintsev, G. (1989). "Iz rabochikh tetradei." *Iskusstvo Kino* 3:96–106.

——— (1990) "Iz rabochikh tetradei)." *Iskusstvo Kino* 8:69–76, 95–105.

——— (1992) "Iz rabochikh tetradei)." *Iskusstvo Kino* 10:70–82.

Kozlov, L. (1992). "Ten' Groznogo." *Nezavisimaia Gazeta* (29 April).

Kracauer, S. (1960). *Theory of Film: The Redemption of Physical Reality*. New York: Oxford University Press.

Kuhn, T. (1970). *The Structure of Scientific Revolutions*, 2nd ed. Chicago: University of Chicago Press.

Kuleshov, L. (1935). *Report of the All-Union Conference of Cinematographers, Moscow, January*. Moscow: Partizdat.

Lawton, A. (ed.) (1987). *An Introduction to Soviet Cinema*. Washington: Kennan Institute for Advanced Russian Studies.

——— (1988). *Russian Futurism through Its Manifestos, 1912–1928*. Ithaca, NY: Cornell University Press.

Lenin, V. *Poln. Sobr. Soch.*, 5th ed., vol. 44. Moscow: Progress.

Levada, Iu. (ed.) (1990). *Est' mnenie*. Moscow: Progress.

Levin, E. (1990). "Piat dnei in 1949." *Iskusstvo Kino* 2:93–101.

Lovell, T. (1980). *Pictures of Reality: Aesthetics, Politics, Pleasure*. London: BFI.

Lukshin, I. (1991). "Mifologia chernoi volny." *Iskusstvo Kino* 3: 12–15.

MacBean, J. (1975). *Film and Revolution*. Bloomington: Indiana University Press.

MacDonald, D. (1938). "The Soviet Cinema: 1930–1939." *Partisan Review* (July):37–50; (August & September):35–61.

—— (1939). "Soviet Society and Its Cinema." *Partisan Review* 6:80–95.

Mamatova, L. (1990). "Model kinomifa 30-kh godov." *Iskusstvo Kino* 11:103–11.

Mannheim, K. (1966). *Ideology and Utopia: An Introduction to the Sociology of Knowledge.* New York: Harcourt, Brace and World.

Marshall, H. (1983). *Masters of the Soviet Cinema.* Boston: Routledge and Kegan Paul.

Matskin, A. (1992). "Plenniki dogmy." *Nezavisimaia Gazeta* (2 April).

May, L. (1980). *Screening Out the Past: The Birth of Mass Culture and the Motion Picture Industry.* New York: Oxford University Press.

Maynard, R. (ed.) (1975). *Propaganda on Film: A Nation at War.* Rochelle Park, NJ: Hayden.

McBride, J. (1992). *Frank Capra: The Catastrophe of Success.* New York: Simon & Schuster.

McClellan, D. (1986). *The Essential Left: Five Classic Texts on the Principles of Socialism.* London/Boston: Unwin.

McGilligan, P. (1991). *George Cukor: A Double Life: A Biography of the Gentleman Director.* New York: St. Martin's Press.

Melentiev, U. (1986). *Glazami Naroda.* Moscow: Sovremennik.

Mitry, J. (1963). *Esthetique et Psychologie du Cinema.* Paris: Editions Universitaires.

Monaco, J. (1981). *How to Read a Film.* New York: Oxford University Press.

Murian, V. (1976). *Sotsialisticheskii realizm i sovremennyi kinoprotsess.* Moskva: Iskusstvo.

Neale, S. (1985). *Cinema and Technology.* London: Macmillan Education.

Nesterov, F. (1984). *Sviaz' Vremen,* 2nd ed. Moscow: Molodaia Gvardia.

Nichols, B. (ed.) (1985). *Movies and Methods.* Berkeley: University of California Press.

O'Connor, J. E., and Jackson, M. A. (eds.) (1979). *American History/American Film: Interpreting the Hollywood Image.* New York: Ungar.

Ogle, P. (1985). "Technological and Aesthetic Influences on the Development of Deep-Focus Cinematography in the United States." Pg. 58–82 in *Movies and Methods,* Vol. 2, edited by B. Nichols. Berkeley: University of California Press.

Ol'khovyi, B. (ed.) (1929). *Puti Kino.* Moscow.

Pervyi Vsesoiuznyi S'ezd Sovetskikh Pisatelei (1934). Stenographic report of the Congress of Soviet Writers, Moscow. Moscow: Khudozhestvennaia Literatura.

Prokhorov, A. M. (ed.) (1983). *Sovetskii entsiklopedicheskii slovar'.* Moskva: Sov. entsiklopediia.

Pronay, N., and Spring, D. W. (1982) *Propaganda, Politics and Film, 1918–45.* London: MacMillan Press.

Pudovkin, V. (1975). *Sobranie Sochinenii.* Moscow: Iskusstvo.

Quinney, R. (1982). *Social Existence: Metaphysics, Marxism, and the Social Sciences.* Beverly Hills, CA: Sage.

Rachuk, I., and Kutorga, Z. (eds.) (1971). *Sotsiologicheskie Issledovaniia Kinematografa.* Moscow: Institut Kinematografii.

Raizman, I. (1988). "Ia nikogda ne byl politikom." *Sovietskaia Kul'tura* (4 June).

Reed, J. (1926). *Ten Days That Shook the World.* New York: International Publishers.

Riazanov, E. (1990). "Kak raz na zhizn svoboda opazdala." *Moskovskie Novosti* (12 May).

Rimberg, J. (1973). *The Motion Picture in the Soviet Union.* New York: Arno Press.

Romanov, A. (1971). *Nravstvennyi ideal v sovetskom kinoiskusstve. Stat'i i ocherki.* Moscow: Iskusstvo.

Schnitzer, J., Schnitzer, L., and Martin, M., (eds.) (1973). *Cinema in Revolution: The Heroic Era of the Soviet Film.* London: Secker & Warburg.

Schuman, H. (1981). *Questions and Answers in Attitude Surveys: Experiments on Question Form, Wording, and Context.* New York: Academic Press.

Shipman, D. (1984). *The Story of Cinema,* Vol 2. London: Hodder and Stoughton.

Shkaratan, O. (1982). "Peremeny v sotsial'nom oblike gorozhan." In *Sovietskaia Sotsiologia,* Vol. II, edited by T. Riabushkin and G. Osipov. Moscow: Nauka.

Shlapentokh, V. (1985). *Sociology and Politics: The Soviet Case.* Falls Church, VA: Delphic Associates.

——— (1986). *Soviet Public Opinion and Ideology: Mythology and Pragmatism in Interaction.* New York: Praeger.

——— (1987). *The Politics of Sociology in the Soviet Union.* Boulder, CO: Westview.

——— (1988). *Soviet Ideologies in the Period of Glasnost.* New York: Praeger.

——— (1990). *Soviet Intellectuals and Political Power.* Princeton, NJ: Princeton University Press.

Shmyrov, V. (1989). *Iskusstvo Kino* 8:80–90.

Shtein, E. (1987). "Moie pokolenie." *Sovietskaia Kul'tura* (23 May).

Shulgin V. V. (1991). *Tri Stolitsy.* Moscow: Sovremennik.

Shusharina, G. (1992). "Disneyland in the Lont Room." *Nezavisimaia Gazeta* (7 March):5.

Sirivlia, N. (1991). "Temnyie sily nas zlobno gnetut." *Iskusstvo Kino* 3.

Smelser, N. (ed.) (1989). *Handbook of Sociology.* Newbury Park, CA: Sage.

Smith, P. (ed.) (1976). *The Historian and Film.* Cambridge: Cambridge University Press.

Sobchack, V. (1992). *The Address of the Eye: A Phenomenology of Film Experience.* Princeton, NJ: Princeton University Press.

Solzhenitsyn, A. (1963). *One Day in the Life of Ivan Denisovich.* New York: E. P. Dutton.

Spoto, D. (1992). *The Art of Alfred Hitchcock: Fifty Years of His Motion Pictures.* New York: Doubleday.

Steudler, R. (1987). "Representations of Drinking and Alcoholism in French Cinema." *International Sociology* 2:45–59.

Steven, P. (ed.) (1985). *Jump Cut.* New York: Praeger.

Strugatskii, A. (1987). "Kakim ia ego znal." *Ogoniok* (29 July):7–8.

Tarkovskii, A. (1992). "Martirolog." *Nezavisimaia Gazeta* (8 April):5.

Taylor, R. (1971). "A Medium for the Masses: Agitation in the Soviet Civil War." *Soviet Studies* (April):562–74.

Taylor, R., and Christie, I. (eds.) (1988). *The Film Factory and Soviet Cinema in Documents, 1896–1939.* London: Routledge and Kegan Paul.

Timofeievskii, A. (1992a). "Adam v pogonakh." *Moskovskie Novosti* (5 April).

——— (1992b). "Ne zhdali." *Moskovskie Novosti* (28 June).

TsSU SSSR (1987). *Narodnoie Khoziastvo SSSR za 70 Let.* Moscow: Finansy i Statistika.

Turner, G. (1988). *Film as Social Practice.* London: Routledge.

Vail, P., and Genis, A. (1990). "Netraditsionnyi vzgliad na taksista i dzhazista." *Literaturnaia Gazeta* (28 November).

Vakhametsa, A., and Plotnikov, S. (1968). *Chelovek i Iskusstvo.* Moscow: Mysl'.

Vidal, G. (1992). *Screening History.* Cambridge, Mass.: Harvard University Press.

Vorontsov, I., and Rachuk, I. (1980). *The Phenomenon of the Soviet Cinema.* Moscow: Progress.

Voslenski, M. (1980). *La Nomenclature: Les privileges en URSS.* Paris: Pierre Belfon.

White, D., and Averson, R. (1972) *The Celluloid Weapon.* Boston: Beacon.

Zaslavskaia, T. (1988). "O Strategii sotsial'nogo upravlenia perestroikoi." In *Inogo Ne Dano*, edited by Iu. Afanasiev. Moscow: Progress.

Zhabskii, M. (1976). *Metodologiia Prikladnogo Sotsiologicheskogo Issledovaniia (Problemy Sotsiologii Kino).* Moscow: Institut Teorii i Istorii Kino.

———— (1989). *Sotsiologia Kino: Istoki Predmet, Perspektivy.* Moscow: Znanie.

Zinin V., and Diskin, I. (eds.) (1985). *Kul'tura i Sredstva Massovoi Informatsii: Sotsial'no ekonomicheskie Problemy.* Moscow: Economika.

Zorkaya, N. (1989). *The Illustrated History of Soviet Cinema.* New York: Hyppocrene Books.

Little Vera
(1988)

Servant (1988)

Юрий Демич
„Ленфильм", 1989

The Extraordinary Event of District Importance (1988)

Black Rose Stands for Sadness, Red Rose Stands for Joy (1989)

Fountain (1988)

The Cold Summer
of 1953 (1987)

Intergirl (1989)

My Friend Ivan Lapshin (1984)

Little Doll (1989)   To Whom Do You Belong, Old People? (1988)

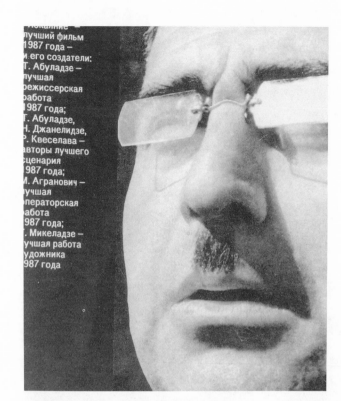

Локалние —
лучший фильм
1987 года —
и его создатели:
Т. Абуладзе —
лучшая
режиссерская
работа
1987 года;
Т. Абуладзе,
Н. Джанелидзе,
Р. Квеселава —
авторы лучшего
сценария
1987 года;
М. Агранович —
лучшая
операторская
работа
1987 года;
. Микеладзе —
лучшая работа
удожника
987 года

Repentance (1984)

Taxi-Blues (1990)

256

Filmography

Academician Ivan Pavlov [*Akademic Ivan Pavlov*], 1949, Grigorii Roshal'
Accuse Klava of My Death [*V moiei smerti proshu vinit' Klavu*], 1980, Nikolai Lebedev
Actress from Gribov, The [*Aktrisa iz Gribova*], 1988, L. Kvirinadze
Aelita, 1924, Iakov Protazanov
Aerograd, 1935, Alexander Dovzhenko
Agony [*Agonia*], 1981, Elem Klimov
Alexander Nevskii, 1938, Sergei Eisenstein
All Ahead [*Vse vperedi*], 1990, Nikolai Burliaev
All Is Left to the People [*Vse ostaietsia liudiam*], 1963, Georgii Natanson
Amusements of Youth [*Zabavy molodykh*], 1987, Evgenii Gerasimov
And What If It Is Love [*A esli eto liubov*], 1962, Iulii Raizman
And Life, and Tears, and Love [*I zhizn' i sliezy i liubov'*], 1983, Nikolai Gubenko
And to Hell with Us [*I chert s nami*], 1991, Alexander Pavlovskii
Andrei Rublev, 1971, Andrei Tarkovskii
Anna Karamazoff, 1990, Rustam Khamdamov
Anna Karenina, 1968, Natan Zarkhi
Arinka, 1940, Nadezhda Kosheverova and Iurii Muzykant
Armavir, 1991, Vadim Abrashitov
Art of Living in Odessa, The [*Iskusstvo zhit' v Odesse*], 1990, Georgii Iungwal'd-
  Khil'kevich'
Asia, 1978, Iosif Kheifits
Assa, 1988, Sergei Soloviev
Asthenic Syndrome [*Astenicheskii sindrom*], 1990, Kira Muratova
Autumn [*Osen'*], 1975, Andrei Smirnov
Autumn Marathon, The [*Osennii marafon*], 1979, Georgii Danelia
Avaria—A Cop's Daughter [*Avaria—doch menta*], 1989, Mikhail Tumanshvili
Back Home [*Domoi*], 1983, Gavriil Egiazarov
Ballad of a Soldier [*Ballada o soldate*], 1959, Grigorii Chukhrai
Baltic Deputy [*Deputat Baltiki*], 1937, Natan Zarkhi, and Iosif Kheifits
Battle of Stalingrad, The [*Stalingradskaia bitva*], 1949, Vladimir Petrov
Battleship Potemkin [*Bronenosets Potemkin*], 1925, Sergei Eisenstein
Beast [*Zver'*], 1990, A. Muratov
Because of a Change of Job [*V sviazi s perekhodom na druguiu rabotu*], 1986, S. Linkov
Beginning, The [*Nachalo*], 1970, Gleb Panfilov
Beware the Car! [*Beregis' avtomobilia*], 1966, El'dar Riazanov
Bezhin Meadow [*Bezhin lug*], 1935–1937, Sergei Eisenstein
Big Family, The [*Bol'shaia semia*], 1954, Iosif Kheifits
Bindiuzhnik and the King [*Bindiuzhnik i korol'*], 1990, Vladimir Aleinikov

257

Bitch's Children [*Sukiny deti*], 1990, Leonid Filatov
Black Castle [*Chiernyi zamok*], 1980, Mikhail Ptashuk
Black Days of Kronstadt, The [*Chernye dni Kronshtada*], 1921, Eduard Tisse
Black Rose Stands for Sadness, Red Rose Stands for Joy [*Chernaia roza—roza pechali,*
   krasnaia roza—emblema liubvi], 1989, Sergei Soloviev
Blackmailer [*Shantazh*], 1986, director unknown
Blia, 1990, Efim Gal'perin
Blonde around the Corner, The [*Blondinka za uglom*], 1984, Vladimir Bortko
Body [*Telo*], 1990, N. Khutov
Bogdan Khmelnitsky, 1941, Igor Savchenko
Bold Seven, The [*Semero smelykh*], 1936, Sergei Gerasimov
Bonus, The [*Premia*], 1975, Sergei Mikaelian
Bright Road [*Svetlyi put'*], 1940, Grigorii Alexandrov
Brothers Karamazov, The [*Bratia Karamazovy*], 1969, Ivan Pyriev
Business of the Heart [*Dela serdechnyie*], 1974, Adzhar Ibragimov
By the Lake [*U ozera*], 1970, Sergei Gerasimov
Carnival Night [*Karnaval'naia noch'*], 1956, El'dar Riazanov
Case of the Death of Russia, The [*Delo ob ubiistve Rossii*], 1992, Stanislav Govo-
   rukhin
Cavalier of the Gold Star, The [*Kavaler zolotoi zvezdy*], 1951, Iulii Raizman
Chairman, The [*Predsedatel'*], 1964, Alexei Saltykov
Chapaiev, 1934, Vasiliev brothers (pen name)
Checkpoint [*Proverka na dorogakh*], 1987, Alexei German
Children's Home [*Detskii dom*], 1982, V. Mosenko
Children's Playground [*Detskaia ploshchadka*], 1987, S. Proskurin
Chosen Heaven [*Nebesa obetovannyie*], 1991, El'dar Riazanov
Circus, The [*Tsirk*], 1936, Grigorii Alexandrov
Close to the Edge of Danger [*U opasnoi cherty*], 1983, V. Georgiev
Cloud Paradise, The [*Oblako rai*], 1991, Nikolai Dostal'
Club of the Big Deed (S.V.D.), The [*Soiuz velikogo dela*], 1927, Grigorii Kozintsev
Cold Summer of 1953, The [*Kholodnoie leto 1953*], 1987, A. Proshkin
Color of Pomegranate, The [*Tsvet granata*], 1970, Sergei Paradzhanov
Commissar, The, 1989, Alexander Askol'dov
Communist, The [*Kommunist*], 1958, Iulii Raizman and Evgenii Gabrilovich
Confrontation [*Protivostoianie*], 1985, Iulian Semenov and Tatiana Lianozova
Consolidation [*Uplotnenie*], 1918, Alexander Panteleev, D. Pashkovskii, and A.
   Dolinov
Conspiracy of the Doomed, The [*Zagovor obrechennykh*], 1950, Mikhail Kalatozov
Corruption [*Korruptsia*], 1990, A. Poliakov
Cosmic Voyage [*Kosmicheskoie puteshestvie*], 1936, Vasilii Zhuravlev
Countryside [*Derevnia*], 1930, Ilia Kopalin
Court of Honor, The [*Sud chesti*], 1945, Abram Room
Cranes Are Flying [*Letiat zhuravli*], 1957, Mikhail Kalatozov
Cranky People [*Choknutye*], 1990, Alla Surikova
Crazy Love [*Sumashedshaia liubov'*], 1992, Avtandil Kvirikashvili
Crime and Punishment [*Prestuplenie i nakazanie*], 1970, Lev Kulidzhanov
Criminal Talent [*Kriminal'nyi talant*], 1988, S. Ashkenazi

Cynics [Tsiniki], 1992, Dmitrii Meskhiev

Damned Days Again in Russia [Okaiannyie dni opiat'v Rossii], 1990, V. Vasil'kov

Danger Zone, The [Zapretnaia zona], 1988, Nikolai Gubenko

Day of the Ghost, The [Dukhov den'], 1991, Nikolai Makarov

Dear Elena Sergeevna [Dorogaia Elena Sergeevna], 1988, El'dar Riazanov

Death Ray [Luch smerti], 1925, Lev Kuleshov

Declaration of Love [Ob'iasnenie v liubvi], 1978, Ilia Averbakh

Defeat [Razgrom] 1931, scriptwriter Alexander Fadeiev

Defense of Tsaritsin, The [Oborona Tsaritsyna], 1942, (pen name) Vasiliev brothers

Desert [Pustynia], 1991, M. Kats

Destiny of Man, The [Sud'ba cheloveka], 1959, Sergei Bondarchuk

Director of a Children's Home [Khoziaika detskogo doma], 1984, Iosif and Victor Olshanskii

Do Not Shoot the White Swans [Ne streliaite v belykh lebedei], 1982, Rodion Nakhapetov

Dog's Feast [Sobachii pir], 1990, Leon Menaker

Dog's Heart [Sobachie serdtse], 1988, Vladimir Bortko

Don Diego and Pelageia [Don Diego i Pelageia], 1928, Iakov Protazanov

Donbass Miners [Donetskie Kharaktezy], 1951, Leonid Lukov

Dream of Taras, The [Son Tarasa], 1919, Lev Kuleshov

Encounter with My Youth [Svidanie s molodost'iu], 1982, V. Popov

End of St. Petersburg, The [Konets Sankt-Peterburga], 1927, Vsevolod Pudovkin

Enemy of the People—Bukharin, The [Vrag naroda—Bukharin], 1989, L. Mariagin

Engineer Berezhkov [Inzhener Berezhkov], 1988, A. Beck and A. Misharin

Everyday Life and Holidays of Serafima Gliukina, The [Budni i prazdniki Serafimy Gliukinoi], 1988, R. Goriaev

Extraordinary Event of District Importance, The [Chrezvychainoie sobytie raionnogo mashtaba], 1988, S. Snezhkin

Failure to Return [Nevozvrashchenets], 1991, S. Snezhkin

Fall of Berlin, The [Padenie Berlina], 1950, Mikhail Chiaureli

Fantasy on Love Themes, A [Fantazia na temu liubvi], 1981, Aida Manasarova

Far Away from Moscow [Daleko ot Moskvy], 1950, Alexander Stolper

Fast Train [Skoryi poezd], 1988, B. Ianshin

Father Sergei [Otets Sergii], 1918, Iakov Protazanov

Fell in Love at My Own Request [Vliublen po sobstvennomu zhelaniu], 1982, Sergei Mikaelian

Female Rivals [Sopernitsy], 1980, Victor Sadovskii

Few Days from the Life of Oblomov, A [Neskol'ko dnei iz zhizni Oblomova], 1980, Nikita Mikhalkov

Fighter Planes [Istrebiteli], 1939, Alexei Pankratiev

First Echelon, The [Pervyi eshelon], 1956, Mikhail Kalatozov

Flights in the Night and Daydreams [Poliety vo sne i naiavu], 1983, Roman Balaian

For Matches [Za spichkami], 1980, Leonid Gaidai

For the Harvest [Za urozhai], 1929, Ilia Kopalin

Foreign Case, A [Chuzhoi sluchai], 1985, V. Dosortsev

Forgotten Melody for Flute and Orchestra [Zabytaia melodia dlia fleity s orkestrom], 1987, El'dar Riazanov

Forty-First, The [*Sorok pervyi*], 1927, Iakov Protazanov

Forty-First, The [*Sorok pervyi*], 1956, Grigorii Chukhrai

Foundling [*Podkidysh*], 1940, Tatiana Lukashevich

Fountain [*Fontan*], 1988, Iurii Mamin

Fragment of the Empire, A [*Oblomok imperii*], 1929, Fridrikh Ermler

From the Four Winds [*Na semi vetrakh*], 1962, Stanislav Rostotskii

From the Life of the Head of the Prosecutors' Office [*Iz zhizni nachal'nika ugolovnogo rozyska*], 1983, S. Puchinian

Front Line behind Front Line [*Front bez flangov*] 1975, Igor' Gostev

Front Line without Front Line [*Front za liniei fronta*], 1978, Igor' Gostev

Gambrinus, 1991, Dmitrii Meskhiev

Games for Teenagers [*Igry dlia detei shkol'nogo vozrasta*], 1986, Leina Laus

Garage, 1980, El'dar Riazanov

Gardener [*Sadovnik*], 1989, V. Buturlin

Georgii Saakadze, 1942–1943, Mikhail Chiaureli

Girl Hurries for Her Date, The [*Devushka speshit na svidanie*], 1936, Andrei Bulinskii

Girl with a Temper, The [*Devushka s kharakterom*], 1939, Konstantin Iudin

Girlfriends, The [*Podrugi*], 1936, Leo Arnshtam

Girl's Mountains [*Dev'i gory*], 1918, Alexander Sanin

Goalie [*Vratar*], 1936, Semien Timoshenko

Grandmother's Flat [*Babushkina kvartira*], 1991, Anchugov

Grasshopper, The [*Kuznechik*], 1986, V. Grigoriev

Great Citizen, A [*Velikii grazhdanin*], 1938–1939, Fridrikh Ermler

Great Dawn [*Velikoe Zarevo*], 1938, Mikhail Chiaureli

Great Life [*Bol'shaia zhizn'*], 1940–1946, Leonid Lukov

Hamlet, 1964, Grigorii Kozintsev

Happiness [*Shchast'e*], 1935, Alexander Medvedkin

Happy Days [*Shchastlivyie dni*], 1990, Alexei Balabanov

Heir to Genghis Khan, The [*Potomok Chingis Khana*], 1928, Vsevolod Pudovkin

Hotel Eden, 1991, V. Liubomudrov

House I Live In, The [*Dom v kotorom ia zhivu*], 1957, Lev Kulidzhanov and Iakov Segel'

House under the Starry Sky, The [*Dom pod zviezdnoi kryshei*], 1991, Sergei Soloviev

How Do You Do, Carps? [*Kak zhivete, Karasi*], 1992, Mikhail Shveitser and Sofia Mil'kina

How Steel Was Tempered [*Kak zakalialas' stal'*], 1942, Mark Donskoi

Humble Cemetery [*Smirennoie kladbishche*], 1989, A. Itychikov

I Am Twenty [*Mne dvadtsat' let*], 1965, Marlen Khutsiev

I Took Control of the City [*Vzial komandu nad gorodom*], 1979, V. Maksakov

Idiot, The [*Idiot*], 1958, Ivan Pyriev

If There Should Be War Tomorrow [*Esli zavtra voina*], 1938, Efim Dzigan and Lazar Antsi-Polovski

In the Intoxication of NEP [*V ugare Nepa*], 1925, Boris Svetozarov

Inner Circle, The [*V uzkom krugu*], 1991, Andrei Mikhalkov-Konchalovskii

Intergirl [*Interdevochka*], 1988, Piotr Todorovskii

Invasion [*Nashestvie*], 1945, Abram Room

It's Not Easy to Be Young [*Legko li byt' molodym*], 1987, Iuris Podniesk

Iudushka Golovlev, 1934, Alexander Ivanovskii
Ivan the Terrible [*Ivan Groznyi*], 1945, Sergei Eisenstein
Ivan's Childhood [*Ivanovo detstvo*], 1962, Andrei Tarkovskii
Jackals [*Shakaly*], 1991, Khabibulat Faiziev
Journalist, The [*Zhurnalist*], 1967, Sergei Gerasimov
Joyful Fellows [*Vesielye rebiata*], 1934, Grigorii Alexandrov
Julian the Apostate [*Iulian Otstupnik, part 1*], 1918, director unknown
Kharms's Old Woman [*Starukha Kharmsa*], 1990, Avtandil Kvirikashvili
Kicks, 1991, Livnev
Kidnapping of the Century [*Pokushenie veka*], 1981, V. Makarov
Kind People [*Dobriaki*], 1980, scriptwriter L. Zorin
Kinfolk [*Rodnia*], 1982, Nikita Mikhalkov
King of the Jews [*Tsar' Iudeiskii*], 1917, scriptwriter Konstantin Romanov
Komsomolsk, 1938, Sergei Gerasimov
Kremlin Secrets of the Seventeenth Century, The [*Kremlievskie secrety semnadtsatogo veka*], 1991, Victor Merezhko
Kuban Cossacks [*Kubanskie kazaki*], 1950, Ivan Pyriev
Kutuzov, 1944, Vladimir Petrov
Lady Tailor [*Damskii portnoi*], 1990, L. Gorovets
Lady with the Little Dog, The [*Dama s sobachkoi*], 1960, Iosif Kheifits
Land [*Zemlia*], 1930, Alexander Dovzhenko
Late Date [*Pozdneie svidanie*], 1986, director unknown
Law [*Zakon*], 1991, V. Naumov
Law of Life, The [*Zakon zhizni*], 1940, Alexander Stolper and Ivanov
Legend of Suram Fortress, The [*Legenda o Suramskoi kreposti*], 1984, Sergei Paradzhanov
Lenin in 1918 [*Lenin v 1918*], 1939, Mikhail Romm
Lenin in October [*Lenin v Octiabre*], 1937, Mikhail Romm
Lenin in Paris [*Lenin v Parizhe*], 1981, Sergei Iutkevich
Lenin in Poland [*Lenin v Pol'she*], 1966, Sergei Iutkevich
Lermontov, 1987, Nikolai Burliaev
Lethargy [*Letargia*], 1983, V. Zheleznikov and V. Lonskii
Leveret [*Zaichik*], 1985, Rolan Bykov
Liberation [*Osvobozhdenie*], 1970–1972, Iurii Ozerov
Life of Vacationers, The [*Iz zhizni otdykhaiushchikh*], 1981, Nikolai Gubenko
Little Doll [*Kukolka*], 1989, Isaak Friedberg
Little Vera [*Malen'kaia Vera*], 1988, V. Pichul
Long Road to Herself, The [*Dolgaia doroga k sebe*], 1983, Natalia Troshchenko
Lost in Siberia [*Poteriannyie v Sibiri*], 1991, Alexander Mitta
Lost Time [*Kanuvsheie vremia*], 1989, Shuster
Love [*Liubov'*], 1991, Valerii Todorovskii
Love and Pigeons [*Liubov' i golubi*], 1984, Vladimir Menshov
Lover's Romance, A [*Romans o vliublennykh*], 1974, Andrei Mikhalkov-Konchalovskii
Lullaby [*Kolybel'naia*], 1934, Dziga Vertov
Man from the Restaurant, The [*Chelovek iz restorana*], 1927, Iakov Protazanov
Man Was Born [*Chelovek rodilsia*], 1956, Vasilii Ordynskii

Man with a Gun [*Chelovek s ruzhiem*], 1938, Sergei Iutkevich
Marked [*Mechennyie*], 1991, Viacheslav Sorokin
Married Bachelor [*Zhenatyi kholostiak*], 1983, Vladimir Rogovoi
Married for the First Time [*Vpervyie zamuzhem*], 1980, Iosif Kheifits
Marshal Bliukher, 1989, V. Eisner
Maxim's Return [*Vozvrashchenie Maxima*], 1937, Grigorii Kozintsev and Leonid Trauberg
Maxim's Youth [*Iunost' Maxima*], 1935, Grigorii Kozintsev and Leonid Trauberg
May I Have the Floor [*Ia proshu slova*], 1976, Gleb Panfilov
The Medal on the Neck [*Anna na sheie*], 1954, Isidor Annenskii
Meeting on the Elbe [*Vstrecha na El'be*], 1949, Grigorii Alexandrov
Member of the Government, A [*Chlen pravitel'stva*], 1940, Iosif Kheifits and Natan Zarkhi
Merry Christmas in Paris [*Schastlivoie Rozhdestvo v Parizhe*], 1991, Ol'ga Zukova
Michurin, 1949, Alexander Dovzhenko
Mimino, 1978, Georgii Danelia and R. Gabriadze
Minin and Pozharsky [*Minin i Pozharskii*], 1939, Vsevolod Pudovkin and Mikhail Doller
Mirror [*Zerkalo*], 1975, Andrei Tarkovskii
Most Charming and Attractive [*Samaia ocharosatel'naia i privlekatel'naia*], 1985, G. Bazhanov
Mother, The [*Mat'*], 1926, Vsevolod Pudovkin
Mother, The [*Mat'*], 1990, Gleb Panfilov
Movie Eye [*Kino glaz*], 1924, Vertov Dziga
Murder on Dante Street, The [*Ubiistvo na ulitse Dante*], 1956, Mikhail Romm
Musorgskii, 1950, Grigorii Roshal'
Muzhiks [*Muzhiki*], 1981, Iskra Balich
My Dear Edison [*Moi dorogoi Edison*], 1986, Isaak Friedberg
My Friend Lapshin [*Moi drug Lapshin*], 1984, Alexei German
My Motherland [*Moia rodina*], 1933, Iosif Kheifits
My Name Is Arlekino [*Moie imia Arlekino*], 1988, V. Rybarev
Nice Little Mug [*Mordashka*], 1990, Andrei Razumovskii
Night Accident [*Nochnoie proishestvie*], 1981, Veniamin Dorman
Nine Days of One Year [*Deviat' dnei odnogo goda*], 1962, Mikhail Romm
Oh, You Geese [*Oi, vy gusi*], 1990, Lidia Bobrova
Objective Circumstance [*Obiektivnyie obstoiatel'stva*], 1988, G. Pavlov
October [*Oktiabr'*], 1927, Sergei Eisenstein
Office Romance, An [*Sluzhebnyi roman*], 1977, El'dar Riazanov
Offspring of the Devil [*Potomok diavola*], 1917, Kharitonov
Old and the New, The [*Staroie i novoie*], 1929, Sergei Eisenstein
Old Debts [*Staryie dolgi*], 1980, Ilia Gurin
Only One, The [*Edinstvennaia*], 1976, Iosif Kheifits
One Hundred Days after Childhood [*Sto dnei posle detstva*], 1975, Sergei Soloviev
Ordinary Fascism [*Obyknovennyi fashizm*], 1966, Mikhail Romm
Our Armored Train [*Nash bronepoezd*], 1989, Mikhail Ptashuk
Overcoat, The [*Shinel'*], 1926, Grigorii Kozintsev and Leonid Trauberg

Papa, Santa Claus Is Dead [*Papa, ded Moroz umer*], 1991, Evgenii Iufit
Parisian Cobbler [*Parizhskii sapozhnik*], 1928, Fridrikh Ermler
Parrot That Speaks Yiddish, The [*Popugai govoriashchii na idishe*], 1990, Efrem Sevela
Party Card [*Partinyi bilet*], 1936, Ivan Pyriev
Pass for Life, A [*Putevka v zhizn'*], 1931, Nikolai Ekk
Passing Twice [*Dvoinoi obgon*], 1979, Alexander Gordon
Passport [*Pasport*], 1990, Georgii Danelia
Pavel Korchagin, 1957, Alexander Alov and Vladimir Naumov
Peace to Those Who Enter [*Mir vkhodiashchemu*], 1961, Alexander Alov and Vladimir Naumov
Peasants [*Krestiane*], 1935, Fridrikh Ermler
Peculiar People [*Strannyie liudi*], 1970, Vasilii Shukshin
Peter and Alexis [*Pietr i Alexei*], 1918, Alexander Sanin
Peter the First [*Pietr pervyi*], 1937–1939, Vladimir Petrov
Photograph for Remembrance, A [*Fotografia na pamiat'*], 1985, R. Muradian
Please Be My Husband [*Bud'te moim muzhem*], 1981, scriptwriter E. Akropov
Please Meet Baluiev [*Znakom'tes' Baluiev*], 1963, Dmitrii Meskhiev and Veniamin Levitin
Please, Say a Good Word about Poor Hussar [*O bednom gusare zamolvite slovechko*], 1981, El'dar Riazanov
Pliumbum, 1986, Vadim Abdrashitov
Plump Girl [*Pyshka*], 1934, Mikhail Romm
Poet and the Tsar, The [*Poet i Tsar'*], 1927, Evgenii Cherviakov
Prank [*Rozygrysh*], 1977, Vladimir Menshov
Professor Mamlok, 1938, Herbert Rapport
Prolong the Enchantment [*prodlis' ocharovan'ie*], 1984, Iaropolk Lapshin
Publication [*Publikatsia*], 1988, Victor Volkov
Quarantine [*Karantin*], 1983, Ilia Frez
Que Viva Mexico! [*Da zdravstvuiet Mexica!*], 1931, Sergei Eisenstein
Rain in July [*Iul'skii Dozhd'*], 1967, Marlen Khutsiev
Rainbow [*Raduga*], 1944, Mark Donskoi
Red Arrow [*Krasnaia strela*], 1986, I. Khamraiev
Red Bells [*Krasnyie kolokola*], 1982, Sergei Bondarchuk
Red Snowball Tree [*Kalina krasnaia*], 1974, Vasilii Shukshin
Rejuvenated Labor [*Obnovlennyi trud*], 1930, Ilia Kopalin
Repentance [*Pokaianie*], 1984, Tengiz Abuladze
Resurrection [*Voskresenie*], 1960–1962, Mikhail Shveitser
Return of Vasilia Bortnikova, The [*Vozvrashchenie Vasilia Bortnikova*], 1953, Vsevolod Pudovkin
Rich Bride, The [*Bogataia nevesta*], 1938, Ivan Pyriev
Rumyantsev's Case [*Delo Rumiantseva*], 1956, Iosif Kheifits
Rural Detective, A [*Derevenskii detectiv*], 1969, Ivan Lukinskii
Rural Doctor [*Sel'skii vrach*], 1952, Sergei Gerasimov
Russia, Which We Lost [*Rossia, kotoruiu my poteriali*], 1992, Stanislav Govorukhin
Russian Question, The [*Russkii vopros*], 1948, Mikhail Romm
Satan [*Satana*], 1991, Victor Aristov
Satan Triumphant [*Satana likuishchii*], 1917, Iakov Protazanov

School Waltz [*Shkol'nyi val's*], 1989, Pavel Liubimov
Second Time in Crimea [*Vtoroi raz v Krymu*], 1984, Pavel Liubimov
Secret Mission [*Sekretnaia missia*], 1950, Mikhail Romm
Secretary of the District Committee [*Sekretar' raikoma*], 1942, Ivan Pyriev
Seduction [*Soblazn*], 1987, Viacheslav Sorokin
Seekers of Happiness, The [*Iskateli shchastia*], 1936, Vladimir Sablin
Sensitive Militiaman, The [*Chuvstvitel'nyi militsioner*], 1990, Kira Muratova
Servant [*Sluga*], 1988, Vadim Abdrashitov
Seventeen Moments of Spring [*Semnadtsat' mgnovenii vesny*], 1973, Iulian Semenov
    and Tatiana Lianozova
Sex Fairy Tale [*Seks-skazka*], 1991, Elena Nikolaieva
Shadows of Our Forgotten Ancestors, The [*Teni zabytykh predkov*], 1965, Sergei Parad-
    zhanov
Shchors, 1939, Alexander Dovzhenko
She Defends Her Country [*Ona zashchishchaet rodinu*], 1943, Fridrikh Ermler
Sholom Aleichem 40 [*Ulitsa Sholom Aleichem 40*], 1987, Alexander Tovstonogov
Shooting Stars [*Zvezdopad*], 1982, Igor Talankin
Shop Crumbs [*Pechki-lavochki*], 1972, Vasilii Shukshin
Shore, The [*Bereg*], 1984, Alexander Alov and Vladimir Naumov
Shtemp, 1991, G. Ivanov
Siberiade, 1979, Andrei Mikhalkov-Konchalovskii
Silence [*Tishina*], 1964, Vladimir Basov
Single Woman Wants to Date Someone [*Odinokaia zhenshchina zhelaiet poznakomitsia*],
    1989, V. Krishtovich
Sinner [*Greshnik*], 1988, V. Popkov
Sixth of July, The [*Shestoie Iiulia*], 1968, Iulii Karasik
Small Favor [*Malen'koie odolzhenie*], 1988, B. Konunov
Soldier's Father, The [*Otets soldata*], 1965, Revaz Chkheidze
Soliaris, 1972, Andrei Tarkovskii
Solovetskaia Power [*Vlast' Solovetskaia*], 1988, Marina Goldovskaia
Song Thrush [*Pevchii drozd*], 1970, Otar Ioseliani
Sophia Petrovna, 1989, A. Sirenko
Sportloto-82, 1982, Leonid Gaidai
Spring in Zarechnaia Street [*Vesna na Zarechnoi ulitse*], 1956, Marlen Khutsiev and
    Felix Mironer
Stalin's Funeral [*Pokhorony Stalina*], 1990, Yevgeni Yevtushenko
Stalin's Trip to Africa [*Puteshestvie tovarishcha Stalina v Afriku*], 1990, Iraklii
    Kvirikadze
Star [*Zvezda*], 1949, Alexander Ivanov
Stories about Lenin [*Rasskazy o Lenine*], 1958, Sergei Iutkevich
Storm, The [*Groza*], 1934, Vladimir Petrov
Story of a Real Man, The [*Povest' o nastoiashchem cheloveke*], 1948, Alexander Stolper
Story of Asya Kliachina, Who Loved But Did Not Marry, The [*Istoria Asi Kliachinoi,*
    kotoraia liubila no ne vyshla zamuzh], 1967, Andrei Mikhalkov-Konchalovskii
Story of Siberian Land, The [*Skazanie o zemle Sibirskoi*], 1948, Ivan Pyriev
Story of the Nonexistent Moon, The [*Povest' o nepogashennoi lune*], 1991, Evgenii
    Zymbal

Strike [*Stachka*], 1925, Sergei Eisenstein

Sunday at Six-Thirty [*Voskresenie, polovina sed'mogo*], 1988, Vadim Zlobin

Sunset [*Zakat*], 1990, Alexander Zel'dovich

Suvorov, 1941, Mikhail Doller and Vsevolod Pudovkin

Swineherd and Shepherd [*Svinarka i pastukh*], 1941, Ivan Pyriev

Taming of Fire, The [*Ukroshchenie ognia*], 1972, Daniil Khrabrovistkii

Tass Is Authorized to Announce [*Tass upolnomochen zaiavit'*], 1986, Iulian Semenov

Taxi-Blues [*Taxi-bliuz*], 1990, Pavel Lungin

Theme [*Tema*], 1986, Gleb Panfilov

They Could Not Get Along [*Ne soshlis' kharakterami*], 1989, V. Shevelev

Thieves in Law [*Vory v zakone*], 1988, Iurii Kara

Third Meshchanskaya, The [*Tretia Meshchanskaia*], 1927, Abram Room

Third Strike, The [*Tretii udar*], 1948, Igor Savchenko

Thirteen [*Trinadtsat'*], 1937, Mikhail Romm

Three People on the Red Rug [*Tri cheloveka na krasnom kovre*], 1989, (first names not available) Brovkin and Solntsev

Three Percent Risk [*Tri protsenta riska*], 1984, E. Orashchenko

Tight Knot [*Tugoi uzel*], 1957, Mikhail Shveitser

To Die from Love [*Umeret' ot liubvi*], 1990, Tofik Shakhverdiev

To Die Is Not Frightening [*Umirat' ne strashno*], 1991, Lev Kulidzhanov

To Whom Do You Belong, Old People? [*Vy chie, starichie?*], 1989, Iosif Kheifits

Top Class [*Vyshii klass*], 1991, Mikhail Mel'nichenko

Top Guy, The [*Pervyi paren'*], 1986, A. Sirenko

Tovarich Abraham [*Tovarishch Abram*], 1919, Feofan Shipulinskii

Tower [*Bashnia*], 1989, V. Tregubov

Tractor Drivers [*Traktoristy*], 1939, Ivan Pyriev

Train Station for Two, A [*Vokzal dlia dvoikh*], 1983, El'dar Riazanov

Trek of Comrade Chkalov through the North Pole, The [*Puteshestvie tovarishcha Chkalova cherez severnyi polius*], 1990, M. Pezhemskii

Tsar's Murder, The [*Tsareubitsa*], 1991, Karen Shakhnazarov

Turksib, 1928–1929, Victor Turin

Turning Point, The [*Povorot*], 1979, Vadim Abdrashitov

Twenty-Six Commissars [*Dvadtsat' shest' komissarov*], 1933, Nikolai Shengelaia

Uncle Vanya [*Diadia Vania*], 1971, Andrei Mikhalkov-Konchalovskii

Uneasy Sunday [*Trevozhnoie Voskresenie*], 1983, scriptwriter B. Medova

Valentin and Valentina, 1983 [*Valentin i Valentina*] scriptwriter Roshekin

Valtasar's Feast or the Night with Stalin [*Piry Valtasara ili noch' so Stalinym*], 1989, Iurii Kara

Vanity of Vanities [*Sueta suet*], 1979, Alla Surikova

Village Teacher, A [*Sel'skaia uchitel'nitsa*], 1947, Mark Donskoi

Volga-Volga, 1938, Grigorii Alexandrov

Vow, The [*Kliatva*], 1946, Mikhail Chiaureli

Vyborg Side, The [*Vyborgskaia storona*], 1939, Grigorii Kozintsev and Leonid Trauberg

Wandering Stars, The [*Bluzhdaiushchie zvezdy*], 1991, Vsevolod Shilovskii

War and Peace [*Voina i mir*], 1966–1967, Sergei Bondarchuk

Wartime Romance [*Voenno-polevoi roman*], 1984, Piotr Todorovskii

We Are from Kronstadt [My iz Kronshtadta], 1936, Efim Dzigan
We Cannot Live This Way Anymore [Tak zhit' nel'zia], 1990, Stanislav Govorukhin
We, the Undersigned [My, nizhepodpisavshiesia], 1981, Alexander Gel'man
Welcome, or No Admittance! [Dobro pozhalovat' ili postoronnim vkhod vospreshchen!],
    1964, Elem Klimov
We'll Get By Till Monday [Dozhivem do ponedel'nika], 1968, Stanislav Rostotskii
Whiskers [Bakenbardy], 1990, Iurii Mamin
White Snow of Russia [Belyi sneg Rossii], 1980, S. Vronskii
Who's Knocking at My Door? [Kto stuchitsia v dver' ko mne], 1983, scriptwriter
    T. Kholopliankina
Wind, The [Veter], 1959, Alexander Alov and Vladimir Naumov
Wings of a Serf, The [Krylia kholopa], 1926, Iurii Tarich
Winter Cherry-2 [Zimniaia vishnia-2], 1990, I. Maslennikov
Worried Youth [Trevozhnaia molodost'], 1955, Vladimir Naumov
Yakov Sverdlov, 1940, Sergei Iutkevich
Young Guard, The [Molodaia gvardia], 1948, Sergei Gerasimov
Your Contemporary [Tvoi sovremennik], 1968, Iulii Raizman
Your Son, Earth [Tvoi syn, zemlia], 1981, Revaz Chkheidze

Director List

Abdrashitov, Vadim: *Armavir* (1991), *Pliumbum* (1986), *Servant* (1988), *The Turning Point* (1979)
Abuladze, Tengiz: *Repentance* (1984)
Akropov, E., scriptwriter: *Please Be My Husband* (1981)
Aleinikov, Vladimir: *Bindiuzhnik and the King* (1990)
Alexandrov, Grigorii: *Bright Road* (1940), *The Circus* (1936), *Joyful Fellows* (1934), *Meeting on the Elbe* (1949), *Volga-Volga* (1938)
Alov, Alexander: *Pavel Korchagin* (1957), *Peace to Those Who Enter* (1961), *The Shore* (1984), *The Wind* (1959)
Anchugov (first name not available): *Grandmother's Flat* (1991)
Annenskii, Isidor: *The Medal on the Neck* (1954)
Antsi-Polovski, Lazar: *If There Should Be War Tomorrow* (1938)
Aristov, Victor: *Satan* (1991)
Arnshtam, Leo: *The Girlfriends* (1936)
Ashkenazi, S.: *Criminal Talent* (1988)
Askol'dov, Alexander: *The Commissar* (1989)
Averbakh, Ilia: *Declaration of Love* (1978)
Balabanov, Alexei: *Happy Days* (1990)
Balaian, Roman: *Flights in the Night and Daydreams* (1983)
Balich, Iskra: *Muzhiks* (1981)
Basov, Vladimir: *Silence* (1964)
Bazhanov, G.: *Most Charming and Attractive* (1985)
Bobrova, Lidia: *Oh, You Geese* (1990)
Bondarchuk, Sergei: *The Destiny of Man* (1959), *Red Bells* (1982), *War and Peace* (1966–1967)
Bortko, Vladimir: *The Blonde around the Corner* (1984), *Dog's Heart* (1988)
Brovkin (first name not available): *Three People on the Red Rug* (1989)
Bulinskii, Andrei: *The Girl Hurries for Her Date* (1936)
Burliaev, Nikolai: *All Ahead* (1990), *Lermontov* (1987)
Buturlin, V.: *Gardener* (1989)
Bykov, Rolan: *Leveret* (1985)
Cherviakov, Evgenii: *The Poet and the Tsar* (1927)
Chiaureli, Mikhail: *The Fall of Berlin* (1950), *Georgii Saakadze* (1942–1943), *Great Dawn* (1938), *The Vow* (1946)
Chkheidze, Revaz: *The Soldier's Father* (1965), *Your Son, Earth* (1981)
Chukhrai, Grigorii: *Ballad of a Soldier* (1959), *The Forty-First* (1956)
Danelia, Georgii: *The Autumn Marathon* (1979), *Mimino* (1978), *Passport* (1990)
Dolinov, A.: *Consolidation* (1918)

267

Doller, Mikhail: *Minin and Pozharsky* (1939), *Suvorov* (1941)
Donskoi, Mark: *How Steel Was Tempered* (1942), *Rainbow* (1944), *A Village Teacher* (1947)
Dorman, Veniamin: *Night Accident* (1981)
Dosortsev, V.: *A Foreign Case* (1985)
Dostal', Nikolai: *The Cloud Paradise* (1991)
Dovzhenko, Alexander: *Aerograd* (1935), *Land* (1930), *Michurin* (1949), *Shchors* (1939)
Dziga, Vertov: *Movie Eye* (1924)
Dzigan, Efim: *If There Should Be War Tomorrow* (1938), *We Are from Kronstadt* (1936)
Egiazarov, Gavriil: *Back Home* (1983)
Eisenstein, Sergei: *Alexander Nevskii* (1938), *Battleship Potemkin* (1925), *Bezhin Meadow* (1935–1937), *Ivan the Terrible* (1945), *October* (1927), *The Old and the New* (1929), *Que Viva Mexico!* (1931), *Strike* (1925)
Eisner, V.: *Marshal Bliukher* (1989)
Ekk, Nikolai: *A Pass for Life* (1931)
Ermler, Fridrikh: *A Fragment of the Empire* (1929), *A Great Citizen* (1938–1939), *Parisian Cobbler* (1928), *Peasants* (1935), *She Defends Her Country* (1943)
Fadeiev, Alexander, scriptwriter: *Defeat* (1931)
Faiziev, Khabibulat: *Jackals* (1991)
Filatov, Leonid: *Bitch's Children* (1990)
Frez, Ilia: *Quarantine* (1983)
Friedberg, Isaak: *Little Doll* (1989), *My Dear Edison* (1986)
Gabriadze, R.: *Mimino* (1978)
Gabrilovich, Evgenii (scriptwriter): *The Communist* (1958)
Gaidai, Leonid: *For Matches* (1980), *Sportloto-82* (1982)
Gal'perin, Efim: *Blia* (1990)
Gel'man, Alexander: *We, the Undersigned* (1981)
Georgiev, V.: *Close to the Edge of Danger* (1983)
Gerasimov, Evgenii: *Amusements of Youth* (1987)
Gerasimov, Sergei: *The Bold Seven* (1936), *By the Lake* (1970), *The Journalist* (1967), *Komsomolsk* (1938), *Rural Doctor* (19523), *The Young Guard* (1948)
German, Alexei: *Checkpoint* (1987), *My Friend Lapshin* (1984)
Goldovskaia, Marina: *Solovetskaia Power* (1988)
Gordon, Alexander: *Passing Twice* (1979)
Goriaev, R.: *The Everyday Life and Holidays of Serafima Gliukina* (1988)
Gorovets, L.: *Lady Tailor* (1990)
Gostev, Igor': *Front Line behind Front Line* (1975), *Front Line without Front Line* (1978)
Govorukhin, Stanislav: *The Case of the Death of Russia* (1992), *We Cannot Live This Way Anymore* (1990), *Russia, Which We Lost* (1992)
Grigoriev, V.: *The Grasshopper* (1986)
Gubenko, Nikolai: *And Life, and Tears, and Love* (1983), *The Danger Zone* (1988), *The Life of Vacationers* (1981)
Gurin, Ilia: *Old Debts* (1980)
Ianshin, B.: *Fast Train* (1988)

Ibragimov, Adzhar: *Business of the Heart* (1974)

Ioseliani, Otar: *Song Thrush* (1970)

Itychikov, A.: *Humble Cemetery* (1989)

Iudin, Konstantin: *The Girl with a Temper* (1939)

Iufit, Evgenii: *Papa, Santa Claus Is Dead* (1991)

Iungwal'd-Khil'kevich', Georgii: *The Art of Living in Odessa* (1990)

Iutkevich, Sergei: *Lenin in Poland* (1966), *Lenin in Paris* (1981), *Man with a Gun* (1938), *Stories about Lenin* (1958), *Yakov Sverdlov* (1940)

Ivanov (first name not available): *The Law of Life* (1940)

Ivanov, Alexander: *Star* (1949)

Ivanov, G.: *Shtemp* (1991)

Ivanovskii, Alexander: *Iudushka Golovlev* (1934)

Kalatozov, Mikhail: *The Conspiracy of the Doomed* (1950), *Cranes Are Flying* (1957), *The First Echelon* (1956)

Kara, Iurii: *Thieves in Law* (1988), *Valtasar's Feast or the Night with Stalin* (1989)

Karasik, Iulii: *The Sixth of July* (1968)

Kats, M.: *Desert* (1991)

Khamdamov, Rustam: *Anna Karamazoff* (1990)

Khamraiev, I.: *Red Arrow* (1986)

Kharitonov (first name not available): *Offspring of the Devil* (1917)

Kheifits, Iosif: *Asia* (1978), *Baltic Deputy* (1937), *The Big Family* (1954), *The Lady with the Little Dog* (1960), *Married for the First Time* (1980), *A Member of the Government* (1940), *My Motherland* (1933), *The Only One* (1976), *Rumyantsev's Case* (1956), *To Whom Do You Belong, Old People?* (1989)

Kholopliankina, T., scriptwriter: *Who's Knocking at My Door?* (1983)

Khrabrovistkii, Daniil: *The Taming of Fire* (1972)

Khutov, N.: *Body* (1990)

Khutsiev, Marlen: *I Am Twenty* (1965), *Rain in July* (1967), *Spring in Zarechnaia Street* (1956)

Klimov, Elem: *Agony* (1981), *Welcome, or No Admittance!* (1964)

Konunov, B.: *Small Favor* (1988)

Kopalin, Ilia: *Countryside* (1930), *For the Harvest* (1929), *Rejuvenated Labor* (1930)

Kosheverova, Nadezhda: *Arinka* (1940)

Kozintsev, Grigorii: *The Club of the Big Deed (S.V.D.)* (1927), *Hamlet* (1964), *Maxim's Return* (1937), *Maxim's Youth* (1935), *The Overcoat* (1926), *The Vyborg Side* (1939)

Krishtovich, V.: *Single Woman Wants to Date Someone* (1989)

Kuleshov, Lev: *Death Ray* (1925), *The Dream of Taras* (1919)

Kulidzhanov, Lev: *Crime and Punishment* (1970), *The House I Live In* (1957), *To Die Is Not Frightening* (1991)

Kvirikadze, Iraklii: *Stalin's Trip to Africa* (1990)

Kvirikashvili, Avtandil: *Crazy Love* (1992), *Kharms's Old Woman* (1990)

Kvirinadze, L.: *The Actress from Gribov* (1988)

Lapshin, Iaropolk: *Prolong the Enchantment* (1984)

Laus, Leina: *Games for Teenagers* (1986)

Lebedev, Nikolai: *Accuse Klava of My Death* (1980)

Levitin, Veniamin: *Please Meet Baluiev* (1963)

Lianozova, Tatiana: *Confrontation* (1985), *Seventeen Moments of Spring* (1973)
Linkov, S.: *Because of a Change of Job* (1986)
Liubimov, Pavel: *School Waltz* (1989), *Second Time in Crimea* (1984)
Liubomudrov, V.: *Hotel Eden* (1991)
Livnev: *Kicks* (1991)
Lonskii, V.: *Lethargy* (1983)
Lukashevich, Tatiana: *Foundling* (1940)
Lukinskii, Ivan: *A Rural Detective* (1969)
Lukov, Leonid: *Donbass Miners* (1951), *Great Life* (1940–1946)
Lungin, Pavel: *Taxi-Blues* (1990)
Makarov, Nikolai: *The Day of the Ghost* (1991)
Makarov, V.: *Kidnapping of the Century* (1981)
Maksakov, V.: *I Took Control of the City* (1979)
Mamin, Iurii: *Fountain* (1988), *Whiskers* (1990)
Manasarova, Aida: *A Fantasy on Love Themes* (1981)
Mariagin, L.: *The Enemy of the People—Bukharin* (1989)
Maslennikov, I.: *Winter Cherry-2* (1990)
Medova, B., scriptwriter: *Uneasy Sunday* (1983)
Medvedkin, Alexander: *Happiness* (1935)
Mel'nichenko, Mikhail: *Top Class* (1991)
Menaker, Leon: *Dog's Feast* (1990)
Menshov, Vladimir: *Love and Pigeons* (1984), *Prank* (1977)
Merezhko, Victor: *The Kremlin Secrets of the Seventeenth Century* (1991)
Meskhiev, Dmitrii: *Cynics* (1992), *Gambrinus* (1991), *Please Meet Baluiev* (1963)
Mikaelian, Sergei: *The Bonus* (1975), *Fell in Love at My Own Request* (1982)
Mikhalkov, Nikita: *A Few Days from the Life of Oblomov* (1980), *Kinfolk* (1982)
Mikhalkov-Konchalovskii, Andrei: *The Inner Circle* (1991), *A Lover's Romance*
    (1974), *Siberiade* (1979), *The Story of Asya Kliachina, Who Loved But Did Not
    Marry* (1967), *Uncle Vanya* (1971)
Mil'kina, Sofia: *How Do You Do, Carps?* (1992)
Mironer, Felix: *Spring in Zarechnaia Street* (1956)
Misharin, A. Beck A.: *Engineer Berezhkov* (1988)
Mitta, Alexander: *Lost in Siberia* (1991)
Mosenko, V.: *Children's Home* (1982)
Muradian, R.: *A Photograph for Remembrance* (1985)
Muratov, A.: *Beast* (1990)
Muratova, Kira: *Asthenic Syndrome* (1990), *The Sensitive Militiaman* (1990)
Muzykant, Iurii: *Arinka* (1940)
Nakhapetov, Rodion: *Do Not Shoot the White Swans* (1982)
Natanson, Georgii: *All Is Left to the People* (1963)
Naumov, Vladimir: *Law* (1991), *Pavel Korchagin* (1957), *Peace to Those Who Enter*
    (1961), *The Shore* (1984), *The Wind* (1959), *Worried Youth* (1955)
Nikolaieva, Elena: *Sex Fairy Tale* (1991)
Olshanskii, Iosif and Victor: *Director of a Children's Home* (1984)
Orashchenko, E.: *Three Percent Risk* (1984)
Ordynskii, Vasilii: *Man Was Born* (1956)
Ozerov, Iurii: *Liberation* (1970–1972)

Panfilov, Gleb: *The Beginning* (1970), *May I Have the Floor* (1976), *The Mother* (1990), *Theme* (1986)
Pankratiev, Alexei: *Fighter Planes* (1939)
Panteleev, Alexander: *Consolidation* (1918)
Paradzhanov, Sergei: *The Color of Pomegranate* (1970), *The Legend of Suram Fortress* (1984), *The Shadows of Our Forgotten Ancestors* (1965)
Pashkovskii, D.: *Consolidation* (1918)
Pavlov, G.: *Objective Circumstance* (1988)
Petrov, Vladimir: *The Battle of Stalingrad* (1949), *Kutuzov* (1944), *Peter the First* (1937–1939), *The Storm* (1934)
Pavlovskii, Alexander: *And to Hell with Us* (1991)
Pezhemskii, M.: *The Trek of Comrade Chkalov through the North Pole* (1990)
Pichul, V.: *Little Vera* (1988)
Podniesk, Iuris: *It's Not Easy to Be Young* (1987)
Poliakov, A.: *Corruption* (1990)
Popkov, V.: *Sinner* (1988)
Popov, V.: *Encounter with My Youth* (1982)
Proshkin, A.: *The Cold Summer of 1953* (1987)
Proskurin, S.: *Children's Playground* (1987)
Protazanov, Iakov: *Aelita* (1924), *Don Diego and Pelageia* (1928), *Father Sergei* (1918), *The Forty-First* (1927), *The Man from the Restaurant* (1927), *Satan Triumphant* (1917)
Ptashuk, Mikhail: *Black Castle* (1980), *Our Armored Train* (1989)
Puchinian, S.: *From the Life of the Head of the Prosecutors' Office* (1983)
Pudovkin, Vsevolod: *The End of St. Petersburg* (1927), *The Heir to Genghis Khan* (1928), *Minin and Pozharsky* (1939), *The Mother* (1926), *The Return of Vasilia Bortnikova* (1953), *Suvorov* (1941)
Pyriev, Ivan: *The Brothers Karamazov* (1969), *The Idiot* (1958), *Kuban Cossacks* (1950), *Party Card* (1936), *The Rich Bride* (1938), *Secretary of the District Committee* (1942), *The Story of Siberian Land* (1948), *Swineherd and Shepherd* (1941), *Tractor Drivers* (1939)
Raizman, Iulii: *And What If It Is Love* (1962), *The Cavalier of the Gold Star* (1951), *The Communist* (1958), *Your Contemporary* (1968)
Rapport, Herbert: *Professor Mamlok* (1938)
Razumovskii, Andrei: *Nice Little Mug* (1990)
Riazanov, El'dar: *Beware the Car!* (1966), *Carnival Night* (1956), *Chosen Heaven* (1991), *Dear Elena Sergeevna* (1988), *Forgotten Melody for Flute and Orchestra* (1987), *Garage* (1980), *Office Romance, An* (1977), *Please, Say a Good Word about Poor Hussar* (1981), *A Train Station for Two* (1983)
Rogovoi, Vladimir: *Married Bachelor* (1983)
Romanov, Konstantin, scriptwriter: *King of the Jews* (1917)
Romm, Mikhail: *Lenin in October* (1937), *Lenin in 1918* (1939), *The Murder on Dante Street* (1956), *Nine Days of One Year* (1962), *Ordinary Fascism* (1966), *Plump Girl* (1934), *The Russian Question* (1948), *Secret Mission* (1950), *Thirteen* (1937)
Room, Abram: *Invasion* (1945), *The Court of Honor* (1945), *The Third Meshchanskaya* (1927)
Roshal', Grigorii: *Academician Ivan Pavlov* (1949), *Musorgskii* (1950)

Roshekin, scriptwriter: *Valentin and Valentina*(1983)
Rostotskii, Stanislav: *From the Four Winds* (1962), *We'll Get By Till Monday* (1968)
Rybarev, V.: *My Name Is Arlekino* (1988)
Sablin, Vladimir: *The Seekers of Happiness* (1936)
Sadovskii, Victor: *Female Rivals* (1980)
Saltykov, Alexei: *The Chairman* (1964)
Sanin, Alexander: *Girl's Mountains* (1918), *Peter and Alexis* (1918)
Savchenko, Igor: *Bogdan Khmelnitsky* (1941), *The Third Strike* (1948)
Segel', Iakov: *The House I Live In* (1957)
Semenov, Iulian: *Confrontation* (1985), *Seventeen Moments of Spring* (1973), *Tass Is Authorized to Announce* (1986) .
Sevela, Efrem: *The Parrot That Speaks Yiddish* (1990)
Shakhnazarov, Karen: *The Tsar's Murder* (1991)
Shakhverdiev, Tofik: *To Die from Love* (1990)
Shengelaia, Nikolai: *Twenty-Six Commissars* (1933)
Shevelev, V.: *They Could Not Get Along* (1989)
Shilovskii, Vsevolod: *The Wandering Stars* (1991)
Shipulinskii, Feofan: *Tovarich Abraham* (1919)
Shukshin, Vasilii: *Peculiar People* (1970), *Red Snowball Tree* (1974), *Shop Crumbs* (1972)
Shuster (first name not available): *Lost Time* (1989)
Shveitser, Mikhail: *How Do You Do, Carps?* (1992), *Resurrection* (1960–1962), *Tight Knot* (1957)
Sirenko, A.: *Sophia Petrovna* (1989), *The Top Guy* (1986)
Smirnov, Andrei: *Autumn* (1975)
Snezhkin, S.: *The Extraordinary Event of District Importance* (1988), *Failure to Return* (1991)
Solntsev (first name not available): *Three People on the Red Rug* (1989)
Soloviev, Sergei: *Assa* (1988), *Black Rose Stands for Sadness, Red Rose Stands for Joy* (1989), *The House under the Starry Sky* (1991), *One Hundred Days after Childhood* (1975)
Sorokin, Viacheslav: *Marked* (1991), *Seduction* (1987)
Stolper, Alexander: *Far Away from Moscow* (1950), *The Law of Life* (1940), *The Story of a Real Man* (1948)
Surikova, Alla: *Cranky People* (1990), *Vanity of Vanities* (1979)
Svetozarov, Boris: *In the Intoxication of NEP* (1925)
Talankin, Igor: *Shooting Stars* (1982)
Tarich, Iurii: *The Wings of a Serf* (1926)
Tarkovskii, Andrei: *Andrei Rublev* (1971), *Ivan's Childhood* (1962), *Mirror* (1975), *Nostalgia* (1983), *Sacrifice* (1986), *Soliaris* (1972), *Stalker* (1980)
Timoshenko, Siomen: *Goalie* (1936)
Tisse, Eduard: *The Black Days of Kronstadt* (1921)
Todorovskii, Piotr: *Intergirl* (1988), *Wartime Romance* (1984)
Todorovskii, Valerii: *Love* (1991)
Tovstonogov, Alexander: *Sholom Aleichem 40* (1987)
Trauberg, Leonid: *Maxim's Return* (1937), *Maxim's Youth* (1935), *The Overcoat* (1926), *The Vyborg Side* (1939)

Tregubov, V.: *Tower* (1989)
Troshchenko, Natalia: *The Long Road to Herself* (1983)
Tumanshvili, Mikhail: *Avaria—A Cop's Daughter* (1989)
Turin, Victor: *Turksib* (1928–1929)
Vasiliev brothers: *Chapaiev* (1934), *The Defense of Tsaritsin* (1942)
Vasil'kov, V.: *Damned Days Again in Russia* (1990)
Vertov, Dziga: *Lullaby* (1934)
Volkov, Victor: *Publication* (1988)
Vronskii, S.: *White Snow of Russia* (1980)
Yevtushenko, Yevgeni: *Stalin's Funeral* (1990)
Zarkhi, Natan: *Anna Karenina* (1968), *Baltic Deputy* (1937), *A Member of the Government* (1940)
Zel'dovich, Alexander: *Sunset* (1990)
Zheleznikov, V.: *Lethargy* (1983)
Zhukova, Ol'ga: *Merry Christmas in Paris* (1991)
Zhuravlev, Vasilii: *Cosmic Voyage* (1936)
Zlobin, Vadim: *Sunday at Six-Thirty* (1988)
Zorin, L., scriptwriter: *Kind People* (1980)
Zymbal, Evgenii: *The Story of the Nonexistent Moon* (1991)

Index

Accommodation, 153–154
Alexander (prince of Novgorod), 79, 100–102
Alienation, 190–191
American movies, 14–16, 200–201, 240–241
American social literature, 4
Anti-Bolshevik movies, 44–47
Anticosmopolitan campaign, 29, 30–31
Antiutopian themes, 45–46
Art, 130–131 (*See also* Literature; Movies)

Beggars, 217–218
Besprisornik, 87–88
Bolshevik Revolution, 39
Bolsheviks, 45–46, 49, 54–55
Bourgeoisie, 224–225
Brezhnev's time, movies of
  accommodation in, 153–154
  bureaucracy as major actors in, 150–153
  demagoguery in, 154–155
  ethnic Russians in, 166
  intellectuals as fighters of bureaucracy in, 159–160
  intellectuals in, 158
  intellectuals in Russophile movies and, 160–162
  masses in liberal movies and, 166
  masses in non-Russophile movies and, 169–171
  negative images of intellectuals in, 162–166
  positive images of bureaucracy in, 155–158
  positive images of intellectuals in, 158–159
  Russians during peacetime in, 168–169
  Russians during wartime in, 166–167

Bureaucracy
  control of filmmakers and, 25–31
  crime and, 216–217
  economic control and, 83–86
  glasnost and, 185–187
  intellectuals as fighters against, in movies of Brezhnev's time, 159–160
  as major actors in movies of Brezhnev's time, 150–153
  members of, 18
  positive images of, in movies of Brezhnev's time, 155–158
Bureaucrats, 185–188

Capitalism, 49–51, 92
Children (*See* Youth)
Cinema (*See* Movies)
Cinematographers (*See* Filmmakers)
Coding works of literature and art, 130–131
Cognitive realism, 4
Cold war, first thaw of, 129–131
Collectivization, 23, 83–88
Cosmos, 204–206
Covert values, 10
Crime
  bureaucracy and, 216–217
  mafias and, 216
  organized, 216
  origins of, 214–215
  scope of criminality and, 214
  youth and, 193–194
Criminals, 213–216
Critics, 64–65, 200–201
Cruelty, 191–192
Cynicism, 191–192

Dead bodies, 226
Decoding works of literature and art, 130–131
Deconstructionism, 5
Degenerated revolutionaries, 60

274